8⁹⁵

THE
GARDEN
TRIUMPHANT

DAVID STUART

THE
GARDEN
TRIUMPHANT

A VICTORIAN
LEGACY

1817

HARPER & ROW, PUBLISHERS, New York

Cambridge, Philadelphia, San Francisco, London
Mexico City, São Paulo, Singapore, Sydney

CONTENTS

LIST OF COLOUR
ILLUSTRATIONS

1. Cragside.

2. Zonal pelargoniums gave handsome foliage as well as luxurious flowers.

3–6. Nasturtiums, tiger-lilies, dahlias and the tulip 'Prince Albert'.

7. Stone and gravel: the parterre at Trentham.

8. Windy magnificence on the parterre at Eaton Hall.

9. Rustic work and tasteful climbers around the arbour at Shrublands.

10. Nasturtiums and Italian cypresses at Shrublands.

11. Calla lilies and ferns in this elegant Wardian case for the drawing-room window.

12, 13. Carpet bedding ideas from the *Gardener's Chronicle* of the 1860s.

14. *Lapageria,* ferns and fruit used on a centrepiece for a dinner-table of 1863.

15. Ivies, coleus and lily in a Gothic windowbox.

16. A lush climbing rose, 'Princess Louise Victoria'.

17–20. Indian pinks, petunias, orchids and tender primulas.

21. Shattered peaks and miniature glaciers surrounded the flower garden at Hoole House.

22. A bouquet of exotic foliage.

23, 24. Exuberant fussiness on the parterre at Wilton contrasts with bleak magnificence at Castle Howard.

25–28. Victorian favourites, from 'florist's' flowers like chrysanthemums, ranunculuses and cyclamen to hot-house stephanotis and belamcandas.

29. A bouquet of late-Victorian roses.

INTRODUCTION

THE VICTORIAN AGE WAS ASTONISHING, VAST and multifarious. The cult of the garden was only the tiniest part of it and yet, perhaps more than at any time before or since, gardening became inextricably linked to the turmoils and aspirations of the times. Gardening suddenly became a substantial market: for plants, for seeds, for gardeners, for magazines and newspapers, for gadgets of innumerable sorts and variable utilities. Gardening reached whole new classes of consumer for the first time. Middle-class housewives in freshly built terrace houses discovered garden flowers, garden crafts, flower-arranging. The new rich could now display their new wealth with as much spectacle as they could possibly wish, for they were now and forever freed from the Georgian canons of 'chaste' good taste. The fast-expanding industrial classes could, if they were lucky, garden their new allotments or tiny back yards, or wander through the innumerable, though still bald and newly planted, public parks. All classes could buy some of the new gardening books, whether as penny pamphlets, as mid-price part-works filled with hand-coloured prints, or as expensive productions devoted to new orchids, camellias, lilies or roses. Everyone could buy gardening newspapers, or some of the many magazines.

7

This new excitement was reflected in new directions in garden design. The visual revolution in garden taste of the previous century needed land, and therefore wealth, for its expression, but by the mid nineteenth century gardening was available and relevant to almost everyone. This was not just to do with mere changes in fashion, but was intimately associated with the whole economic and political fabric of the time (gardening always is). The social shifts that made all the astonishing changes in gardens possible may be glimpsed behind every advance, whether apparently trivial (like the supplanting by mass-produced rubber hoses of the old handmade leather ones, or the introduction of cast-iron plant vases), or more plainly important (like the flood of South American plants as that subcontinent was opened up, or the growth of garden societies to improve the gardens of the rural destitute).

The whole Victorian age, here, is only just visible beyond the greenery, and is seen entirely through its gardens and gardeners. More gardeners, of more sorts, were more vocal than ever before, and the pages of the new publications designed for them burst with their voices. Through their own words, through the commercial world that battened upon them (quack medicines, Doulton aspidistra holders, false teeth, interior decorators, emigration societies, subscription pleas to save widows and children from the workhouse, dinner table designers, chrysanthemum shades, two-horse lawnmowers), we can build up a picture of how many of them lived.

For the first time in the history of gardening, it is possible to know almost as much about the elderly weeding-women who cleared caterpillars from the cabbages, and the obscure Scottish plant collectors stationed in Nepal or the jungles of Brazil, as about the new 'media stars', whether surgeons' wives, gardeners from the humblest backgrounds who won for themselves rank and fortune, or great magnates pacing their Italian terraces and French parterres.

Of course not all Victorian gardens were beautiful, though many, both in Europe and America, were. Some were quite preposterous. In previous epochs, when the changes of taste and style were usually worked out for aristocratic and often visually-educated patrons, sometimes by designers or gardeners of great sophistication, there were still, no doubt, terrible visual disasters. Modern books about seventeenth- or eighteenth-century gardens usually appeal for the conservation or restoration of what remains from those periods. For the Victorian one, with so many partial remains left to us of both the nasty and the marvellous, the problem of conservation is more complex. It is difficult to know whether it would be worth recreating, somewhere, the tightly packed Lawrencian villa gardens (see p. 32) or the vast sequence of circular flower beds at Wimbledon House, let alone the immense bedding schemes at Sydenham, the rock gardens that modelled the Matterhorn (the most important of these still exists beneath a grove of sycamores), or Scottish glens decked out to look like Japan.

However, there were also a large number of beautiful gardens – the Victorian period produced innumerable highly talented gardeners, and many of their gardens still exist, even though some lie, half-vanished, in their own jungles of American rhododendron and laurel. At a less grand level, thousands of small Victorian houses could look delightful if framed once again by Victorian gardens and the rooms decorated with Victorian flower arrangements. Here the problems are fewer, and this book can be used to find good plants and planting schemes.

Lastly, it is worth pointing out that this book is largely based on British and, to a lesser extent, American sources. There is enough of those to swamp a dozen writers and produce a score of books. However, it was not only in those countries that the enthusiasm for gardens took hold. It was international. All over Europe and Russia gardeners were looking for new plants and new ways of putting them together, and their triumphs were transmitted by the presses and copied elsewhere. Japanese nurserymen exported plants to California, where they were bought by gardeners who experimented with Spanish garden styles but ignored the annual plants of their own deserts. These, like *Eschscholtzia* and *Clarkia*, were grown in every back yard in Peckham or Solihull. Chinese gardeners, with their own wonderful garden flora still being exported to Europe, fell crazily in love with the new roses being shown in London or Paris, and paid huge prices for a single twig.

It was all quite extraordinary. Yet it was in Britain that everything seemed to be finally brought together. It was here too, maybe for cultural or climatic reasons, that the first blows against the triumphant high-Victorian styles of gardening were struck, and here that the compromises which created the next style of gardening were worked out, compromises with which we are still, mostly, perfectly happy.

Of course, the new victory wasn't absolute. Wherever you see blue and white alyssum or lobelia alternated around the outside of a flower-bed, or red salvias surrounding a thin clump of canna lilies, the high-Victorian garden, though muted, is still alive. Wherever you see a vast monkey-puzzle tree dwarfing a red brick terrace house, a country rectory or a manse, some vanished winter bedding scheme is still remembered.

However, at Hidcote, at Sissinghurst, in every sophisticated 'cottage' garden filled with herbs and old roses, in every border where the colour schemes are carefully worked through, and even in those nasty island beds filled with ericas and dwarf conifers, the late Victorian compromises are alive and well. We are all still late Victorians, even now.

BELHAVEN, 1987

CHAPTER

I

GARDENS OF CROESUS

THE VAST IRON WHEEL OF TASTE THAT HAD spun, for much of the eighteenth century, with such speed and precision that it seemed scarcely to move began to slow down towards the century's end. As it began to swing on its axis like the wheel of a gyroscope, it threw out small showers of tiny sparks: a cluster of picturesque gardens, a sudden brilliant flower garden, an American garden, a few rose arbours, or a heart-shaped flower-bed filled with a mixture of simple annuals.

As the swings became wider and wilder in the 1830s, the showers of sparks became more and more showy and more and more unpredictable. There were sudden bursts of Italianate, or French, or Chinese, or Egyptian gardens, or vast and brilliant parterres filled with exotic plants from the swamps of South America, or immense rockeries intended to model the Alps, with glaciers of crushed marble and spar, populated with real alpine plants and model chamois goats in tin. There were sudden showers of back-to-nature gardens, of gardens filled only for a season with palms and Indian lilies, or of gardens so refined and chilly and classical that they were inhabited only by painted iron casts of Roman antiques.

As the glare from the slowing wheel's streams of sparks increased, it was possible to see more than the gardens of the rich and the stylish. There were gardens everywhere: in dark industrial

cities where artisans cherished the latest variety of
rose or auricula, in front of cramped terraced
houses, in parks and pleasure grounds and tea
gardens. There were even plots of gaudy
bedding plants amongst fresh grey tombstones.
Gardens invaded windowsills, drawing-rooms,
dirty closes and courtyards of ancient cities, or spawned ideas
of ideal 'garden cities' with which to replace them. Gardens

became places where the rich could be even more extravagant, places to be given to the turbulent masses to placate them, or places to store the incredible flood of plants that poured into Britain from all over the world.

It seemed, throughout much of Victorian Britain, that everyone gardened, from great aristocrats and magnates, vying with each other to produce ever vaster conservatories, terraces, and parterres all planted with ever rarer flowers and shrubs, to obscure spinsters, dying curates, artisans, labourers, tradesmen. More surprisingly, almost everyone seems to have written about gardening. The dying curates wrote brave best-sellers completed by an anonymous 'fair hand', the spinsters (from the marvellous muscular Miss Hope of Edinburgh to the egregious 'Rosa' of the *Cottage Gardener*'s pages) charted the changing role of women from delicate flower to muddy painter and designer; artisans and labourers joined florists' societies and sent letters and papers to the increasing number of gardening magazines. Garden books poured from the presses: books for gardening children, for bored housewives, for new-minted members of the middle class in crisp 'third rate' houses in Fulham or Manchester or Goole; books by plant collectors, travellers, gardeners to the peerage (so many of these seemed either to write or to edit that they must scarcely have had time to manage their employers' no doubt very weedy gardens). Reverends wrote comfortable garden books in the home counties, and ministers wrote them in the dampest and remotest parts of Scotland. Landowners' younger brothers wrote penny pamphlets for the destitute cottagers of their brother's estates, half-mad men wrote impossible books for the impossible urban poor.

Though most of this book is about the more modest classes of garden and gardener, and almost everybody with but the tiniest scrap of ground had at least a few flower-beds and a rockery scattered with seashells and broken porcelain, the very rich naturally produced the grandest and often most extraordinary examples. To get a flavour of the period, it is simplest to look at the great prodigies of Victorian gardening first.

Of these vast gardens – like Chatsworth, Trentham, Wimbledon, Cragside, Drummond Castle and Castle Kennedy – there are an enormous number of examples. It sometimes seems as if every great house spent much of the age surrounded by mud, scaffolding and plant baskets. In some of them, the grandee owners evoked memories of their families, or at least of their house's past grandeurs, either by supposedly copying rediscovered designs for its garden or by re-creating gardens based on their own, or their gardener's, reading of early English garden books.

Others, and especially the new magnates of America, who had provided themselves with new houses in Gothic or French style, chose to see themselves as Renaissance or seventeenth-century princelings and adopted only moderately Victorianized schemes culled from European sources. Some, whether owning old or new money, chose the fashionable style of the early Victorian period, which they called, without an enormous amount of justification, 'Italianate', and surrounded their mansions with immense terraces, astonishing fountains, box-edged parterres, statuary, orange trees, and gravel walks that stretched to the horizon. Greedy magnates wanted, and got, everything. Some gardens had alpine rockeries, Elizabethan knot gardens, models of the Great Wall of China, miniature Scottish glens, two-acre conservatories, American gardens, grottoes and Swiss cottages, all in alarming abundance.

The magnificence and expense of some of these gardens was quite remarkable. Probably one of the most astonishing was Trentham Hall, an early seventeenth-century site, renowned for its dullness, owned by the Marquis of Stafford. Work on a vast new scheme began as part of the development of the house undertaken by Sir Charles Barry from 1833, and was prodigious. There were proposals for an immense stone and glass conservatory that was to equal the house in size and form an entire wing. The gardens, whose initial plans were also by Barry, began to take shape almost as soon as the house was begun. An account from a few decades after their partial completion describes the terraces, created from almost flat ground:

2. Italianate magnificence at Trentham, shown on the estate's letterhead. Only the portico now remains.

... the first level is about 200 feet square, and is divided from the second by a stone balustrade. In the centre is a circular plot with a fountain and pond. A flight of circular steps leads to the second level, an oblong enclosure 700 feet long by 500 feet in breadth, divided by a broad gravel path, bordered with trees in tubs, and on each side are ponds. At the far end, overlooking the lake, is a handsome stone terrace 460 feet long, with a statue of Perseus, and a circular stone landing.

The site had been considered very inauspicious for such magnificence. John Claudius Loudon, an influential author and an arbiter of taste, thought that 'We could not help doubting whether even Mr Barry could make anything of this great dull flat place, with its immense mansion, as tame and spiritless as the ground on which it stands; we have seen the plan, however, for the additions and alterations. Let no man henceforth ever despair of a dead flat.' No rich one at any rate – the plans Loudon had seen were very spectacular indeed, and included an island garden in the lake, modelled on Isola Bella. Much of the practical work was at first left to the gardener, Mr Fleming, who had already worked for the Duke of Sutherland at Dunrobin. Though the Italian garden was begun the year before Fleming was appointed, he soon took both practical and design matters in hand. It was he who altered the course of the River Trent (it flowed into one end of the lake), not only as part of a massive drainage system he determined to have for the rather boggy site but also because it rather muddied what had to be clear water.

Mr Fleming also had to enrich the very poor soil of the entire area; it took several years of work to get even the kitchen garden going satisfactorily. That comprised about five acres, a size not unusual for an exceptionally grand household of the day. However, it was an extraordinarily grand five acres. As one contemporary writer remarked: 'Although in every sense of the word a Kitchen-garden, it may nevertheless be traversed by ladies in any weather, so perfectly hard and impervious are the walks.' Over each of these walks was either a pear tunnel (ladies, as we shall see in Chapter 3, were not supposed to get the slightest tan from the sun), or trellis to support Mr Fleming's trained peaches, nectarines and apricots.

On the vast terraces were vast parterres filled with geraniums and pansies, and the conservatory, in its final state as designed by Fleming (no doubt in an attempt to out-do another famous gardener), was held up by no less than forty cast-iron columns. The window sashes of the structure were counterbalanced by large hanging baskets of plants, though it is not clear if the windows closed once these began to dry out and so became lighter.

There was such an enormous acreage of gravelled walks in the garden that it taxed even the resources of the colossal Trentham staff to keep them all clean and weedfree. Undaunted, the head gardener developed a unique piece of machinery to do just this. He put it on show at the Great Exhibition at the Crystal Palace, and it began to save his employer at least part of the £100 a year (that was two men, full-time) that it took just to keep moss from the paths. The new machine was a boiler on wheels, and looked remarkably like one of the equally new railway engines. However, the boiler contained water, with two pounds of salt to every gallon, and the gravel was watered with the boiling mixture.

In an entirely different and rather earlier style was the astonishing flower garden at Wimbledon House. This was another ancient and notable garden site, having been owned by Charles I, then by General Lambert. Inventories over the centuries list astonishing rarities, some of the tougher of which were discovered, gone wild, when Victorian collectors searched the locality.

3. Rustic arbour and plant stand at Wimbledon House, and some of the 200 flower-beds.

Whatever beauties Wimbledon House may once have shown, by the early nineteenth century it occupied a rather ambiguous position – it was on such a scale that few commentators felt themselves in a position to make any but the most oblique criticism. The house, described with some understatement as 'first rate', was set in an undulating park, with lakes and groves of trees. All this was reasonably standard. What was extraordinary was the astonishing flower garden, with the ground totally covered with oval, round and moon-shaped beds, stuffed tight with plants. A contemporary noted:

But the grand feature of the place, in a gardening point of view, is the flower-garden, which occupies upwards of three acres, and contains about two hundred flower beds. These beds are of different shapes and sizes, and they are scattered over the surface with very little regard to regularity or symmetry; the object being, apparently, to get as many beds as possible into the given space, allowing a small strip of grass between them. In point of general design, therefore, this flower-garden has little to recommend it; but, from the great number of beds, and almost endless variety of the kinds and colours of the flowers they contain, it presents a dazzling surface, of the most brilliant colours, mingled together in confusion.

Two hundred flower-beds up to about fifteen feet in diameter might contain approximately 60,000 plants, all, in this case, either annuals or not winter hardy, and often replanted twice or even three times a year. This was a fairly modest requirement.

For sheer scale, some of the Scottish estate gardens, where land was rather cheaper than in the south of Britain, won the palm. When Queen Victoria visited Scotland in 1841 and journeyed to Drummond Castle, passing through villages decorated with the new red or yellow dahlias, her arrival was witnessed by a local journalist, James Buist of Perth. Lord Willoughby d'Eresby, Drummond's owner, had adorned the main entrance not with dahlias but simply with heather. Beyond that, Gaelic-speaking tenants, carefully selected for their looks, were lined up along the immense drive. The journalist, captivated, wrote:

The policy (a Scottish word for pleasure grounds) extends to two miles every way ... On the North there is a beautiful artificial lake, with the foliage depending to the water's edge, and rendered animated and gaudy by the troops of swans ... On the south side, and immediately fronting the principal face of the Castle, lie the matchless flower gardens of Drummond, which, though situated in the north, are as well known by repute to every florist, and every man of cultivated taste in London, as the lion of Northumberland at Charing Cross ... We have no meaner authority than the Duchess of Sutherland for saying that these gardens are unequalled in Europe . . . They have been called Dutch; but the fact is, that the old common garden of Drummond has been transformed by Lord Willoughby into the floral gem which it now is.

He went on, with an entirely Victorian lack of embarrassment at using flattery, 'It reminds the writer of the hanging gardens of Babylon', and he proceeded to describe Drummond terrace by terrace. On the lowest level there was, and still is, if now rather debased, the 'nearly level expanse of the Drummond gardens, laid out in every conceivable form of beauty, containing every floral treasure known in our clime, interspersed with beautiful pieces of statuary, and the walks shorn by the scythe, and levelled by the roller, till they have contained the BEAU IDEAL of a velvet sward . . .'

However, if Drummond or Taymouth had scale to help them, one English garden had, above any other, wealth to ensure its fame, and a gardener of genius to ensure its beauty: Chatsworth. This was, and still remains, stupendous. Its gardener, whom we shall meet often in these pages, was Joseph Paxton. Here, in a garden already containing magnificent seventeenth-century features, he created for the Duke of Devonshire a new paradise of immense rocky waterfalls, shaded gorges, nearly two acres of conservatory constructed on entirely new principles, formal canals with astonishing fountains, and parterres in the newest taste. Although the conservatory's builder, poor Mr Mankey, despite desperate advertising throughout the 1840s, eventually went bankrupt, the conservatories he built saw the first flowers of the astonishing waterlily *Victoria regia*. The Chatsworth glasshouses also saw the first flowering of innumerable new introductions, whether huge specimens of exotic orchids like the one eventually named *Dendrobium paxtonii*, or plants like some of the *Verbena* species that went on to become popular bedding plants in the tiniest of gardens.

Curiously, for all the magnificence and expense of these colossal structures and the interest of the plants that they contained, glasshouses, at least in the early part of the Victorian period, were a masculine preserve, and for an odd reason. It was believed that perfume had an adverse effect on the health, particularly of ladies, but also of anyone of refined breeding. A writer, probably Paxton himself, suggested of orchid houses that: 'Not one in ten of the houses expressly devoted to their culture, can be entered by the most robust among the higher classes, much less by delicate persons or by ladies, without experiencing highly uncomfortable and overpowering sensations, and entailing unpleasant and even dangerous consequences. Everyone will acknowledge that this is a state of things which urgently demands some remedial measures, if such can be applied consistently with the safety and prosperity of the plants.'

Of course Chatsworth, too, had its vast bedding schemes, and outdoors was entirely in keeping with the conservatory interiors. The bedding arrangements were designed early in the century by Paxton himself. He began to popularize his own geometrical plans by publishing rather watered-down variants in the horticultural press, so that even middle-class readers could emulate at least part of the gardens of those socially far above them.

Bedding plants were the mainspring of high-Victorian gardening. By mid century there were hordes of nurserymen selling job lots of bedding plants for middle- and lower-class gardens (one London nurseryman sent out, each season, 80,000 plants of any one variety of geranium, and most nurserymen stocked at least 100 varieties – then there were verbenas, calceolarias, fuchsias, and so on), but grand gardens almost always used plants from their own glasshouses. Indeed, the new engineering possibilities of cast iron and cheaper glass (once the associated taxes were repealed) made the propagation and overwintering of all the new bedding plants, and so bedding itself, possible. It was estimated in the 1850s that even an ordinary middling landowner's garden, with a fairly simple design, might need something approaching 100,000 bedding plants a year.

For example, at Thornham Hall in Suffolk, all the flower-beds contained between 200 and 300 plants each, and there were about seventy-five beds. They contained all the usual plants, though the gardeners also put out more interesting things like *Felicia*,

Gaillardia, *Cuphea*, *Lantana* and *Gazania*. Throughout most of the 1850s there were also seventy-five smaller beds, and each of those contained between twenty-five and thirty plants, so the total for an average summer planting must have been a very modest 16,000 plants. If that isn't too surprising, it is important to remember not only that they were all planted in a very short space of time, often a week or so in early June (they lasted until the end of September, and were then rehoused under glass for the winter), but that there was often a spring and a winter bedding scheme as well.

4. The parterre at Castle Ashby, using 20,000 plants and some subtle colours.

By 1871 the Thornham Hall bedding scheme included not only tender plants from South America but also some of the brand new pansies like 'Sandbeck Gem' or 'Pride of Stafford'. The gardener planted 4,000 of them in 1870, and planned for 8–10,000 in 1871. Although critics of violas claimed that they didn't flower much in bad seasons, he maintained that they did if they were well fed. He mixed them with Mangle's pelargonium (still to be found) or 'Beaton's Variegated Nosegay' (now lost). Though the colours must have clashed, 10,000 visitors admired the whole ensemble very much, and ladies especially were reported to have liked the pansies, calling them 'beautiful and so sweetly innocent'.

Thornham Hall was modest indeed. The tremendous parterre at Castle Ashby was designed for the Marquess of Northampton by Joseph Newton of Oxford Terrace. It was planted up on what Newton hoped to establish as a new 'shading principle'. It isn't now clear how this was done, though presumably each section of the parterre was planted with various shades of one colour to get a needlework effect. Each of the parterre's squares had sides of 110 feet and was filled with curlicue box-work. Each square needed 5,000 flowering plants every time it was planted.

Newton was, understandably, a strong supporter of the parterre. Its design provided him with an income, and its possession sometimes flattered the ancient lineage of his patrons. While some merely alluded to such things by their fake 'historicism', others actually copied, in flowers, the family coat of arms (some aristocratic gardeners still do this, though the sight of so many not too dissimilar municipal 'flower clocks' should put them off).

Victorian prodigiousness was shown not only by the quantities of plants put in the ground, or by the cost of the conservatories built, but also in the pretensions of the work undertaken. One aspect of this was shown in the constant attempts by some gardeners to recreate or even out-do the gardens of the past. Naturally in a garden like Chatsworth, owned by someone as enormously rich and aristocratic as the Duke of Devonshire, no particular need was felt to recreate lost grandeur; the duke was perfectly content to create grandeur now. Other less grand persons had, though, a less simple attitude to the past, and felt their past reflected too poorly on their present status.

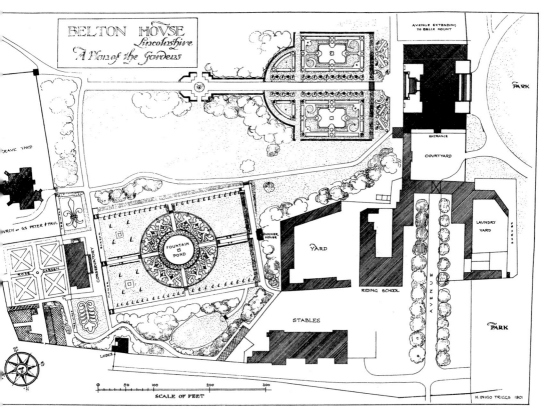

5. The Victorian garden at Belton, formal, but a shadow of the original scheme.

Belton House, owned by Lord Brownlow, had had a notable formal garden in the late seventeenth century, one quite grand enough to have been illustrated by the topographical artists Kypp and Knyff. By the end of the eighteenth century, the park had been rather well landscaped, but in 1850 Lord Brownlow, following one aspect of the taste of his time, wanted a formal environment once more for his lovely house. As he knew what the gardens had looked like in the seventeenth century, it seemed an easy matter to recreate them. He certainly claimed that he was making a replica of what had once been there.

The results were rather surprising, and considerably less grand than the original. Photographs show a very Victorian-looking scheme indeed. A few ideas from the original plan have indeed been used, but they ended up giving little idea of the original richness of effect. The alternate obelisks and balls made of yew were set in the sort of carpet bedding that would have quite horrified seventeenth-century owners. Elsewhere, modern tea roses were mixed with fairly modern herbaceous flowers giving borders that immediate look, to modern eyes, of the mid nineteenth century.

Rather similar recreations even took place at Hatfield, the seat of the ancient Cecil family. There, the immense parterres were based on designs taken from seventeenth-century books. The results were more satisfactory. However, even there was seen the age's passion for piling embellishment upon embellishment. Not only are the surrounding balustrades entirely Victorian, but the beds, properly seventeenth-century in shape, were studded with central standard tea roses, yuccas or cordylines.

The flower-bed and the conservatory were not the only garden elements used as badges of wealth and extravagance. Whatever the style of the garden, and whether aristocratic or suburban, everyone had to have certain elements which have become identified almost as *the* Victorian garden: rockeries, rustic summer houses, arboreta, ferneries and rose gardens.

Of these, the rockery gave rise to some of the most astonishing prodigies of all. Books and articles in praise of rockeries show the quite extraordinary lengths to which Victorian self-deception could be taken. Of all the other garden elements, the rockery has had by far the longest life (it is still with us). It is dealt with in more detail in Chapter 6, but it is worth looking at just a few examples here.

In the 1840s the rockery was commonly made out of almost any sort of junk – broken porcelain plates, broken bricks, flints, tattered statuary. By 1853 the *Book of the Garden* suggests that it should be made more tastefully of

stones, the fused masses of brick procured from brick kilns, or indeed, any coarse material most convenient to be got. These are built up in the most rugged and mis-shapen forms imaginable and afterward covered over with Roman cement, and formed into recesses, projections, and overhanging crags, according to the taste of the artist. Sufficient apertures are left for receiving soil, in which rock plants are planted. When the whole is perfectly dry and set, it is painted with oil paint to represent veined or stratified granite, or any other kind of natural rockwork that may be desired. Here is no unnatural mixture of shells, fossils, petrifications, architectural remains, and natural masses of stone huddled together, as if it were the omnium-gatherum of the vestiges of creation.

6. The rock garden at Hoole House, once the most fashionable in Britain, encircling the rows of round flower-beds.

Rockeries were soon so important a part of the garden scene that there were, for a while, hordes of rockery designers. Even so, in the capital, most rockeries were, at mid-century, often just a pile of stones around the roots of a tree, or a heap of stone, broken bricks, glass debris or old tree roots. Elsewhere, some were already extraordinarily grand.

While many rockeries were unashamedly unnatural in appearance (deliberate artifice, as we shall see, was a sought-for quality in the century's early years and the taste hung on till its end), one of the most natural-looking examples was at Redleaf near Tunbridge Wells. This was made of real rocks, set together to look as if they were part of a natural outcrop (the sort that garden books still suggest).

The most unnatural rockery was in the Duke of Marlborough's private garden at Blenheim. Though this was actually formed on a scar of natural rock, it had been hewn into zig-zag paths with numerous hand-cut niches on each side to receive plants. However, most of the niches were cased in spar, a richly coloured, expensive and rather glittery natural rock. The final result was a rich and sparkling effect, which can have done little to make the plants it contained look at home.

Hybrid in effect was the rockery at Syon Park, where a pile of only moderately large granite stones had been shipped from Scotland. Assembled, they were compared by most London journalists 'to the scenery of a Highland glen'. Only Jane Loudon was brave enough to 'confess there does not appear to me the slightest resemblance. In fact, the Syon rockwork is so over-powered by the magnificent conservatory in front ... that it becomes quite a secondary object ... It consists of masses of granite, intermixed with broken capitals planted with ornamental flowering plants, principally exotic...' However, in her books she approved of some which must, in their hey-day, have appeared equally odd. She much admired

the most remarkable of all ... that of Lady Broughton, at the Hoole, Cheshire, which, indeed, stands quite alone, the only one of its kind. The design for this rockwork was taken from a small model, representing the mountains of Savoy, with the valley of Chamouni ... The plants are all strictly alpine – the only liberty taken being the mingling of the alpine plants of hot and cold countries, or rather of different elevations, together, and this is contrived very ingeniously, by placing fragments of dark stone to absorb the heat, round those that require most warmth, and fragments of white stone to reflect the heat, round those that require to be kept cool.

Attempts to reproduce natural mountain scenery in more or less miniature form remained a theme throughout the nineteenth century, and eventually gave rise to some splendid gardening rows.

Another major badge of wealth, even for suburban gardens (it is important to remember that the early Victorian concept of 'suburban' included properties most of which are now used as golf clubs, nursing homes or borstals), was the arboretum or pinetum.

An arboretum, vaguely considered, is merely a collection of indigenous or exotic trees, disposed according to the taste of the proprietor ... In modern arboretums, every genus or tribe of plants is grouped together, more or less densely in estates of considerable circuit, or in botanical or other public gardens. Such departments create a variation, and sometimes a pleasing one. They also furnish the beholder, at one gaze, with a knowledge of the hardy ligneous species of every genus, tribe or order of plants, and their position in the natural system of botany.

All very laudable, and many surviving arboreta are today very beautiful. However, they were also wonderful places to show wealth (it takes a lot of space to collect trees) and status (the first specimen of such and such a species in the country, or one planted by a member of the royal family – a social gambit which still continues).

Even without a rockery or an arboretum, garden mania soon invaded the actual house itself and in unlikely and new ways, partly made possible by new technology, partly by a wider spread of the new wealth. For middle-class homes, nice hardy plants became, at least for a few months at a time, denizens of the drawing-room. It is quite common to find pictures of, for example, 'Yuccas, New Zealand Flax, Palms, India-rubber, and Ivy grouped around a Sofa Arbour in the Drawing-room'. To do this sort of thing properly there was a thriving trade in curious metal frames, rather like garden arches on castors, to place over each over-stuffed neo-classical sofa.

At the grandest social levels, things were correspondingly expensive. At a ball given at Bridgewater House, St James, attended by the Prince and Princess of Wales, the public rooms were turned into a jungle, apart from the incongruous crimson baize carpet and grey granite columns. On this occasion new technology, money and gardening combined. A magazine correspondent wrote:

> During the past season, Mr John Wills, one of our most extensive floral decorators, has used huge blocks of real ice tastefully arranged in the form of obelisks and rockeries. These, when illuminated from behind and wreathed in *Ficus repens*, Creeping Jenny, Ivy, *Lygodium scandens* or Virginia creeper, are very beautiful, and give a most delicious idea of coolness even during the hottest summer weather.

Fun though all this must have been, not all the taste shown by even the richest of patrons was universally admired. Bizarre rockeries were common, but the vogue for the 'rustic', which started in Regency times, went on to produce some equally odd structures. 'Rustic work' made use of odds and ends collected from the forest to make seats, tables, plant baskets, pergolas, even whole summerhouses or hermit's huts. All these were supposed to look enchantingly natural, and in fact probably did make a refreshing if uncomfortable change from the over-upholstered and densely furnished main rooms of the house. However, the Victorian urge to decorate took over even these 'toys', and numbers of 'craft' techniques became devoted to their beautification. Rustic sofas became so covered in twigs, roots and cones that they began to look like pieces of woody coral. By the 1850s arbours, moss houses and covered seats were similarly elaborated. Thousands of such things still exist, now usually lop-sided and half rotten. Some are very pretty indeed, but all are just a tiny fraction of the enormous quantities that once graced almost every garden. The vogue was so strong that 'rustic' seats, vases, bird baths, sundials were soon appearing, made in all sorts of entirely non-rustic materials like cast iron, terracotta and concrete. Most seem to have been designed for urban consumers, whose contact with the countryside and therefore with the sources of the materials for construction was slight: few of them are in the least attractive.

If the rich were inexorably drawn to the excess that their wealth allowed, it was impossible for those within, if even partly, their orbit not to emulate them. Some of the gentry gardens became places to visit in their own right, and made their owners well known in the gardening world. The most extraordinary of these even had a waiting room built to accommodate those who arrived on open days too early to be allowed in. Biddulph Grange had such a garden, and was the subject of a series of articles in the *Gardener's Chronicle* of 1862. It was quite extraordinary. Parts of the scheme remain today much as they were then, though enough has vanished to remove the remarkable density of garden 'features' crammed into a rather small area.

Biddulph Grange had a lean-to greenhouse for tender rhododendrons and camellias, as well as glasshouses for all the fruit crops that could be cultivated in them; terraces; private gardens (the general public were not allowed access to these); a couple of parterre gardens, one for coloured sand (an idea taken from some seventeenth-century gardens, which caught a number of Victorian imaginations), one devoted to all the new verbenas being bred by the nurserymen; a large patch of hardy rhododendrons surrounding a pond with an islet set in its middle; narrow winding walks and tunnels; endless rockwork, part of which was an imitation of the Great Wall of China, planted about with bamboos and some of the newly imported hostas; a pinetum (an arboretum devoted to pine species, with its conifers planted, for some reason, on irregular banks); a bowling green; a quoit ground; a raised terraced crescent, again possibly modelled on seventeenth-century features, and planted with strips of rhododendrons (as in the

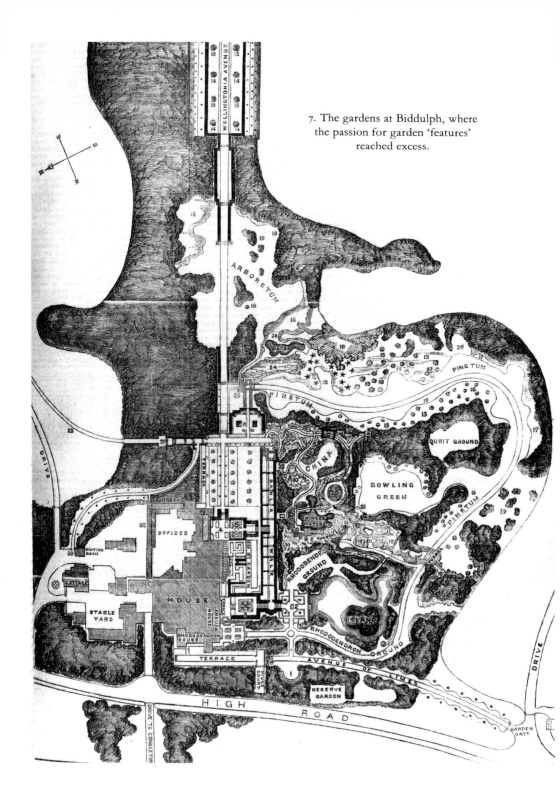

7. The gardens at Biddulph, where the passion for garden 'features' reached excess.

grandest of the surviving and full-scale seventeenth-century examples at Castle Kennedy); and an Italian parterre built around four very un-Italian araucarias (monkey-puzzle trees, see page 153). However, after all that, what impressed one journalist most of all was that

after leaving the *Wellingtonia* avenue, which is stopped by a very large and handsome vase, this walk ascends a hill so abruptly, through a mass of old plantation, that being covered with the yellow sandstone of the district, and terminated by a rocky knoll, through which there is a winding, invisible tunnel, the walk presents the appearance of a large obelisk, backed by a dark hill, and has a most curious and startling effect.

Even more lay in wait. The writer went on:

Between figs. 4 and 6 is an ornamental cherry orchard, the trees being planted on little mounds, surrounded and supported by closely clipped *Cotoneaster*, and turned into a pretty pendant bell shape, the intermediate spaces being grass ... [then] ... we enter the Egyptian court, shut in by yew hedges and decorated by stone sphinxes ... a yew pyramid over the tunnel to the east, which last is entered through a fine Egyptian doorway [this still exists and is indeed very handsome]. This tunnel leads to a somewhat darkened apartment, with cavern views etc., and there are some adjoining rooms adapted for rural fêtes. The whole opens, but through a porch in the style of an old Cheshire black and white timbered cottage, towards the Pinetum ...

Yet still it wasn't finished:

By another route from the terrace to the west of the Egyptian Court, a singular and most characteristic Chinese scene is approached, through an admirable root garden ... A Chinese temple and terrace occur ... some ruins and part of a supposed Chinese wall ... [with] elevated rockwork ... Moutan paeonies.

The Chinese garden was full of idols, joss houses, and the so-called great wall (really a rather elongated rockery complete with

31

towers), temples, winding paths, winding ponds, and even a couple of dragon-shaped beds filled with red gravel. The whole area was planted with hostas, skimmias, bamboos, ferns, Japanese maples, aucubas and *Cardiocrinum giganteum*, and also various American plants and purple beeches. Every part of the garden was kept to a meticulous standard, perhaps financed by the entrance fee. It must have been rather like an American theme park, and was open free on the first Monday of each summer month, though any other day cost 5s. It was, of course, closed on Sunday.

While Biddulph was the result of the gardening mania of a county family, the same sort of passion for excess took place in the suburbs of almost every major city. Slightly earlier than Biddulph, the best known of the London prodigy gardens was that of a Mrs Lawrence (see page 253), the wife of a surgeon, who transformed twenty-eight acres near Drayton Green in the late 1820s and 30s. The house, known as the Lawrencian villa, had a garden that was 'unquestionably the most remarkable of its size in the neighbourhood of London, on account of the great variety and beauty which have been created in it, under the supervision of Mrs Lawrence, F.H.S., the lady of the celebrated surgeon of that name'. It contained four separate decorative gardens, a small farm, and a rather compressed sort of parkland. Loudon thought that 'the secret of producing this variety consists in introducing numerous small groups of trees and shrubs, sometimes combined with flowers or climbers etc., other times with rockwork, and with statues, fountains, basketwork and so on'.

Mrs Lawrence was fortunate in having six gardeners '... with one or two women for collecting insects and dead leaves, and during winter, three. It is only further necessary to add, that all the different scenes in these gardens, all the beds of flowers, pieces of rockwork, etc., as well as the greenhouses, and hot-houses, were designed by Mrs Lawrence herself, and executed under her direction.' She plainly liked the picturesque style, for Loudon's woodcuts show dense and intertwined planting, often with details like a rustic arch framing a vase with a view of the paddock behind. However, she also had a long Italian walk dotted with statuary, urns, and an awful fountain, a so-called French parterre with rather little French about it, a pond in a wirework basket swathed with roses and with a tented Turkish pavilion beyond, and even a rockwork arch with a fountain at either side, surmounted by a kneeling Cupid.

8. The Italian Walk at Mrs Lawrence's villa near Drayton Green.

A later edition of the *Suburban Gardener* (edited by Loudon's wife, Jane) went on:

... this villa may be considered as a model of its particular kind ... Everyone cannot have so many fountains or form rockwork of spars, fossil organic remains, and other geological specimens brought from distant parts of the country, but everyone may sink in the ground a few small wooden cisterns lined with lead, and supply them with water by hand, as it evaporates in the summer season. Some of these may serve as brilliant spots to attract the eye, and others as habitats for aquatic plants. The margins of basins of this sort can be effectually disguised with rockwork.

Jane Loudon describes some of the new additions, such as rockwork fountains supporting weird figures, more paths, more flower baskets, one backed by a pair of simpering nymphs arising out of a picturesque planting. However, her tastes were sharper than those her husband had allowed himself. 'We are aware,' she wrote,

that there are many persons, of a simple and severe taste, who will think that the Lawrencian Villa is too highly ornamented with statues and sculptures; but allowance must be made for individual taste, for devotion to the subject, and for the limited extent of the place. Were Mrs Lawrence in possession of a villa of one hundred acres, there can be no doubt that she would display on her lawn a taste as appropriate to a residence of that extent, as the taste she has displayed at Drayton Green.

Mrs Lawrence may not have noticed the barbs, but she did get a larger garden.

But whatever opulent gardens had in the way of armies of gardeners, parterres the size of football pitches, or rockeries like scaled-down Mont Blancs with glaciers of crushed marble, the richness of the garden culture (if it can be so called) is also expressed by the diversity of people who care about gardens and gardening, and by the diversity of the things they do. Victorian Britain and, later in the century, America, seems to have teemed with energetic gardeners. This energy was fuelled not only by a proliferation of business ventures, from publishers of garden part-works to manufacturers of gadgets like the essential 'Flor-umbra' (see page 177) or the patent earwig catcher, but also by extraordinary gardeners like Mr Thomson of Clovenfords near Gala-

shiels, who, when he retired, built himself at that village a vast
glassed-over vineyard and produced many tons of ripe grapes for
the London market.

There was an explosion of gardening at all social levels. This
is best shown by the sudden burst of excitement about gardening
societies. These ranged from those devoted to special plants, like
the Ipswich Cucumber Society which had its first show in 1842,
the Pelargonium Society set up on 14 June of the same year, or
the Pansy Society, based in Falkirk, which had its first show in
1844, to more generalized societies like the York Grand Floricultural and Horticultural Society, at whose great exhibition of
1842 a first prize of £100 was offered for the best stand of twenty-
four dahlia blooms (the prize was approximately the salary for a
head gardener for an entire year), and, of course, the London
Horticultural Society, whose shows were famous and remain so,
under a different title.

While most of the horticultural societies were set up for town-
based enthusiasts, 'cottage garden societies' sprang up to encourage rural gardeners. Some societies were set up by the local gentry
to teach the local workers how to use their small gardens to
improve their living conditions; others sprang from humbler
origins and less worthy motives. By 1860 there were such societies
scattered liberally over the countryside, often carefully kept separate from the local horticultural group, especially during the
show season. At most local shows, fancy fruit and flowers from
the gardens of the gentry usually won (still often the case, except
perhaps for dahlias and chrysanthemums). At cottagers' shows
the rural middle class were sometimes allowed to enter, as at a
show in Wales in 1861, when 'a few plants and fruits for decoration were sent by the neighbouring gentry, but in no case was
a farthing of the funds applied to any but its legitimate use, for
though farmers and village tradesmen were invited to compete,
it was perfectly understood that if any prize was awarded to their
productions, the value reverted to the funds of the Society. Prizes
were given for collections and also for each kind of vegetable
and fruit; for window plants in collections of three, and single
specimens of cut flowers.' One contemporary wrote: 'Some of

35

the collections of cut flowers were very beautiful, and I recollect a bouquet of these (in an old china vase) composed of Ferns, Foxgloves, Grasses, Orchids, Honeysuckles, Eglantine etc. managed so artfully and elegantly that the Queen herself would have been proud of it.'

Another example was the charmingly named Bletchingley and Nutfield Cottage Garden Society; this consisted of just two parishes covering about 9,000 acres. The whole area was agricultural and contained about 250 cottages with gardens, all inhabited by agricultural workers, mechanics and gardeners. The membership

9. The ideal cottager's house; beehives, climbing roses and a little bedding.

was divided into classes so that the latter didn't always win. All the cottagers' gardens were inspected by the judges (no doubt the local gentry) and there were four winners per class; each was awarded a grand 5s. prize. Entries included potatoes, cabbages, carrots, peas, onions, parsnips, turnips, rhubarb, red and white beans, blackcurrants, gooseberries and raspberries (about thirty crops in all).

In Lincolnshire the Sleaford Cottage Garden Society had yet another set of rules: the winner on two consecutive years was debarred from further entry (something that many modern flower shows should still consider), but got a 10s. prize if his or her garden was still up to scratch. Entry classes for that society included the amusing 'Basket of fruit, vegetables and flowers, arrangement to matter'. The reporter inclined to the view that the society had actually improved local cottage gardens.

However, perhaps the main energies of the whole society-forming movement were directed to the florists' societies. There had, of course, been 'florists' flowers', that is, groups of flowers such as hyacinths, tulips and anemones, which had attracted passionate admirers since the seventeenth century. In Victorian Britain the number of newly imported flower species was so vast that all sorts of new things had caught the florist's eye. Suitable groups of plants needed, above all, to be easily crossed, with plenty of resultant variations. It didn't matter too much about the actual scale of the plants, or even the ease with which they were grown. Mid-Victorian grandees took up rhododendrons, camellias and orchids as their florists' group; poorer folk took up violas and pansies, calceolarias, dahlias and chrysanthemums, or kept going on with their pinks, picotees, sweet williams and auriculas.

While the old florists' flowers were continually said to be going out of fashion, they were never entirely eclipsed, and some of the old societies devoted to their culture still exist. However, the superstructure of nurserymen/breeders built upon them did decay, though as many of the nurseries that closed down were on the outskirts of major cities, the owners of the land no doubt retired to reasonable prosperity. New nurseries, devoted to new flowers, sprang up to replace them, like Mr Chater's which specialized in hollyhocks, or others growing new gladioli, geraniums, penstemons and paeonies.

All this pressure for new varieties (partly economic, for second-season varieties were worth almost nothing) caused an extraordinarily fast development of new types of flower. John Claudius Loudon wrote in the late 1830s:

Floriculture is, at present, unquestionably the most flourishing department of gardening; and nothing in this way can be more remarkable than the immense number of roses, dahlias, and hearts-eases raised and sold by commercial growers in Britain, France and Germany. Even the Chinese chrysanthemum has been subject to British improvement, and a number of new and beautiful varieties have lately been raised from seeds saved at Oxford, and other places in England, and in Guernsey. The establishment of flower shows by the London Horticultural Society, at their garden, has been the means of producing some splendid specimens of what may be called botanical floriculture.

Only a decade later some sophisticated gardeners were beginning to find it all too much, and one agonized writer proclaimed in 1842:

What in the name of moderation, is one to do with 'four thousand new seedling, shrubby calceolarias, all named varieties', beautiful as they undoubtedly are? ... Woe unto the flower that becomes the fashion! It is as sure to be spoilt as the belle of the season. How well I remember the coming out, the first introduction, of that brilliant little creature, the scarlet verbena! It was engaged a hundred deep the moment it appeared; the gardening world was utterly infatuated, and fifteen florists, balked in their possession of it, hanged themselves in their own potting-houses.

Rules for how a perfect flower should look were of tremendous importance to the florists and to the nurserymen. Varieties that won at the shows sold at great premiums, and various attempts were made at standardizing the sorts that won throughout the country. Naturally, what was the 'perfect' flower aroused considerable debate, even acrimony. Various writers claimed to have put forward the 'correctest' set of rules, none more vociferous than William Glenny. This gentleman, who advertised himself as an 'improver of estates, sale and purchase of property, advisory work on fruit, flowers and vegetables, as well as design of grounds, planting, construction of conservatories etc.', wrote *Gardening for the Million* in 1847. A snappy title like this covered all sorts of topics, including the statement that florists' flowers take up too much time, and working men should grow only useful plants! This didn't discourage him from going on to proclaim: 'THE STANDARDS OF PERFECTION FOR THE PROPERTIES OF FLOWERS AND PLANTS ORIGINATED AND DEFINED BY GEORGE GLENNY F.H.S.'

I believe that there are many old florists, who would give their ears had the idea of publishing certain rules for judging flowers by a perfect model, instead of by comparison with general favourites crossed their mind instead of mine; they would make great sacrifices to be the author of 'The Properties of flowers and Plants'.

He does, among the fogs of delusion, admit that Maddock and Loudon have already published some ideas. However, he says of most of these that they contradict themselves; this, in the light of his next few pages, is quite surprising.

However, it is not to be disputed, that Maddock was much before the cultivators of his day in defining the 'criterion' of a flower, as I have been before other people of my day. Nobody can question the fact, that I struck out into a new path; the only point they have to settle is whether I am in the right or the wrong road.

Let me ask some who feel inclined to detract from my merit, if there be any, of originating any standards, where they will find the criterions for the Geranium? the Pansy? Rose? Fuchsia? Chrysanthemum? Verbena? Cineraria? Rhododendron? Azalea? and half a score others, which none had ventured to mention? And why was I to be the subject of constant injustice and robbery by persons who ought to be the last to take so mean an advantage?

Mr Wood of Nottingham, Mr Slater, of Manchester, and some others, gave the properties of certain flowers, which had previously been mentioned by Maddock, Loudon, and others, as if they were fair game. It was unkind, however, and unhandsome, not to give the authority on THE POINTS WHICH I ORIGINATED.

When examined, the standards of which he was so proud seem to have been more or less the same in every flower – perfect circularity, and either perfectly flat, or only half-globular. This applied to tulips (concave) as well as to dahlias and chrysanthemums (convex). All sorts of flower had to have smooth-edged petals, and some of his systematizations seem deliberately outrageous. How can anyone have grown a hollyhock thus: '... there is not fixed height for the plants; but the flowers should begin one foot from the ground, and open all at once'? His botanical perceptions were equally bizarre, and often just plain wrong. Of hollyhocks again: 'The centre, which is composed of florets, should form half a ball, and the more it covers the principal or guard petals the better.' Hollyhock flowers are not composed of florets. However silly a lot of the book was, it sold and sold, reaching its seventeenth edition in as few years.

In spite of the consequent millions of confused gardeners, whole new sorts of floristic endeavour arose, some directly pre-figuring the flower-arrangers of today, and flowers and their arrangement soon became an important preoccupation of nineteenth-century hosts and hostesses. At least in London, it gave rise to competitions in the new 'art' form, as well as to quantities of professional table and room decorators.

By the 1870s London had popular shows for the competitive exhibition of 'dinner table arrangements'. Elaborate rules were given for the size of table; it had to have settings for between twelve and twenty guests (nothing smaller or larger was possible!). Competition exhibitors had to provide their own cutlery, dishes and glasses. Tables had to be three feet ten inches high, so that the inspectors were at same height as if they were sitting. No lamps or candles were allowed.

While Victorian domestic life developed, a whole series of crafts developed around the garden, designed to fill the hours of idle ladies. There was also a vast and rapidly increasing urban working class. These people, often gardenless and often recruited from the countryside, where they had once had gardens of their own, or at least with some degree of tenure, also needed to be catered for. If these city dwellers were not totally destitute, then some of the great new dark cities began to provide green places for them to go.

For private use, the growth of the allotment movement was of immense importance both in London and in the provinces. However, those who felt disinclined (or much too tired) to garden for themselves could visit the 'tea garden', or, as the century progressed, some of the new urban 'parks'.

The 'tea garden' was an ancient institution; some of them dated from Elizabethan times, and many still offered an Elizabethan diet of cakes and ale. However, many of them also offered more exciting fare, and had done so throughout the eighteenth century. Many allowed patrons, even the poorest, a whole variety of carnal pleasures, and even some dangers, for wherever purses and jewels (however simple) could be taken, and modesty be surrendered, thieves and thugs gathered.

Some of the sites of these tea gardens have marvellous histories. There was, for instance, the notorious Highbury Barn, a vast and ancient barn on a site once owned by Priors of the Knights of St John of Jerusalem. A place of resort by the eighteenth century, it had by the century's end charming gardens, bowling greens, with courts for all manner of ball games. As its owners became prosperous, more land and more buildings were added, until the main barn became a sort of conference centre for clubs and societies as well as for chance visitors. By 1800 it could accommodate up to 800 diners, and had kitchen facilities large enough to cope with seventy geese in front of the fire. By 1841 it was even larger, and when the Licensed Victuallers held a dinner, more than 3,000 people attended.

Vauxhall Gardens, a place of resort for Londoners for several centuries, advertised, apart from the attractive gardens, 'various objects of attraction, the principal of which is the representation of the late fire at Hamburgh, painted by Mr Marshall. The scale upon which it is painted may be judged when it is known that the spire of St Nicholas is nearly one hundred and fifty feet tall, and may be seen from the different bridges.'

Similar establishments, if less grand and less respectable, could be found in most parts of the teeming capital. One in north London had, by 1858, a vast dancing platform 4,000 feet square, with orchestra, ironwork roof with gas lamps, and yet more lamps on railings and on pillars in the centre. Vast throngs assembled there on summer evenings.

For dancers tired of the heat, or inflamed in other ways, there was a more secluded part of the garden, with an avenue flanked by female statues holding less brightly lit lamps. This led to even darker parts of the five acres.

There were, of course, other public entertainments to be had as well as just music to dance to. Leotard the gymnast performed daily all summer in 1862, Blondin in 1868, and the Siamese twins in 1869. However, that part of north London was becoming rapidly respectable, aided by the growth of the suburban railways, and the Gardens' neighbours finally got its licence revoked in 1870. It closed down soon after.

At other gardens, some of the public shows were extraordinary. Chabert the fire-eater, in 1826, '. . . after swallowing arsenic, oxalic acid, boiling oil and molten lead without, it is said, feeling any inconvenience . . . entered a large heated oven, supported by four pillars, and there cooked a leg of lamb and rump steak, which he proceeded to divide amongst the spectators . . .'

At the disreputable Flora Gardens in Camberwell, shows like 'Lady Godiva' were staged (in 1854), with a torchlight procession to follow the naked lady. The almost equally riotous 'Montpelier Tea Garden' at Walworth staged an unpleasant cricket match between eleven one-legged pensioners (from Greenwich), and eleven one-armed ones. Attendant gentry placed bets of up to 1,000 guineas on the outcome.

Many provincial towns had similar institutions (for instance, there was what must have been a very sedate tea garden at Enderby, near Leicester, which had a strawberry garden, a plant nursery and a wilderness with serpentine walks, all being advertised for sale in 1849).

However, the various public disturbances of 1830 and 1848 began to frighten the more prosperous patrons away. So the tea garden, which had been important in forming the public taste in gardening (perhaps it was in one of those that Mrs Lawrence developed her passion for gimcrack and glitter), began to lose influence to the more sober pleasures of the park, or other sorts of urban garden. Though we shall look at the formations of these in more detail in Chapter 6, it is worth noting here just how grand some of the public spaces designed for the urban masses

10. The second grand terrace below Paxton's Crystal Palace at Sydenham.

could be, and the important role that they played in forming Victorian taste.

As the tea gardens declined, London parks like that at Battersea became increasingly popular and increasingly opulent. The capital accumulated new parks throughout the century, and most big cities, particularly the wealthy industrial ones, followed suit. The most stupendous of all was that around the Sydenham Crystal Palace. Although that building was designed by the century's greatest gardener, and although it contained innumerable plants, because it was first set in Hyde Park its immediate environs were left as parkland and so not gardened. The first Crystal Palace therefore played rather little part in the development of popular gardening taste.

Once it was dismantled, re-designed and enlarged, then re-assembled at Sydenham by the Crystal Palace Company, the

surrounding gardens became vastly important. Designed by
Paxton himself, no expense was spared in the assembling of plants.
In 1852, the fabulous collection of rare trees and shrubs owned
by the once famous nursery of Loddiges was purchased and
replanted in its entirety. It represented one of the most complete
collections in the country. Paxton commissioned huge amounts
of garden statuary, urns, fountains, seats, edgings and balustrades.
It was all stupendous. The new palace was larger than the original
by 50 per cent. There were sixteen and a half miles of iron
columns, and twenty-five acres of glass. The whole building was
treated as a gigantic conservatory, with, at the south end, vast
plantings of rhododendrons, azaleas and camellias. There were
huge clumps of rather incongruous aloes near the Pompeian court
(South Africa mixed with Roman Italy), new and rare Norfolk
Island pines near the Birmingham Industrial Court. Some fashionable palms grew in gardens facing the Egyptian Court, and also
'Two fine India-rubber plants – a plant that has lately acquired a
considerable interest and value, on account of the variety and
importance of the use to which its sap is applied' (gutta percha
was soon to be found throughout the garden, as hose pipes,
sheeting, boots, waterproofs and so on).

Elsewhere, the building was filled with potted pomegranates,
olives, oranges, *Drimys winteri*, date palms and the whole panoply
of Victorian conservatory flora. Outdoors, there were sheets of
the old yellow calceolaria bought in from every nursery in London
and beyond, together with thousands upon thousands of other
plants, all set out in the 'massing system' (we call it 'bedding').
Bands of these plants were used to edge shrubberies of rhododendrons, camellias, azaleas and roses.

Old tree stumps were hollowed out and used as rustic flower-
pots. Thousands of iron seats were provided. The Crystal Palace
was hailed as truly the 'people's own garden'.

So, in 1854, as war raged in the Crimea, the Queen opened the
new building:

On the central platform there stood a royal family unequalled by any
of its contemporaries whether regarded as an illustration of English

domestic happiness, or as an example of a monarch wisely careful to provide the home improvements and pleasures of her subjects, whilst as discreetly directing their energies in the waging of one of the most world-wide wars that ever impended over Europe. That group told by its example, that however high the public duties, however difficult and weighty the cares with which our nature can be called upon to sustain, there are sympathies within the home circle that sustain, and encourage and aid – upon which the heart, as well as the mind, can lean with a certainty of being strengthened... The group further gave evidence that those possessed of power, almost without limit, to command all that is rare and vivid of enjoyment, still felt that this enjoyment would be purchased too dear if it excluded the quieter pleasures of home; that the enjoyment would be scarcely worthy of the name if it could not be shared by all members of the circle...

The Crystal Palace was a tremendous success commercially and socially. One writer of 1854 saw it in political terms, writing

that the more people have of new plants, and the more they delight in them, the happier and the better they will be; we let them in to Kew Gardens unwatched, and yet not a leaf is rifled; we build, or they build for themselves, Crystal Palaces, and we make for them parks and gardens, where they may walk unrestrained and roll upon the grass even, and bask in the sunshine, and revel in pure air. And what is the consequence of this? We must condense the reply into one sentence – We have had no Revolution.

That was true, in a sense. However, there was at least a revolution in gardening...

THE
BACKGROUND

F OR ALL THE IMAGES OF GRACE, ELEGANCE AND
serenity conjured up by the Georgian Age (and indeed,
heavily promoted by the Georgians themselves), it was
a period of considerable turmoil. Even in the apparently rather
trivial side-issue of garden design, arguments about it raged
fiercely from at least the 1730s onwards. The way in which those
arguments developed ensured that garden design began to move
into a far more important position among the visual arts than it
had ever held before. So although the gyroscope of taste remained
stable and upright, for at least the middle years of the century its
movement was fuelled by acrimony and antagonism.

The arguments were mostly about what was 'right', for it was
a widely held belief among people rich enough to care about such
matters, and to indulge their visual tastes, that there were real
and absolute standards of taste and beauty, and that the laws of
fashion were quite as real as some of the scientific 'laws' that were
beginning to be discovered. It was as if skirt length, car design
or golf shoes were to be given a philosophical dimension; many
people felt that adhering to such rules and standards of taste, once
they were discovered and proved to be true, was both socially
and even morally necessary. It was all, of course, fairly ridiculous,
even though some of the gardens produced by the new theories
were marvellous.

There had been, in the eighteenth century, a tremendous break with tradition. By the 1750s the old standards of the formal garden, which descended in an almost direct line from the ancient classical world, had been destroyed; a number of rival theories now began to gain currency and often became associated with other rival sets of opinions, both moral and political.

The old formal garden had been entirely based on artifice and symmetry, and grand ones often consisted of immense formal walks, centred on house or gates, flanked by formal and rectangular gardens of flowers, box hedges, topiary, or even statuary. In larger establishments, the gardens near the house were almost always enclosed by walls, though these were sometimes, at least late in the life of the formal garden, pierced with sections of decorative railings so that the countryside beyond could be admired. Beyond the garden wall, the surrounding parkland often had vast straight rides cut through it, both for the convenience of huntsmen and also for sheer magnificence. Where a number of these rides crossed one another, formal pools (in the grandest, surrounding some marvellous pavilion) mirrored the avenues.

Many fragmentary remains of these gardens can still be found in Britain, notably at Hampton Court, Wrest Park, Hall Barn and Newliston, but thousands of good examples were illustrated by the topographical artists of the day, or visited by diarists like Celia Fiennes. For the lesser ones, a glance at almost any modern ordnance survey map of suitable scale will show remains of avenues, rides, canals, fishponds, even parterres, around almost every country house built before the early eighteenth century.

Even tiny gardens consisted of a few formally arranged flowerbeds, box-edged and centred on a sundial, a tank of water or a pot of carnations. Some had summerhouses, or a small wooden loggia covered with trained apples or, in warmer parts, a vine. Naturally there were important changes in style over the centuries, but always within a formal framework and often using much the same elements and often the same plants.

By the early eighteenth century some British gardeners were beginning to long for something different. Already a few 'wildernesses' had begun to appear; these were playful attempts at mimicking 'nature', where trees and bushes were left unpruned, though the paths, sometimes in daring curves, still had neat hedges or were bordered by rows of flowers. To the dissatisfied gardener, they seemed to offer hints of a way forward.

However, those with an itch for the new were at a loss to know what any proposed new sort of garden should actually look like; simply making the wildernesses larger wasn't enough. There were no informal models available, though the scholarly dissatisfied knew that some ancient Roman gardens had had parts that were supposed to look like the natural landscape. The rich among them had also begun to collect landscape paintings, mostly Italian, and mostly by masters of the previous century. These paintings came to play an important role in garden theory for the next century and a half, even though all the landscapes in them were those of the imagination, and even though there were other, and more architectural, factors at work.

In the 1730s wealthy patrons, having, at least since the Renaissance, built themselves houses only rather loosely based on ancient Roman models, began to want houses that used columns, porticoes and decorative detailing which were copied directly from proper Roman fragments. They were becoming art historians.

Curiously, instead of searching out real Roman houses themselves, they preferred to copy someone else who had looked at Roman remains – the sixteenth-century architect Andrea Palladio. He had used his knowledge of Roman architecture to design some quite marvellous villas and town palaces in the countryside and towns near Venice. Eighteenth-century British travellers, visiting these hardly very ancient houses yet much preferring them to the only slightly Romanized houses they had at home, wanted similar things for themselves.

Palladio's buildings were often designed as grand summer retreats, and so were not especially suited either to British winters, or to the ways in which British houses were used. British architects therefore had to adapt and develop them, eventually producing a delightful and flexible style that could cope perfectly with a tiny country house or a vast mansion.

Once the owners had moved into these new and more fully Roman houses, they were faced with the garden 'problem'.

Renaissance or Baroque houses, whether of Corinthian or Ionic orders, grand or small, had had Renaissance or Baroque gardens. As we have seen, these were always formal, proclaiming the artificial nature of the garden, whether beyond it lay a magnificent hunting park or only the lane that led to the village high street.

Now the great *avant garde* patrons of eighteenth-century Britain began to want suitably Roman gardens in which to set their new houses. Managing to ignore the fact that the formal gardens with which they were so bored were only a few steps away from what Roman gardens had actually looked like, they hunted for other sources of information. They were already passionately in love with the historical and topographical paintings of several seventeenth-century artists, most notably Claude, but also Nicolas Poussin and Salvator Rosa. It seemed as if their canvas landscapes could be the model for new gardens.

In the work of Claude and Poussin, figures from classical mythology, of all ranks from proper gods to fairly simple shepherds, were often shown amid sumptuous but calm landscapes which usually contained equally sumptuous but fantasticated Roman buildings; sheep and cattle often grazed on perfect meadows in the middle distance, and beyond them was a perfect view of distant blue hills and the sea. There was not a garden wall, a piece of topiary or a box hedge to be seen.

Beguiled, the grandees wanted something similar for their houses. While none wanted to go as far as dressing in togas, they had soon swept away their garden walls, every scrap of box, most of the flowers, every sundial, neighbouring villages, indeed even nearby hills, so that they could take their carriages over neatly scythed lawns into the misty distance, along the margins of new lakes, to play cards or take tea (or to have wild banquets) in expensive miniaturizations of the Pantheon, the Temple of the Winds, or, later in the century, the Doric temples of southern Italy or of Greece itself.

There are a few early landscape gardens left (Chiswick and

Rousham are two examples), but the great age of the landscape is associated with 'Capability' Brown and a few of his imitators. Good landscape gardens became, in expert hands, like extended sculptures, carried out upon the basic 'geological' landscape with trees, water and grass. Almost every Georgian landowner at once wanted one, and with justification. They can be thrilling places to be in, and to walk along the lake edge at Sherborne Castle or Bowood, or along the approaches to Longleat, Alnwick Castle and dozens of others, especially on a misty summer morning, is an exciting experience.

Perfection, of course, is uncommon. Many landscape gardens were so overloaded with walks, urns, temples, Turkish tents, hermit's grottoes, obelisks, cheap copies of Roman tombs, and so on, that quite a number looked like rather lush fairgrounds. Fortunately, a lot of these garden features were so gimcrack that they did not last, and gardens like Stourhead are now more tasteful than they may once have been.

Because the old sorts of garden had so unequivocally proclaimed 'artifice', the new landscape gardens were believed to proclaim 'nature'. Not all garden owners could refrain, though, from artifice, and there were all sorts of lapses, from elegant bridges that were just 'cutouts' of woodwork which only the birds could use, to entire canvas hoardings painted with a landscape to put at the end of a lake or behind some real trees. Even the influential Horace Walpole used an especially small breed of cow on his fields at Strawberry Hill, to fiddle the laws of perspective and make his grounds look larger.

For a few years, Olympian calm (however artificial and at whatever cost) reigned. It couldn't last; it was soon pointed out that the trim perfections of the great landscape gardens, especially those by Brown, had not only nothing to do with real nature, but little to do with paintings either, and that whatever the cost of their construction, they fell far short of the idealized fantasies of both Claude and Poussin.

The gardens had all sorts of other weaknesses too. First, the style was only adaptable to landowners living in suitably mild terrain (there are few cliffs, ravines, moors or wild mountainsides in Claude's paintings). Those who owned estates filled with such things, or who felt themselves inspired by the popular Gothic novels of the period (which were set not in the home counties, but in the Alps of Switzerland or Italy, or even in remotest Scotland), pointed out that there was plenty of wild terrain to be found in the paintings of the third of the triumvirate – Rosa.

Rosa also portrayed real, even criminal, Romans in his paintings, rarely minor godlings, and so appealed to more democratic tastes. Democrats and those who were unable to indulge in the 'landscape' garden, especially those who were too poor to do so, felt that they should espouse some other style that would suit them better. Further, the purest of the landscape gardens used native trees, open water, far-flung lawns, and expensive stonework. The grass swept elegantly right up to the house and its portico; flowers and shrubs, however lovely, were banished to the walled kitchen garden, or to glades in the distant woodland.

Yet throughout the eighteenth century, new plants began to flood into the country from all the Americas and most of Asia. By the end of the century they were flooding in even faster, yet there was nowhere to put them, no way to integrate them into the garden. Those who owned them, perhaps growing the rarest that could be found, felt that they were quite as status-full as having a summerhouse shaped like the Colosseum, and hankered after a mode of gardening that would allow them to show their wonderful plants to the world.

Consequently, by the end of the eighteenth century, the landscape garden was quite clearly doomed. On the one hand there were the many proponents of what became known as the 'picturesque'; usually of a romantic cast of mind, they were admirers of the paintings of Salvator Rosa, with their shattered trees and wild rock-strewn and bandit-infested landscapes, and wanted more truly 'painterly' gardens, with rough-foliaged plants to give good foregrounds, rotting moss-encrusted fencing instead of neat iron railings or the invisible ha-has necessary for a 'proper' landscape. They claimed that lawns were unpaintable (untrue, in fact, for a number of topographical artists painted them rather well), had nothing to do with real nature (more or less true), and should therefore be banned from anywhere that claimed to be a natural garden.

Rather than parks or dazzlingly elegant landscapes striving to look like ancient Italy, they preferred the natural scene, usually rural, often farmland, though preferably lightly enriched with interesting and foreign trees and flowers, and with a few fake designer-cottages carefully placed by the garden designer to enhance the view rather than help the cottager (some were paid a fuel allowance, so that their chimneys would always sport a picturesque plume of smoke).

On the other hand, there were several influential writers, notably Uvedale Price, who began, in the early years of the nineteenth century, to regret the loss of the formal gardens that he had swept away in his youthful desire to keep his estates in the latest fashion. He wrote, in *Essays on the Picturesque* of 1810:

I may perhaps have spoken more feelingly on this subject from having done myself what I so condemn in others – destroyed an old fashioned garden. It was not indeed in the high style of those I have described, but it had many circumstances of a similar kind and effect. As I have long since perceived the advantage which I could have made of them, and how much I could have added to that effect, how well I could have in parts mixed the modern style and have altered and concealed many of the stiff and glaring formalities, I have long regretted its destruction. I destroyed it, not from disliking it; on the contrary, it was a sacrifice I made against my own sensation to the prevailing opinion. . .

He had destroyed his garden's old walls and terraces, its warm and sheltered walks, smashed its statues and its splendid iron gateways, and pulled down a beautiful summerhouse smothered in ancient creepers, all in an attempt to recreate the grounds' original state of wild nature. He went on:

I probably have in some degree succeeded, and after much difficulty, expense and dirt, I have made it look like many other parts of mine and of all beautiful grounds; but with little to mark the difference

between what is close to the house and what is at a distance from it;
between the habitation of man and that of sheep.

This sort of nostalgia became increasingly widespread. Oddly,
it was an exactly comparable nostalgia, but about seventy or
eighty years in the future, that put paid to the high-Victorian
style of garden that crystallized out of the late Georgian confusion.

Late Georgian gardens did sometimes reach some sort of
compromise, and one on which Humphry Repton (who died in
1818) built a career. His gardens owed much to the picturesque,
but it was he who made having flower-beds, terraces and balus-
traded steps fashionable once more. He pointed out that houses
were entirely 'artificial', therefore there could be no objection to
having the immediate environs artificial as well; grassland did not
need to sweep right up to the drawing-room windows. He saw
the house as a light, whose rays faded with distance. Flowers
faded into lawns, which themselves soon faded into wild (and
preferably picturesque) countryside or parkland. Repton, though,
soon became too absorbed by garden decoration (that was, after
all, what most of his clients wanted), and was eventually disowned
by the most extreme supporters of both traditional and picturesque gardens.

After his death, garden theory took three main directions. One
was towards a more extreme picturesque, in that its proponents
wanted gardens to look much more like paintings (even though
paintings cannot be walked through, viewed at different seasons,
or need replanting). A second stream wanted to hold on to the
informal idea that had so completely overturned the past, but
wanted to throw out the silly and constricting belief in 'nature'
and the natural. The third stream (Uvedale Price's) regretted that
the 'landscape' movement had happened at all, and wanted to go
back to the old certainties and comforts of the past.

Which of these directions would ultimately win was to be
whichever one could adapt itself to the emerging middle classes;
the gorgeous landscape gardens of the middle of the eighteenth
century were perfectly adapted to express the Olympian and
rather self-absorbed state of mind of well-landed aristocrats, but

it was hard to cram a convincing lake, a large temple or two, lawns and forests into two-thirds of an acre. There was an entire class, becoming rapidly more prosperous, who wanted fashionable gardens yet were dispossessed from the prevailing eighteenth-century fashion.

However, the landscape movement was an extremely successful one, wiping out almost every garden, whatever its quality, of any previous epoch. It spread quickly to Europe and America, and in both continents wreaked almost as much devastation as it had at home. In spite of its narrowly defined clientele, and even though it was short-lived (most fashions, even revolutionary ones, usually are), it became the new orthodoxy which, for progress' sake, had to be shattered.

A Georgian landscape garden, with its groves, lakes and temples, is immediately recognizable; quite as easily as a high-Victorian one, with its bedding schemes, rustic seats, iron urns and statuary. Yet the gap in time between the most extreme examples of each style is only about sixty or seventy years. Clearly, a great deal must have been happening in late Georgian gardens for such a radical change to take place with such speed and such thoroughness.

Of course, garden aesthetics were also closely linked to architectural styles. During the eighteenth century some patrons, perhaps not interested in the pomposities of pure Roman, or fed up with the passionate symmetry of such buildings, played with various rather flimsily theatrical styles based either on the buildings of China (a country then becoming better known) or on the 'Gothic' buildings still standing in the countryside, whether medieval castle or Elizabethan country house. However, the use of these styles was only 'playing', with decorative details culled from the Orient or the past being applied to buildings which were otherwise fairly typically 'Georgian'.

All this was great fun, and produced some quite delicious buildings. By the end of the eighteenth century, though, frivolity of that sort came to look rather cheap, and people of true taste and superior morality began to want houses that both reflected their personal attitudes and were truer to the feel of the original buildings, even if they did, naturally, have all modern comforts. Some purists began to feel that as Rome had admired the buildings of Greece, then Greek architecture must be 'purer', and certainly nobler, than that of Rome. The Greek revival was under way, and people soon began to try living in fake Greek temples rather than fake Roman ones (fortunately no one knew anything at all about Greek gardens).

Others wanted to stay with Italy but felt that the idea of copying temple detailing was pretentious. It seemed to them that the villas and farmhouses of the Italian countryside, especially of the sort that were quite often found in the paintings of Poussin, were probably rather close to Roman domestic originals, were often ramshackle and asymmetrical, and were therefore both especially 'picturesque' and adaptable to modern and northern house plans. Thus began the 'Italianate' style of building, with its heavy cornices and pediments, watchtowers, exotic groundplans, loggias and heavily emphasized chimneys. It was soon widely popular, and its idiosyncratic results can be seen in the suburbs of almost every British city and town.

Others again wanted to copy the vernacular architecture of Britain, building vaguely 'gothick' (or 'Old English') cottages, or quite serious Gothic mansions. Others still wondered why such things should stop at the Channel, and were soon building themselves Swiss chalets, German castles, Moorish lodges, or abbreviated versions of the castles of the Loire or of Aberdeenshire. Every one of these houses needed a garden, but there was, by the 1820s, no longer any easy way of deciding what it should look like. All was chaos.

By 1822, whatever sort of house an owner had, there seemed to be only two main sorts of garden available (no one had yet begun to take Uvedale Price's sorrow seriously). In that year John Claudius Loudon published the first of many editions of his great work *The Gardener's Encyclopaedia*. This vast compilation of everything that was then known or thought about gardening and botany offers an absorbing picture of what Regency gardeners liked. The early editions of the encyclopaedia show clearly the two main streams of garden design: the picturesque, and the

11. Greek Revival architecture was often associated with 'picturesque' plantings.

gardenesque (this was a new word, coined by Loudon to denote what he felt was an entirely new direction in garden style). Both these terms became important for early Victorian gardeners, and were further developed by other writers of the period with far less imagination and intelligence than Loudon.

The 'picturesque' (a word still in current use, though no longer much used to describe gardens), was a development of the land-scape garden idea; following Repton's innovations, the house was often anchored to the landscape by the use of a terrace, so that the docks, nettles and burdock (necessary for the 'landscape' part of the style) did not need to obscure the drawing-room or library windows and trip up the denizens of the house. Flowers and decorative bushes were used nearby (the shrubbery often served, undemocratically, to screen the service quarters) and allowed to be as colourful as required.

Still following Repton, once away from the house, 'nature' had full sway and the wilder and more tangled it was, the better. It was also felt that the terrain had to be suitable; it was not possible to have a picturesque garden on the dead flat, and rather immoral (as well as expensive) to create a false landform.

Garden 'props', too, had been popularized by Repton, and were now even more important in emphasizing the garden's allegiance. Loudon thought that without the adjuncts of the picturesque (rustic seats, shelters, urns, and so on), the 'pic-turesque style would be little better than a well-thinned and moderately well-kept sylvan scene'. For most middle-class gardens of the period, it seems that the main characteristic of the style was that the bigger beds (scaled down in size from a 'Brownian' clump so that they would fit into a more modest garden) had trees and shrubs that tried to imitate natural growth patterns. There were usually some exotics, perhaps American kalmias, rhododendrons, or Chinese camellias in the foreground, with these elegant plants backed by plainer but indigenous species.

For garden owners lucky enough to have interesting sites, other sorts of scene could be imitated: 'For example, an old gravel pit, which had become covered with bushes and indigenous trees, and contained a hovel or rude cottage in the bottom, with a natural path worn in the grass by the occupants.'

However, Loudon couldn't leave things alone (and few of his readers would have been happy with merely a rude cottage). For him, the gravel pit could only become a picturesque garden if it

be improved, according to the imaginative art, if foreign trees, shrubs and plants, even to the grasses, were introduced instead of indigenous ones; and a Swiss cottage, or an architectural cottage of any kind that would not be recognized as the common cottage of the country, substituted for the hovel. To complete the character of art, the walk should be formed and gravelled, at least to such an extent as to prevent its being mistaken for a natural path.

That makes it sound very artificial-looking indeed, however 'wild' it was meant to be.

Of course, as it posed a threat to his own ideas of what should be the theoretical basis of gardening, he mused rather grandly in the *Suburban Gardener* of 1838 that the point of

RUSTIC, INDIGENOUS OR FAC-SIMILE IMITATIONS OF NATURAL SCENERY ... [i.e. the picturesque] is to deceive the spectator, and make him believe that the scene produced is of a fortuitous origin; or produced by the humbler exertions of a country labourer ... they can have no merit in design, and only mechanical merit in the execution. They scarcely require the aid of either a professional landscape-gardener, or a professional horticulturalist; but, at the same time, they could not be executed by every common labourer...

Few such 'gardens' were ever built, though the idea must have offered a neat excuse for inept gardeners. Loudon continued that

the imitation of such scenes must be made by a sort of self-taught artist, or a regularly instructed artist who will condescend to accept of this kind of employment ... If the plantation [around the home grounds] were surrounded by a hedge or other fence, and the entrance to the path were through a gap in this fence, the deception would be the more complete.

He didn't manage to kill the style off with these blows, and by the mid-nineteenth century the picturesque had been subdivided into various minutely differentiated sorts. Charles McIntosh took the subdivisions to their most extreme and rather ridiculous lengths. Most of them were even more theoretical than the quarry garden of Loudon, and when he had to describe any actual site he found himself in the most awful, but oddly unrecognized, trouble.

According to McIntosh's classification, all 'picturesque' gardens had to avoid walls or railings but have any necessary divisions made of trellis-work of unbarked wood, or fancy wire-work. The grounds could be decorated with vases, rustic cascades, moss houses, the rosery (as rose gardens were then called; they used early nineteenth-century shrubby roses, not the 'bedding' teas), rockeries and the heathery (a forerunner of the erica garden). All these items, including the rootery (used for growing ferns and wild orchids, and preferably situated in some 'obscure ravine'), were usually sited just beyond the lawn, where many can still be found.

After such basic necessities, the style could be further studied. For a start there was the 'rough picturesque', in which the garden had to look like the 'margin of a forest glade, with shrubs and plants looking as if grazed by cattle' (he doesn't say how this charming effect was to be created). There were also to be rocks, rills, and tangled masses of roots. Then there was the 'refined picturesque', which must use only exotic species of shrubs and trees. If neither rough nor refined were suitable, the baffled gardener could try the 'trivial picturesque'. In this, common native trees and shrubs of the country were placed on grass. All three categories were further divided.

In spite of all this, the word 'picturesque' managed to remain in use for gardens at least until 1878, when William Robinson wrote, of Parisian parks and gardens: 'This [Le Parc des Buttes Chaumont] is as regards garden design, the most distinct and interesting garden in Paris ... It is the boldest attempt at what is called the picturesque style that has been made in any London or Paris garden.'

The park he describes was actually a site once occupied by vast and ancient quarries, and had been nothing but acres of rubbish for centuries. In the nineteenth century the site had been turned into an exotic public park with tall cliffs, reflected in artificial ponds far below. Inside the cliffs were fake stalactite caves. Robinson, with a sharp eye for the sham, disapproved of the latter, though he did like the prettily planted stream that tumbled between the rocks on the floor. Outside, the cliff faces were picturesquely draped with ivy and more exotic plants, which at that time included the rare 'japonica' quince and *Forsythia*.

On the fake cliff summits, the stones were so carefully cemented together that there was no plant growth. There, 'A great mistake has been made in placing a cafe on the edge of the rock, occupying one of the finest central sites in the park ...' The 'picturesque', then, could in fact be as artificial as it pleased, provided that it at

12. 'Rough picturesque', modern conifers and a grand fountain in the Champs Élysées.

least attempted to look natural and romantic and provided that it eschewed any sort of formality.

The 'gardenesque', on the other hand, had, by the time Loudon's new *Encyclopaedia of Cottage Architecture* was published in 1835, become a rather curious style. In this style of informally arranged beds, still using the suburbanized outlines adopted by the picturesque (and still found in today's 'island beds'), artifice was trumpeted aloud.

The natural way that plants tend to grow together was scorned, and the trees, shrubs and herbaceous plants had to be grown so that they remained separate. Loudon insisted that 'every gardenesque group must consist of trees which do not touch each other, and which become groups by being as near together as is practicable without touching ... It is not meant by this that in that case they would not form a whole ...' The idea was that care should be taken to display every aspect of the individual beauty of trees, shrubs and flowers, gravel walks and so on, though he gives no suggestion as to how plants were to be commanded to cease growth lest they touched (and suddenly became 'picturesque').

Later development of the gardenesque became more complex, and even odder. The 'pictorial gardenesque' was used for 'moderately dressed surfaces'. Often to be seen in contemporary garden plans, such gardens contained many irregular flower-beds. These, when large and surrounded by plantations of exotics, were actually built up in the centre to a height of several feet, so that 'when the garden extends over an acre or more space, and the tops of the beds are planted with flowering shrubs, the whole becomes a sort of labyrinth, through which one may wander for hours ...' This sort of garden was thought suitable to a residence in the rural Gothic or cottage style.

However, not all gardenesque beds had wavy outlines. Some gardens had lawns freckled with various sizes of circular beds (like those at Hoole or Wimbledon), planted up with native or exotic plants but all still grown as detached specimens. The earth between each was always kept hoed, and the margins of the bed were neatly cut clear of grass to mark out the beds as being definitely distinct from the picturesque.

By 1850 McIntosh was suggesting that gardenesque beds like these could be 'divided into equal parts ... and the colours so disposed as to produce harmonious arrangements ... The divisions of circles may be into six portions, or into three or six zones, or concentric circles, admitting the three primary colours in succession.'

He goes on, perhaps aware of how strange this could have looked:

We have no doubt that many will be surprised at our recommendation of circular figures only. Those who have seen the unique garden of Lady Broughton at Hoole House near Chester ... will not, we are certain, be amongst the number ... its whole arrangement consists of five straight rows of circles, each 9 feet 5 inches in diameter, and each surrounded by wire basketwork, painted a yellow stone colour, to harmonize with the very tasteful rockwork which surrounds the garden.

There was also, by 1853, a supposedly 'Geometric gardenesque', which McIntosh wanted to call gardenesque only because of its obvious artifice. It was entirely formal, soon becoming the most important style of the times and the third of the design streams carrying Victorian gardens along.

Whether trivial or profound, picturesque or gardenesque, many garden plans were published. Loudon, for instance, from what can be seen of his designs, turns out not to have been a brilliant designer. He specialized in curious 'angel'-shaped beds looking, in plan, very much like stylized birds. These were grouped along straight or curving walks, pushed into the angles of lawns, or clustered around garden 'features'. Close to the house and the windows of the public rooms he preferred rather more formal beds, often shaped like the palmettes so popular in plaster and ironwork decoration of the period.

One of his plans, in the *Gardener's Magazine* of 1835, he described as: 'A Working Plan for laying out and planting a Suburban Flower Garden, containing about $\frac{1}{4}$ of an acre, and situated within Two Miles of St Paul's, London'. Basically it was the usual urban strip, and for it he gives a complete planting scheme down to shrub level (it would, for owners of houses of that date, still be an easy matter to get suitable flowers for the flower-beds), including seating positions, places for vases and the rest. All in all, it is a fairly standard layout with a path inside a narrow boundary of trees and shrubs. The path itself is screened from the central lawn by Loudon's usual angel beds, and was to be planted with smaller shrubs, herbaceous flowers and many of the showy annual plants newly introduced.

At the same time Loudon was also publishing monthly garden plans in *The Architectural Magazine* and even more in the *Encyclopaedia of Cottage Architecture*. Later the same year he managed to squeeze a series of articles out of a garden plan submitted for approbation by a fortunately anonymous reader. Loudon rightly said that it was awful, and invited readers to suggest improvements. He received several from 'knowledgeable amateurs' and published those, together with his own improvements of the latter. The poor owner of the garden in question must have been in complete confusion as to what to do once he (or she) had seen all the suggestions. The amateur ones were extraordinary, crammed with so many irregularly shaped beds that merely to cross the garden would have taken an hour. His own plan was really a modestly picturesque 'landscape' arrangement, with a scattering of flower-beds.

By the close of the Georgian period, and in spite of all Loudon's efforts, there were several alternatives to the descendant of the landscape style (the picturesque) or Loudon's particular brand of the gardenesque. For gardeners not influenced by Uvedale Price and not wanting to recreate the formal gardens of their grandfathers, there were, by the mid-1820s, already a number of attempts at an 'English parterre' (one, that is, in contrast to the formal sort of a hundred years earlier, but which still survived in conservative European gardens and which were thought of by Regency gardeners as 'French'). Really part of the 'gardenesque', these were to be found at various gardens, notably Dropmore, where isolated colourful flower-beds could be found scattered at random over the lawns and clustering near the belts of trees. At Dropmore they were shaped like the 'tadpoles' on Paisley shawls,

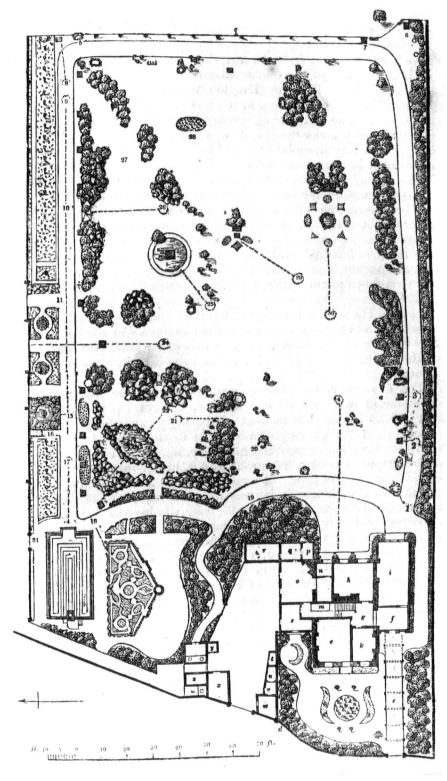

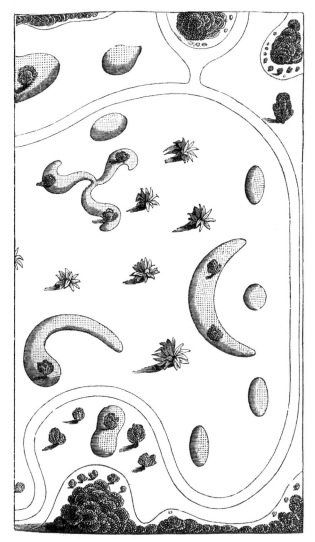

14. The gardenesque at its most alarming.

and in other gardens like the hearts, clubs and diamonds of playing cards.

A contemporary wrote that 'the genius of the English parterre is totally different from that of the French parterre; for while that of the latter is to display forms and lines, the former aims at

Variety and brilliance of colouring by means of flowers, without much regard to forms, and with very little regard to lines ...' It was a difficult design idiom in which to achieve perfection, for 'With respect to the design of English parterres, there are only two or three in the environs of London that we could refer to, as being tolerably perfect ...' This may have been true. How the beds were planted, and the controversy over who planted the first of them, we leave until the following chapters. Of course the word 'parterre' was being used very loosely indeed here. More historically accurate parterres were certainly being built (or even re-built) in the 1820s.

A final aspect of gardening in late Georgian Britain, though one that did not enter into any of the theoretical arguments, was the 'American' garden; these first began to appear in the late eighteenth century, and were places in which to put all the wonderful new introductions from North America and Canada. Many of the first introductions were collected along the main routes of communication, the rivers. They needed, therefore, damp and often peaty soil, which especially suited many of the new rhododendrons, kalmias and cassiopes as well as the exciting and elegant new conifers. This led to them being grouped together, a grouping reinforced by the reluctance of conventional 'landscapers' to admit the exotics to their designs. Even though the specifically American angle of such plantings became weakened once Indian, Himalayan and Chinese plants (especially the oriental rhododendrons and camellias) were found to do well in exactly the same conditions, the name stuck. American gardens became an important element in many large grounds, and went on to become virtually the only sort of Victorian garden in the damper parts of the British isles.

Naturally, some of these various new garden themes were taken up by gardeners not brave or rich enough to convert their entire gardens. This led to some odd scenes, like that at Hendon Rectory, a widely admired garden in the late 1830s, which had a fine formal canal remaining from the early part of the eighteenth century, but bordered with tadpole, oval and star-shaped flower-beds filled with the very latest dahlias and geraniums. It was further elaborated with vases, urns, standard fruit trees in tubs, and rambling roses tumbling over rose arches. It must have been pretty.

In America itself, gardens had been rather conservative in the matter of design. Many of the smaller manor houses and farms seem to have clung to entirely formal arrangements. They also clung to the old garden flora that was fast becoming unfashionable in the wealthier parts of the United Kingdom. The method of planting, too, was conservative, relying on the sort of 'cottage garden' mix of vegetables and flowers once common in England and Scotland. House styles, oddly, seemed more easily exportable, and while builders kept up with European fashions, and Greek, Old English, and Swiss houses began to appear, the garden clung to outmoded, though no longer rigidly formal, styles.

Even by 1849, when the first editions of Andrew Jackson Downing's *Treatise on the Theory and Practice of Landscape Gardening, with a view to the improvement of Country Residences* began to appear, he could still recycle Loudon's work with advantage. In the preface to that work, Downing draws a nice contrast between the pioneers and their precarious lands in the West, and the old and long-cultivated country in the East, where there were fine gardens to be found. He thought, though, that the contemporary economic advances, especially of the late 1830s and early 1840s, would spawn a vast amount of new building and therefore a need for gardens (he must have hoped, therefore, for larger sales).

Downing's work, however closely based on European texts, was the first American book on landscape gardening and an attempt to show the 'correct' taste for the new rich. Ironically, though he freely acknowledges Loudon's help as well as that of various American garden owners, he goes on to give lists of very out-of-date European plants as suitable for American flower borders. In these he includes things like romantic old pasque flowers, hepaticas, violets, polyanthus, pulmonarias, white corydalis, lily of the valley, *Iris florentina*, hemerocallis, double-flowered *Campanula persicifolia*, *Hesperis matronalis*, double catch-flies, and other lovely old plants about to vanish from almost every British garden.

More surprisingly, there were as yet rather few American species in the lists; not much beyond the lovely *Aquilegia canadensis*, various penstemons, *Tradescantia*, wild delphiniums, lupins and cypripediums. So while European gardeners were going frantic to get hold of the latest American plant, American gardeners were still happily growing old European ones. However naïve Downing's garden flora was, he advocated all the latest in new garden decorations, from conservatories, covered seats and rustic pavilions to the charming new moss houses, bridges, rockwork and the rest. America was catching up.

All over Europe, and soon in America, fashion-conscious gardeners eagerly read the latest garden magazines or visited the most lately fashionable gardens. Soon everyone cared about gardening, and much of the population became involved with it in one way or another. With so much interest, with such a vast market for ideas, for plants, and for garden artefacts, it is little surprise that soon any clear threads of philosophical argument (however false, or even silly) became lost in the babel.

CHAPTER
3

THE
NEW MARKETS

WHILE THE MARKET FOR THE EIGHTEENTH-century landscape garden was small, restricting itself to people with sufficient land to express it, much of the style of the Victorian period could be expressed in a tiny front garden just as well as below the terraces of a country mansion. There was, therefore, an entirely new and vast market waiting to be tapped.

The sudden expansion of the economy of late Georgian Britain, which made most parts of the country the envy of Europe, occasioned a widespread increase in personal wealth. This was not only the result of people's direct involvement in trade or industrial development; there were whole new professions that developed (like the vast ranks of clerks who were needed to service businesses, banks, factories). Almost everyone else, whether lawyers, doctors, actors, publicans, hotel owners, prostitutes, professors, bakers or milliners, shared in the rivers of gold that both the city and sometimes the countryside were beginning to generate. Naturally, not all this new money went on daily needs; much of it was spent conspicuously, as today, on houses and land (though we may regret the loss of architectural style between then and now).

By the earliest part of the Victorian period there were huge numbers of owners of comfortable and generally elegant villas

15. Heavily clothed walls, crammed windowsills, and a cosy porch; a contrast with chaste Georgian simplicity.

and terrace houses (of all sizes, from the grand palace-fronted terraces of Regent's Park, or the New Town of Edinburgh, to tiny artisans' houses tucked away in the depths of Fulham or other erstwhile villages ringing the rapidly growing industrial cities). Such dwellings were so packed together, largely as the public transport system allowed, that towns of any importance developed areas that were not characteristically crowded and ugly enough to be called urban, nor were yet properly 'country'. The once grand word 'suburban' came to be applied to these new areas, and the word altered rapidly in its use between 1820 and 1860.

Many of the dwellers in these new communities were 'new rich', even if only modestly so. Their parents, and perhaps they themselves, were quite probably born into rather more humble circumstances. Such people, with their usual ardent desire to meet the perceived social standards of their new class, and to have instantly the appearance of having been there for ever, have always been the butt of the humorist and exploiter. Now, however, there were so many of them that they were no longer funny. They were simply an enormous new market.

Certainly, as they paced their bare drawing-rooms which over-looked small and muddy pieces of ground, many must have felt as much at a loss to know what to do about furnishing the rooms as about furnishing the garden. That is plainly what many publishers felt, too, and soon such houseproud but timorous owners were besieged by books and magazines offering guidance in these vital matters.

The first assault on this juicy new market was, of course, published by John Claudius Loudon. The book appeared in 1838 and was called, equally naturally, *The Suburban Gardener*. The book's full title gives a rather spacious early nineteenth-century interpretation to the word 'suburban', and deals with all aspects of house and garden that might be of help to the reader, from the general sorts of furnishings and architectural details that are appropriate to the reader's means and class (telling the reader everything, from what sort of dressers to have in the kitchen to what sort of upholstery to have on the sofas in the library; it's a fascinating document), as well as how to design the garden.

Loudon was still following a line of thought popular since the early years of the century, when he and others (notably the Edinburgh printer and dilettante gardener Patrick Neill) began a long and rather fruitless attempt to codify what were really 'sumptuary' regulations defining the new class system more clearly. They tried allotting each segment of each class a particular degree of gardening or housing, which they thought socially important to uphold and vulgar to exceed (for instance, farmers were not expected to grow peaches or the better varieties of grape, which should only be found in gentlemen's gardens). Such classificatory attempts were really a symptom of the radical social changes that were under way. The changes are quite clearly mirrored in the garden publishing of the times.

The Suburban Gardener, for instance, gives definitions for the various possible sorts of surburban house. A 'fourth rate' one was suitable for the occupation of mechanics and had two rooms per floor, often with a twelve- to fourteen-foot frontage to the whole house. There was often a rear stair, sometimes open to the elements, and a small back garden. The same 'rate' could also include artisans' dwellings and those of the lowest grades of clerk, though they more commonly lived in houses with a fifteen-foot frontage, a twenty-three foot depth, a basement to keep them dry, a cellar, a washhouse, an inside staircase, a parlour floor of two rooms, two drawing-rooms with folding doors, and two bedrooms.

Third rate houses were grander: a width of seventeen to eighteen feet (enough for a front door and two windows), and a depth of nearly thirty feet (suburbs like Chelsea and Fulham were mostly third rate). They were by far the most numerous new houses ringing all the great cities and boasted a detached washhouse, even a gighouse and stable. Gardens were commonly set at three or four times longer than broad.

Second rate houses were for wealthy tradesmen, for professionals, or even for gentlemen. Two to three bays wide, they had service accommodation and higher and better finished rooms.

16. New markets and new materials gave rise to an unlikely 'acanthus' garden seat.
They're now rare.

Loudon may have been a little too early with his innovatory idea (for marketing a garden book, that is, rather than for the content of the gardening material, most of which had been around for a decade or more). His wife republished much the same information twelve years later in the *The Villa Garden* of 1850. The word 'suburban' had been dropped from the main title, for it was already becoming a liability. It was not dropped altogether, though, and the full title was now: *The Villa Gardener, comprising the choice of suburban villa residence: The laying out of the garden and grounds, and the Management of the Villa Farm, including dairy and poultry yard. Adapted, in extent, for grounds from one perch to fifty acres and upwards, and intended for the instruction of those who know little of gardening and rural affairs, and more particularly for the use of ladies.* However, though there was no change in the text on garden designing (even though styles had moved on), the book dropped any pronouncements about interior decoration. More significantly, it had also dropped much of the classification of 'rates' of house, and indeed much of the suburban angle. As Mrs Loudon

73

now included some examples of fashionable gardens owned by some very fashionable people indeed, she was clearly aiming the book at a rather higher section of the market than the original concept, or at least hoping to flatter more the buyers who had rather less than fifty acres at their disposal.

The work went through several editions, and was successful enough to produce some imitators. Edward Kemp was a notable example, with his *How to Lay Out a Garden*, a popular work in spite of the deep unimaginativeness of the text. It too went through many editions, and clearly filled a great need. In the preface to the first edition he wrote something that will have struck many modern observers just as strongly:

Having spent a good deal of time in passing through the suburbs of large towns (particularly the metropolis), the author ... has been very much impressed with the incongruity and dullness observable in the majority of small gardens, and has been led strongly to wish that the general appearance of such districts were more gratifying to the passer-by, and the arrangement of individual gardens more productive of pleasure to the several occupants.

He was, as the later text shows, writing for a prosperous part of the suburban market, and a very good deal of it at least leans gently upon Loudon's 'suburban villa'.

In Scotland, too, with the sudden growth of the capital but especially of Glasgow and the industrial towns, publishers eyed the new middle-class market with eagerness. A magazine called *The Gardener* appeared in 1861, edited by William Thomson, head gardener at Dalkeith Palace. It was specifically designed for suburban gardeners, whose existence was now made possible by the advent of a network of suburban railways. Further, it was aimed at that section of the middle-class market without full-time gardeners or with only casual help. 'It will be our special aim,' Thomson wrote, 'to make it useful to that large and increasing class of the community who, previous to the development of our railway system, lived in cities, but who now live in the country, and who occupy their hours of relaxation from city business in managing, with or without the help of a common labourer, their suburban gardens.' A parallel exists with a number of the present-day 'glossies' which cater for a new suburban market. Alas for *The Gardener*, there were not enough Scottish gardeners of the right sort to keep it in print.

Nevertheless, throughout the period, publishers of all levels had a generally profitable time. In early Victorian Britain there was an enormous growth in numbers and in the market for magazines and newspapers, as printing costs fell and educational levels rose. The market covered almost all possible fields, from politics and crime (one of the most successful sectors) to issues like 'Cleaves Penny Gazette of Variety and Amusement' (set up in 1837 as a mixture of instruction and jokes, but with regular gardening articles). Some papers did very well indeed: the *Argosy* was launched in 1865 and achieved a circulation of 65,000 in six weeks. Naturally, such rich potential pickings ensured that even in the field of gardening there was a wide range of new weekly and monthly publications, mostly (as today) aimed at the lower ranges of the market.

The indefatigable Joseph Paxton started up *Paxton's Magazine of Botany* in 1834, using the title not so much to boost his personal fame but to distinguish it clearly from the *Botanical Magazine*, which already had an august history. His work was much more carefully aimed at gardeners, and with only four hand-coloured plates to each issue was very much cheaper. There was a lot of what Paxton called 'practical letterpress', much of it written by him. The very first plate, incidentally, was of *Ribes sanguineus*, the flowering currant, soon in every suburban garden and introduced in 1826.

Sensing yet another gap in the market, Paxton and an associate of his, Lindley, founded the still extant *Gardener's Chronicle* in 1841. This was a full-blown newspaper with both national and foreign news, with vast amounts of material sent in by gardeners and scientists and covering every conceivable aspect of gardening. Unsatisfied even with this, Paxton went on to co-edit the *Horticultural Register* with Joseph Harrison of Birkenhead.

By 1851 the circulation of the *Gardener's Chronicle* was 6,500;

this should be compared with that of the far more eminent *Observer* at 6,230, and the *Economist* at 3,826.

The *Gardener's Chronicle* did astonishingly well with its large advertising section, and the year after the Great Exhibition ran page after page of new and very grand adverts for conservatories. Paxton must have been amused to note that many of them made use of the ridge and furrow system that he had developed for the glasshouses at Chatsworth and for the Crystal Palace. The conservatory makers had simply added some pretty Gothic decorative details.

A more minor but almost more fascinating publication was the *Cottage Gardener* of 1849. Its full title was *The Cottage Gardener or, Amateur and Cottager's Guide to Outdoor Gardening and Spade Cultivation . . . conducted by George Johnson (editor of Gardener's Almanac' 'Modern Gardener's Dictionary' etc). Contributors: the Fruit-Garden by Mr R. Errington (Gdnr to Sir P. Egerton, Oulton Park); the Kitchen-Garden, by the editor, and Mr J. Barnes (Gdnr to Lady Rolle, Bicton); the Flower-Garden, by Mr T. Appleby (Floricultural Manager to Messrs Henderson, Edgware Rd); Greenhouse and Window Gardening, by Mr D. Beaton, Gdnr to Sir Wm Middleton, Shrubland Park; the Agrarian Calendar, by Mr. J. H. Payne, author of 'The Bee Keeper's Guide' Vol. I, London 1849.* That took up almost the whole title page.

It was designed to be the first cheap periodical devoted to the small gardener, and appeared every Thursday. It intended to avoid all grand plants, whether pineapples or orchids, and the opening editorial stated that 'we shall claim praise, at all events, not more equivocal, if we know a garden in which the Cabbage has been more productive, the Apples more abundant, and the Mignonette more enduring, from information gathered in our columns'. It was a lovely idea that was soon to fall by the wayside.

The *Cottage Gardener* was also rich in advertising, promoting everything from 'The British Economical Manure Company' to 'Atkinson and Barker's Royal Infant's Preservative', which had as its copy: 'Mothers, call at your Druggists . . . no stupefactive deadly narcotics! but a veritable preservative of infants.' Then there were Heythorn's Hexagon Garden Nets, 'patronized by

Nobility, Clergy, Gentry ... the best and cheapest article for the protection of bloom, fruit and flowers, from frosts, birds, wasps, flies, children and servants ...' and Baker's Poultry Preservative, 'A certain cure for all diseases of Poultry, Pheasants etc'.

By 1854 a note to advertisers stated that the magazine sold 6,000 copies weekly and 'Amongst the subscribers are included GARDENERS, POULTRY BREEDERS and BEE-KEEPERS — Professional and Amateur, — Country Gentlemen and Clergymen. To advertisers desirous of community with these classes, its columns offer EXCLUSIVE advantages ...' However, by that date the title had officially changed to *The Cottage Gardener's and Country Gentleman's Companion*, which made sense of the fact that it was becoming full of articles on both pineapples and orchids as well as hothouses and conservatories to house them. Even renamed, one reader complained to a 'startled' editor:

Living in a cottage, and being fond of gardening, I began, some time ago, to take in THE COTTAGE GARDENER, and purchased some volumes of back numbers. I find, however, that it takes a much higher flight than its name indicates (for though I see, in several columns, it claims also to be a 'Country Gentleman's Companion', that name is at present abandoned). Now, I do not complain of your having articles for country gentlemen, directions for greenhouses, or even hothouses, and disquisitions on articles quite out of the cottager's reach; but I do think that we, who have been induced to become subscribers to the work in consequence of its professed accommodation to our wants and means, ought to be somewhat considered.

He accuses the editor of being absurd; what the reader wants to know about is the best or new sorts of potato and cauliflower, not new orchids or Cochin China pheasants. His feelings must have been shared by many readers, for the magazine soon folded and was merged with others under a new title (not an unknown happening today).

A much more successful attempt to capture the same market was the *Garden Oracle and Economic Yearbook*, edited from 1859 by Shirley Hibberd. Basically a very cheap almanac (packed with tradesmen's costing prices and endless lists of prize florist's flowers), it also had a useful gardener's calendar and oddments on forcing cherries under glass, and such like. It, too, was a mine of fascinating adverts, with pictures of everything from the latest species of *Berberidopsis* or various new calceolarias, to more surprising things like 'A NEW DESCRIPTION OF ARTIFICIAL TEETH, fixed without springs', and 'The Paxton drawing-room Hanging Baskets'. It also contained some of the first coloured adverts, including a glamorous one for the Royal Insurance Company.

A few years later the *Gardener's Chronicle* was selling full page adverts for the vast range of cast-iron garden decorations; everything from fancy tazzas for geraniums and verbenas, to garden seats and statuary. Meanwhile the nursery of William Paul was proclaiming the virtues of roses 'old and new' (famous now for things like 'Paul's Himalayan Musk' and 'Paul's Scarlet'), while Lea and Perrins advertised against fake Worcester sauce. More modern still, there were dozens of quite marvellous advertisements for the latest sort of domestic lawnmowers and rollers.

Shirley Hibberd must have made enough from editing the *Oracle*, or from some of the garden books which we have already looked at, to risk a venture that was almost certainly doomed to make a loss. This was the astonishingly grand new and rare beautiful leaved plants, *containing illustrations and descriptions of the Most Ornamental-Foliaged Plants not noticed in any work on the Subject*. This was the first major work heralding the tropical bedding movement. The pictures were of tremendous quality, still hand coloured (1870), and the preface remarked that 'It is but recently that the beauty of leaves has been fully recognized, and the passion that has arisen [for them] is one of the newest, but is not at all likely to be transient . . .'

Because such things were so expensive to produce they were often published as 'partworks', that is, books which appear in weekly instalments until they are complete. There were so many of them, of variable quality, that the *Gardener's Chronicle* actually published monthly lists of the best of the pictures, so that its readers could keep abreast of the latest introductions.

By the 1880s the market was becoming so demanding of

17. Mangin's 'Babylon' – an entirely Victorian mix of plants.

material that books were even being bought from foreign publishers. *The Famous Parks and Gardens of the World, described and
illustrated* is based on a French book called *Les Jardins* by A.
Mangin. The gardens shown are drawn both from the real world
and from the imagination, and include quite Hollywood-like

plates of the hanging gardens of Babylon (all planted up with incorrectly American opuntias and agaves) and some wonderfully romantic graphics, as well as pictures of ancient Rome, modern Vaux, Versailles and Marly.

Finally, in 1871, the most influential magazine of them all set up in business: *The Garden*. It provided a perfect platform for the crusading energies of William Robinson. Then, in 1875, a dumpy and short-sighted lady gardener walked into the office, and the end of high-Victorian gardens was well in sight. The lady was Gertrude Jekyll.

Long before that happened, though, in thousands upon thousands of suburban gardens, new conventions of gardening developed fast. The 'front garden' (see page 196) became an important phenomenon, where part of the land on which the house stood became devoted to public show, rather than for the private convenience of the inhabitants. It was there that the job lots of bedding plants were assembled around the single seedling of monkey-puzzle, and there where the new cast-iron vase or the collection of conch shells were neatly arranged. It was by its path that the Doulton edging tiles or the 'Patent Ferro-vitreous' edgings kept mud from its pretty tiles to the front door.

Even behind the front door, the middle-class garden market became ever more specialized; inside most of these middle-class houses, whether terraced, semi-detached, or standing in fifty acres, were women. Because the labour of others was so cheap, many women, even in houses that nowadays do not even have a cleaning lady, had almost nothing to do. Apart from deciding perhaps what the family was to have for dinner, no other domestic duty loomed. In large houses there were sisters, sisters-in-law, daughters, nieces, and the whole panoply of Victorian female relatives and friends. All needed occupation; all provided an astonishingly rich market for new ideas and ways of filling the time. Gardening provided an almost perfect outlet. It was healthy, involving slight labours, a little fresh air and a ready access to flowers, with which Victorian ladies were so often compared.

The comparison had also been made for much of the eighteenth century as well. Women had actually studied botany for the last

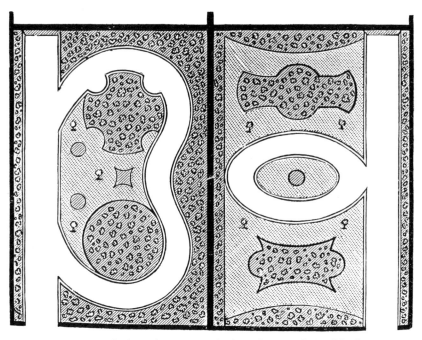

18. Shrubs, flower-beds, and some grass in these front gardens of the late 1830s.

of its decades, even though most botanists were male, and it had been a man who proposed the classification of plants on the number of their sexual parts (it was only in the late Victorian period that flowers for the drawing-room with over-conspicuous parts had such things carefully cut away). There had also been a number of well-known gardening ladies, though none had yet become an authority either on garden design or on the flowers themselves. By the end of the Victorian period, gardening in all its branches was almost a female preserve, from journalism to the highest reaches of garden design, and it is still today very much their province; few men will admit to being interested in more than the lawn and the vegetables.

However, it was two aristocratic Regency ladies whose gardens vied for being the first to use the 'bedding system'. It was another upper-class lady's garden that saw the first of the new violas. Lady Farnborough's garden at Bromley Hill was famous for its beauty, where 'the hollyhocks broke the horizon with their obelisks of colour'. Then there was the famous flower garden of the Hoole, with its extraordinary rockery, and Mrs Lawrence's over-decorated garden which we have already visited.

Such women must have been only the media-conscious tip of a hidden iceberg of interest in gardens, though when contemporary writers mention the difficulties under which women of almost all the polite classes laboured, it's astonishing that any managed to garden at all. All women, however vital, and even if over six feet tall and as healthy as a horse, were conventionally seen as weak and fragile beings, for ever wearing satin slippers on the tiniest of feet, for ever at risk of illness from the merest touch of damp or cold, and for ever decorative (they seem almost to have been as much a piece of upholstery as the expensive sofas in the drawing-room).

Nevertheless, underneath this burden, there must have been sufficient of them prepared to throw off oppression to justify the appearance of a number of Regency garden books designed especially for them. Jane Loudon, too, brought out her own example in 1840. Called *Instructions on Gardening for Ladies*, she starts almost immediately with passages such as:

... the uses of digging having been thus explained, it is now necessary to say something of its practise, and particularly of its applicability to ladies. It must be confessed that digging appears, at first sight, a very laborious employment, and one peculiarly unfitted to small and delicately formed hands and feet ...

She goes on to explain what a spade is for and how it is used:

... a lady, with a small light spade may, by taking time, succeed in doing all the digging that can be required in a small garden, and she will not only have all the satisfaction of seeing the garden created, as it were, by the labour of her own hands, but she will find her health and spirits wonderfully improved by the exercise, and by the reviving smell of fresh earth.

A LADY'S GAUNTLET OF STRONG LEATHER, INVENTED BY
MISS PERRY OF STROUD, NEAR HAZLEMERE.

In a fascinating section on the difficulty of dressing as a lady and yet managing to garden, she shows a picture of 'A lady's gauntlet', conventionally small and delicately formed, holding a rose stem, plus clogs and gaiters. She goes on:

The time for digging should always be chosen, if possible, when the ground is tolerably dry; not only on account of the danger of taking cold by standing on the damp earth, but because the soil, when damp, adheres to the spade ... Every lady should be careful when she has finished digging, to have her spade dipped in water, and then wiped dry, after which it should be hung up in some warm dry shed, or harness room, to keep it free from rust.

Of course digging was most essential for vegetables, which were quite obviously a man's department, for

Whatever doubts may be entertained as to the practicability of a lady attending to the culture of culinary vegetables, and fruit-trees, none can exist respecting her management of the flower-garden, as that is pre-eminently a woman's department. The culture of flowers implies the highest possible kind of garden labour; only indeed enough to give an interest in its effects. This light labour is, in fact, one of the reasons that the culture of flowers is so generally a favourite occupation.

Similar prejudices are expressed by 'Rosa', one of the first female journalists of the Victorian period. In the *Cottage Gardener* of 1849 she writes:

I should advise ladies to have as little DUG ground as possible, amongst shrubs and bushes, for it is a perpetual trouble; weeds spring up incessantly, and it is very difficult to get at them. The rose and the sweet-briar tear our bonnets and collars to pieces, and we tread most vexatiously on our raiment when stooping to avoid them.

She had all her own borders turfed.
She, too, found her clothes difficult:

There is no doubt that a lady's dress is not one very well suited for gardening; all we can do to obviate its disadvantages ... we will still I fear find, that actual work in a garden does not improve its appearance. A large apron, and gloves are some protection; but what I have found better is a dark shirt. Gloves are indispensable to prevent the earth getting in at the wrist. I have seen ladies make gauntlets of strong unbleached linen fastened to the glove; this is quite as effectual for protecting the dress and for preventing that sun-burning of the wrist which is the frequent fate of lady gardeners.

This self-oppression continued almost to the end of the century, though by then it had a very much sharper edge and was clearly doomed. Mrs Earle, writing in 1897 in the best-selling *Pot-Pourri from a Surrey Garden*, said:

I am merely, like so many other women of the past and present, a patient gleaner in the fields of knowledge, and absolutely dependent on human sympathy in order to do anything at all. I cannot explain too much that the object of my book is to try and make everyone think for himself or herself. Women are still behind the other sex in the power of thinking at all, much more so in the power of thinking of several things at once. I hope the coming women may see the great advantage of training their minds early in life to be a practical denial of Swift's cynical assertion that 'mankind are as unfit for flying as for thinking'.

Mrs Earle thought perfectly clearly, and made a lot of money.

The conventions about what a woman could do were naturally reflected in the sort of garden she could have. These were generally small and colourful, especially something in the 'Dutch manner'. By 1850:

These are very suitable for villa-gardens of small extent, but require to be kept exceedingly neat and trim to be effective, and are very proper for the ladies to exercise upon, and keep in order, as the gravel walks will be more frequently in a dry state than the lawn; not that but a garden with grass between the beds may be partially managed by its mistress, as well as the other.

The flora too was restricted, even at the end of the century. Many advertisements appeared for 'Flower seeds for ladies; including everlastings, mignonette ...' and so on. White flowers seem to have been popular, perhaps giving rise to white gardens that were the progenitor of famous modern examples. The flora was also often nostalgic (though why women should be more prone to this feeling than men, or why they had not been prone to it before, is not known). Herbs, columbines and cottage flowers were particularly feminine. Flowers could, of course, be taken

20. The lady of the house, aproned, spraying her flowers.

indoors and arranged, though they could not be admitted to the bedchamber, Rosa pointing out that: 'No highly scented flowers should be permitted there, as they are injurious to health, and affect some persons painfully, but in the open air we can enjoy the strongest perfumes in safety.'

Among the flowers, indoors or out, Rosa goes on:

Woman has much in her power. Wives and mothers have great duties to perform; they are the mainsprings of the moral world: and even among their fragrant flowers they may cull instruction and impart lessons of wisdom, – for nature has many tongues. The holly and the Christmas rose, belonging as they do to former times and customs, teach us to keep the great festival now passing more in the Christian than the Pagan manner. Let this brilliant flower and glossy shrub repay our care by urging us to value more deeply, and commemorate more suitably the great deliverance wrought by Him who came to 'save his people from their sins'.

Flower arranging seems to have been an innovation of the Victorian period. Since medieval times, and probably earlier, everyone had carried with them small posies of flowers to sweeten the air and ward off infection (memories of this tradition can still be found in Mediterranean Europe and the Near East when sprigs of lemon flowers are given to intending travellers). In the seventeenth century flowers had quite often been cut and carried into the house to decorate the table, and in the eighteenth century great social occasions were commonly decorated with greens from the orangery, or hired from commercial nurseries who specialized in such business. However, references to any actual arrangements (apart from one suggesting the use of crown imperials to decorate grand rooms; odd because the leaves smell strongly of 'fox'), or methods of putting flowers together, are extremely rare.

However, the decoration of rooms with cut flowers became increasingly important in the nineteenth century and gave rise, by mid-century, to all sorts of appliances to hold flowers and keep them fresh. Many of the large bell jars found in present-day antique shops will once have been used to cover a bunch of flowers and preserve them from the heat and fumes of the drawing-room (though to protect fresh flowers under glass seems to make pleasure in them worthless).

A popular way of storing flowers in an almost airtight way was the 'Elizabethan vase'. In this, a glass dome fitted into a water-filled collar at the top of the vase. The flowers themselves were not in water, but were held in a suitably artistic pose by wet sand.

'Doing the flowers' was an important part of female duties, and doing them well was a sign that all was well with domestic life. The author of *Domestic Floriculture* (1874) wrote of bouquets, wreaths and vase decorations: 'In every bright and happy house this is peculiarly the ladies' province, and but a few of the sterner sex can hope to rival them on their own grounds.' He goes on: 'Of late years it has been the custom to ornament the dinner table either with living plants or cut flowers. The heavy and costly epergnes, or the great heaps of flowers and fruit formerly tolerated on the festive board, have now been superceded by more pleasing arrangements.'

21. 'A tasteful Dinner-table Decoration, arranged by Miss Annie Hassard' in 1874.

Some of these pleasing arrangements were quite curious; he gives an illustration of a table entirely encompassed by a fancy wirework arch, and suggests that 'The wax-like flowers of both the rosy and the white lapageria may be neatly mounted on wires and suspended from the margins of the vase, or from a light and graceful arch, where they look natural, and have a good effect.' Another extraordinary table arrangement shows a central stand with whole tree ferns at each end, and an even more crowded 'Dinner table decorated with ferns' so heavily vegetated that it must have been quite impossible to see through.

Incidentally, the present-day custom of having a dessert of fruit as part of the decoration of the dining table was new in the 1870s: 'It is considered fashionable now to dine *à la Russe*; and in this

case, the dishes of fruit and floral decoration are grouped together, and serve as ornaments during the earlier portion of the
repast.'

22. Indoor window-boxes screen the harsh world beyond the drawing-room.

The need for ladies to be accomplished flower arrangers
extended to almost all aspects of both life and death. The everlastings now so fashionable were then (as now) mostly imported
from the Continent. In the 1870s they were particularly used at
funerals, and more especially as decorations at the graveside.
Tasteful arrangements were usually put under glass shades, where

they could be expected to last clean and fresh for several years. Burbidge urges the use of plenty of grasses to give the correctly funereal 'look'. Dried flowers were also used as decorations for an unlit fireplace, or as a *garniture de cheminée*. While some amateurs dried their own, the flower-sellers were importing sand-dried roses, pelargoniums (no one seems to do these today), even chrysanthemums and carnations. The empty fireplaces of summer, when not filled with 'drieds', were sometimes treated more exotically, and one illustration of the 1870s shows a 'Fireplace decorated with Ferns and Trailing-plants during the Summer'. It certainly had all of these, but also included a mini-fountain, though how this was supplied isn't made clear.

Arranging dried flowers and glittering grasses for room or tomb was only one of a wide range of garden 'crafts' with which Victorian ladies could fill their time. Such attainments became popular around the middle of the century, and reached their apogee in the seventies.

'Rustic work' garden baskets were, of course, beginning to make their appearance in Regency gardens, though it isn't clear if their owners were also their physical creators. Even in 1850, though Victorian ladies seem to have been even more delicate than Regency ones, Rosa could write: '... the ivy basket may now begin to look gay. Rustic stands, roughly nailed together, look extremely well when filled with flowering plants. These things cannot be formed by a lady's hand, and, therefore, in many cases cannot be obtained.'

By 1870, ladies, even if not yet handy with a large hammer, were busily sand-drying half their garden and assembling the resultant crisped flowers under glass domes, or as flower pictures neatly framed. They were also doing more daring things, like 'fuming' them with sulphur dioxide (covering themselves with newly patented tarpaulins and rubberized gloves). Dried grasses, flattened pansies, roses, fuchsias, lobelias and the rest were used in firescreens, window screens, even as glazed panels for doors (they were carefully sandwiched between two sheets of glass, one sometimes frosted, for boudoir doors).

Then there were all sorts of albums that could be made, perhaps using a little stiff bristled brush to flick droplets of paint around 'a bold leaf such as that of *Ficus elastica*, as a centre, arranging a border of ferns around it; this forms an oblong or heart-shaped space, in which a verse of poetry may either be written or painted and illuminated'.

More experimental ladies could learn how to 'skeletonize' leaves and seed vessels for winter decoration.

The best method is given by Mr Robinson in the GARDEN – 4 oz of washing soda are to be dissolved in a quart of boiling water, then add 2 oz of slaked quicklime, and boil for 15 minutes. The mixture should be cooled and decanted. Reboil the clear liquid and add the vegetation. Boil for an hour. Drain the flowers then carefully rub off the flesh. Bleach the skeleton in chloride of lime.

It was apparently quite easy to do, and some ladies went so far as to have an outbuilding devoted to the hobby. Less wealthy ones must just have annoyed the cook. Good plants to use included vine leaves, fig (useful), beech, ivy, the seed vessels of *Datura*, cape gooseberry and so on. Some of these flowers were later treated with a supersaturated alum solution, poured over bundles of fresh or skeletonized material, then dried so that 'a sparkling crystal glistens from every spray'.

While many middle-class women were content to do a little light digging, or to skeletonize fig leaves amid the fumes of boiling soda, a few took the whole thing much further. By the 1880s a Miss J. Loadstone was advertising the brand new variety of pink called 'Mrs Sinkins' (a lovely thing and still available) and calling herself 'The Lady Florist'. Her business seems to have prospered for several years, and perhaps she had a substantial market in the large numbers of prosperous spinsters who seemed to exist.

By 1897 Mrs Earle could write: 'Yesterday, I paid a visit to the Horticultural College at Swanley, with its branch for women students. It immediately struck me as quite possible that a new employment may be developed for women of small means out of the modern increased taste for gardening.' She goes on to suggest that the trainees would be especially useful for small suburban gardens in which lady gardeners could cope well, and would be even more suitable for large establishments owned by maiden ladies.

Rather fewer ladies went on to become garden 'stars' in their own right. Those that did, did so mostly through the field of design. Earlier, Jane Loudon had pointed out in 1838 that: 'There is scarcely such a thing to be found as a lady who is not fond of flowers; but it is not saying too much, to affirm that there are very few ladies indeed who are competent to lay out a flower garden; though the skill required to do so is within the capacity of every woman who can cut out, and put together, the different parts of female dress.'

One who made herself if not a star, at least a glimmer, was Rosa, who seems to have epitomized the ordinary mid-century lower middle-class lady. She wrote for the *Cottage Gardener* between 1849 and the early 1850s. As far as I can see she is never named, though she seems to have been a spinster with a rather meagre, though private, income. It may be that her father was a nurseryman, for she does say that she was brought up to admire polyanthus and can't now like inferior sorts. Her strange mix of sententiousness and careful charity seem as typical of the period as was her 'sisterly' preaching of the role of 'woman' as keeper of the state's moral fibre. She also seems to have had an engaging desire for drama as well as sentiment, and a barely veiled desire to become a novelist.

Rosa's writings clearly enforced the class system of the day, where the poor had to work for others rather than subsist from their own ground. Rosa thought that 'No right minded English cottager will desire such a state of things as this. A garden is one of the cottager's best helps – it does not FILL his pot every day, but every day it will yield something to put into the pot. No cottager should desire to have more than an eighth of an acre for his garden. A slip of ground, twenty yards wide and thirty one yards long, will be about the size.'

However, the cottager's dwelling should delight the gentry when 'covered with woodbines, roses and jessamines' (she suggests taking cuttings, or buying some at only a few shillings each – a week's wages for any real cottager).

How much of the enjoyment of a happy domestic country house springs from its garden! What tales it may tell, in its silent sweetness, of all that is passing within. It 'Discourses eloquent music'. There are the husband's apple and pear trees, twined by the wife's sweet clematis ... all speaking loudly of the happy union of their hearts and tastes. This is one of England's blessed peculiarities – one of the secrets of her peace and power. Let us foster as much as possible the love of gardening, for it involves that holy feeling, the love of HOME. . . .

Usually the outside of our country cottages [are] bare, desolate and neglected; whereas for the smallest outlay, or rather without any outlay at all, those cottages might be clothed with a never-failing leafy ornament, equalling in beauty any that the most lavish expenditure could obtain ... Whenever we see a well-furnished gable of this character [she means one with a carefully espaliered pear tree] a clean garden and a good boundary hedge: we may always augur well of the moral and industrial character of their possessor. These are not the sort of persons who are ever seeking parish relief. Self-reliance is manifest in the neat and thrifty garden of the humblest cottager. . .

Nothing adds so much to the landscape as the picturesque, well-ordered COTTAGES – nothing delights the feelings more than a neat hamlet of snug, cheerful, bowery-looking cottages, with their little gardens brimful of cabbages, potatoes, and onions; and their wickets and porches shaded over with waving flowers. The residences of gentlemen do not please and interest us half as much, unless it is the parsonage, which, to an English heart, is, and must ever be, second only to the venerable pile near which it stands. There is moral beauty, too, in the cultivated cottage garden. Neatness and attendance bespeak activity, diligence, and care; neglect and untidiness tell of the BEER-HOUSE.

She adds a footnote: 'We recommend to our readers, in connection with this subject, a very excellent tract published this year . . .'

Rosa adored innocent flowers, especially after a morning dew, when 'the shining drops tremble and sparkle so prettily in their tiny cups, and they seem so fully to enjoy their pure repast, that it makes me almost wish I could live on dewdrops too'. She pontificated upon taste, as well: 'I have never been able to decide whether flower beds should be placed upon grass or gravel. In the summer, the coolness of a lawn is delightful to the eye and the foot, but in winter the wet and sponginess of grass frequently prevents a lady venturing among her borders, and thereby she loses much pleasure and employment as the year advances.' She adored plants such as heliotropes, but with grave reservations: 'I have seen them in the open ground, spreading themselves around quite widely, and throwing their spicy shoots across the walk in rich exuberance. They are too fragrant for a room.'

As the years progressed, she became more interested in cottagers' morals than in their gardens, and began to write small serialized and improving tales. By 1854 she was writing moralistic novelettes or horror stories – all about dissolute young noblemen being drowned at sea without a moment's repentance, or poor peasants who had NEVER ENTERED A CHURCH (a phrase she says she can scarcely write, though she does so in capitals). The editors presumably got fed up with such things, and *My Flowers* was dropped after forty-six instalments. She wrote: 'And now "My flowers" close. The evening of their short existence has arrived, but before the last leaf falls they would speak one parting word of warning to our hearts. Let our flowers repeat continuously the solemn truth, confirmed by the fall of thousands in our streets, "Surely the people is grass."'

Rosa was put on to a new series called *Our Village Walls*: 'Much is doing, in many ways, for the poor, but their health and comfort would be greatly increased if their dwellings were improved where it can be effected. I think much would be altered in this, as in every other case, if men would regard everything they possess as a talent committed to them by God. Men would not dare "grind the faces of the poor", nor to neglect even their common daily comforts.' She still managed to slip in some gardening, like this piece on lily-of-the-valley:

Shady nooks and corners, which are sometimes suffered to be neglected, or filled with stones and rubbish, might become green and fragrant with these lovely flowers. Not an inch of cottage ground should be suffered to be idle. As with the heart, so with the garden. If any spot, however small, is left untilled, up springs an evil weed, or it becomes a wilderness. It is worth noticing HOW VERY SOON this happens. Let us, then, plant with diligence and care the garden of the soil, but let us, with far deeper earnestness, tend the garden of our hearts.

The series didn't last, and was replaced first by *Hints for Humble Households*, then by *Home Suggestions*. She remained quite as religiose as ever, and after a first few articles on what to do in suddenly reduced circumstances (perhaps her own were about to be), she vanished for ever.

Even if Rosa became more obsessed with morals than with flowers, there were quite a few ladies of taste who created elaborate and beautiful gardens in the first half of the Victorian period; in the second half, the emotion that seems to have been associated with womanhood, nostalgia, began to play an important part in garden design, so naturally women became some of its main proponents. Even by 1842 nostalgia for a vanished golden age (perhaps when women had a more active role in the household than that of flower arranger) became apparent in the beginnings of a feeling for herb gardens. 'The olitory, or herb-garden, is a part of our horticulture now comparatively neglected; and yet once the culture and culling of simples was as much part of female education as the preserving and tying down of "rasps and apricocks".' Countrified wives of the past were thought to have invented herbal potions without number to enhance their own and their daughters' charms, 'for then the wife was head gardener'. She had a role.

In the 1870s one writer felt that 'To speak of a posy carries us back to quiet country villages where sweet-scented Jasmine and Woodbine, purple Clematis and monthly Roses fight longingly for a place beside the rustic porch; while the little plots in front of white thatch-roofed cottages afforded a variety of bright blossoms for the nosegay of the past.'

Mrs Earle was, by 1897, in full flight of nostalgia, especially when she remembers her old garden. 'The garden had peculiar charms for us, because, though we hardly realized it, such gardens were already beginning to grow out of fashion.' Flower-arranging 'stars' like Mrs Oliphant and Miss Hope collected old-fashioned flowers; Miss Willmott, Mrs Ewing and Miss Jekyll studied the already vanishing ways of the countryside.

Ironically, one woman who seems not to have been publicly interested in gardening was the Queen herself. A mid-century author, writing at a time when gardening was still equated with political harmony, of the exhibitions of the London Horticultural Society (now the Royal Horticultural Society):

But they have done more than this: they have brought together, on one common scene of enjoyment, an orderly and happy mass, from the labourer of the soil to the queen upon the throne. We can only have wished that royalty had been pleased to have paid a public as well as a private visit to the gardens. Her Majesty would have gratified the loyallest and best conducted portion of her subjects ... the cheerful ... thousands of well-dressed and happy-looking people of every degree. If we wished to show an 'intelligent foreigner' what everyday England really is – what we mean by the middle class – what by the wealth, the power, the beauty of the gentry of England – what by the courtesy and real unaffectedness of our nobility – we would take him on a horticultural fete-day to see the string of well-ordered carriages and well-filled omnibuses, the fly, the hackney, and the glass-coach taking up their positions with the britzcha, the barrouche, and the landau, in one unbroken line from Hyde Park Corner to Turnham Green – bid him to look at the good-humoured faces of those who filled them and say whether any other country in the world could, or ever would, turn out a like population.

There were even quite strong attempts to get children into the garden market; a number of vaguely improving children's garden books were written, especially the charming *Mary's Meadow*. But the idea didn't really catch hold of any but the most garden-oriented mothers, though there was the rather curious *Usable Handbook of Gardening* by James Rennie. This is a guide to Linnaean classification for children, and is actually quite fun. The 1834 edition is a new and much enlarged one, with a charming frontispiece of a cottage garden with bee-skeps, slate fences, and round flower-beds.

The writer points out that gardening is taught in Swiss schools and hopes that that will soon be the case in Britain, though he begins with the

ORIGIN OF THE WORK, within a very brief period of time, public attention has been strongly directed to bettering the conditions of our peasantry, and in consequence partly of their wants (real in many cases, imaginary in others), having driven them to commit extensive depredations, and in numerous ways to become formidably troublesome. This public attention has given rise to an almost simultaneous rise in England of the system, of allotting, on a moderate rent, from one-fourth to half an acre to an individual labourer willing to cultivate the same at his own charge; and, in Scotland, where the peasantry are of a greatly different character, to the proposal of a regular system of instruction in gardening...

When I was in Switzerland, in the autumn of 1832, nothing surprised me more ... than the extraordinary neatness of the gardens attached to cottages and farmhouses, far surpassing in this respect anything I had ever seen in Holland or Belgium, much less in England. Scotland, I am sorry to say, is with a few rare exceptions, around Paisley and other manufacturing districts, quite out of the question, being in this respect little better than Ireland or France.

Everyone kept trying, and even in 1884 a writer was hoping to interest children in newly fashionable 'WILD GARDENS for girls and boys', while most of their parents were still in love with verbenas.

However, there were other possible markets if the children's one failed, and among the dead if not among the living. The market for gardens and gardening could naturally be extended to wherever there was a green space, and so gardens for the dead, in cemeteries, became a new area for their expansion. The old graveyards, particularly urban ones, had been pretty frightful, and Loudon describes some in London that had soil so rich in organic material that it was pitch black and almost as sticky. Some of them, too, followed the practice, common in Europe where the pressure of the dead on the space available was equally great, of exhuming the bodies every couple of years and clearing the land for a new set. This outraged Victorian sensibilities, and Loudon, acute as usual, published his interesting *On the Laying out of Cemeteries etc* in 1843. He preferred burials in open soil, as in churchyards like Greyfriars, where even under the grandest tombs, bodies lay in winding sheets alone. The reason for this was that decomposition was much more rapid and complete, even if will-o'-the-wisps (the flames from the methane produced by the process) did occasionally frighten passers-by. 'If men of landed property,' he added, 'however small its extent, were to reflect on this subject, we are persuaded that they would greatly prefer laying their bones in a suitable spot in their own grounds, than having them piled up in any family grave, vault or catacomb whatever.' A fine idea when a property remains in the same family, but embarrassing if it changes hands frequently.

Loudon's book stimulated an interest in the design of cemeteries, and the idea of turning such places into gardens began to take hold. Men like Edward Kemp began to design them for some of the larger cemetery companies; he was even buried in one of his own design.

By 1878 William Robinson was admiring some of the most advanced cemetery gardens in the world – those of America. There, especially in those designed by J. Jay Smith of Pennsylvania, they were beginning to look like parklands, filled with rare trees and flower-beds. Smith had recently been in London looking for sites on which to do something similar. Forty years ago, when Loudon had suggested that this could be done, the idea had provoked horror. However, the idea was now catching on all over America and was beginning to take root in Europe. Robinson obtained photographs of the famous 'Spring Grove', by the American landscape designer T. L. Olmsted, and was impressed that only one monument per family was allowed and that there were complex building regulations to ensure stability (important in a country with such cold winters, when frost-heave could easily destabilize a monument's foundations). He wrote that 'the introduction of varieties of evergreens, whose perennial verdure is particularly appropriate to ornamenting places of sepulture, has contributed much to mitigate the bleak desolation of winter and to render the prospect agreeable at all times'. Soon, of course, gardeners began to think of all evergreens as funereal, one of the reasons why they are too little planted today. He went on to suggest wild gardens in churchyards, with spring bulbs to give an attractive turf. He wanted no flower-beds, but good trees, and roses to drape church walls and tombstones. Soon, all over the country, graves were treated as tiny gardens, with each plot prettified with daisies, lilies, saxifrages and scillas. The rose 'Aimée Vibert' was thought to be the best for twining round a grave's railings.

All of this was, of course, for the middle classes. They, property owners for the most part, had considerable economic strength. However, the working classes, often living in rented housing that varied from the Prince Albert design to cellars of the most dreadful type, were increasingly beginning to wield the political strength of fear.

But what use was the upsurge of interest in gardens to the working classes or to the urban poor? They had no ground, no sunny windowsills on which to grow pelargoniums, and no idle hours to fill with arranging flowers under expensive glass domes; their nearest and dearest were buried in scarcely marked graves, where the planting of roses and forget-me-nots was impossible. The conditions in which many of them lived seriously alarmed their betters. Outbreaks of cholera in overcrowded cities were common, and the terrible epidemic at Exeter, which caused not only vast casualties but also outbreaks of riotous, even libidinous, behaviour among those at risk, concentrated the minds of the propertied classes. Soon surveys of the worst urban areas were being made. One, of Leeds, showed that of 568 streets only sixty-eight were paved and ninety-six were neither paved nor drained nor even cleared of refuse. One street with 176 families had not been touched for fifteen years. Many were permanently flooded with sewage. Two hundred were crossed with clothes lines. Five hundred houses had dark cellars which were actually lived in. All this was combined with 451 pubs, ninety-eight brothels, two churches and thirty-nine meeting houses. The death rate in a clean street was one in thirty-six; in a dirty street it was one in twenty-three.

As gardens and gardening were already thought of as a social stabilizer, it is not surprising that the provision of open spaces in the new industrial cities, or even in the hearts of ancient ones, became a priority. Though there were of course fine gardens surrounded by the terraces and circuses of the grander Georgian developments all over the country, they were mostly for local residents, not for the propertyless poor (as some still remain). London, Edinburgh, and a few other major cities had parklands near the city centres, in some cases former royal or ecclesiastical hunting parks. However, these rarely advanced the stabilizing love of flowers or offered attractive places to promenade, neither did they attract the funds of wealthy philanthropists.

By 1835 the *Botanical Magazine* could say:

Public gardens are just beginning to be thought of in England [there were many more in formation in France, Germany and Holland]; and, like most other great domestic improvements in our country, they have originated in the spirit of the people, rather than in that of the government. On the Continent, the contrary has generally been the case...

The desire for public parks, felt by a portion of the people in England, has given rise to societies for their production; and hence, we have the gardens of the Zoological Society in London, and a few others such as the Botanical Garden in Liverpool, Hull etc. The formation of these gardens by public associations may be regarded as an indication of a rising taste for this kind of enjoyment; and, as a farther indication of it, we may refer to the favourable reception given to the bill brought forward during the last session of parliament, by Mr Buckingham, for establishing a public park at every town and village where a majority of the rate-paying inhabitants expressed a desire to have one...

It was the rate-payers who felt at risk.

In 1851 the need was clearly growing apace, for in that year the predominantly urban manufacturing population had just begun to exceed the less volatile agricultural one. Thirty years later there were twice as many urban poor as rural ones. While for those in the countryside a garden was well known to be essential to their physical survival, no one quite knew what to do for city workers. While the allotment idea took root it was clearly impossible, in spite of the vast expansion in rail (especially) and road investments (which made trade and industry more vigorous and profitable), to provide most urban families with a plot of cultivatable land. However, by the 1880s a town like Nottingham had 10,000 allotments.

Even in the countryside the idea prospered, and various gentlemen or secretaries of committees published their arrangements for such things in the hope that others would follow. One such was SOME ACCOUNT OF A SYSTEM OF GARDEN LABOUR, *acted upon in the Parish of Springfield, Essex, with a few general remarks on Cottage-Gardening by Rev. Arthur Pearson 1837*. The author describes how eight acres were divided into allotments at six shillings for each of the sixty. They were allotted to men of the village by draw, and were thought big enough to help the cottagers' finance without taking up too much of their employers' time. At least in the early part of the period, and particularly during the Chartist excitements, this rate of return per acre was almost more profitable to the proprietor than farming the land, and there were various proposals for breaking up entire estates into cottagers' holdings (those proposals don't seem to have been taken up).

For at least some allotment holders it all worked, and all sorts of new pleasures were discovered. One correspondent to the *Cottage Gardener* in 1850 wrote that he had '. . . a habit of drinking intoxicating drinks to excess; and at the time I first saw the placards announcing your publication, I was in a state of great nervous debility. So much was my whole frame ennervated that my arms hung almost paralysed by my side . . . Such was my state then; thank God, it is not so now. I became a subscriber, and have since succeeded in getting an allotment of four hundred yards. . .' His health and vigour were restored. Others had to go abroad for 'allotments', and in 1842 the New Zealand Company was offering allotments in that country at rents of £300 for 150 acres in the countryside, or fifty acres in the suburbs, or for a single acre near the centre of Wellington.

Apart from allotments in the modern form, various hybrids developed, including some thought up by Joseph Paxton (though his were hardly designed for the urban poor). In *Design for forming Subscription Gardens in the Vicinity of large Commercial Towns* (1834) he proposed a sort of allotment scheme for tradesmen and others who, because of their business, had to live in the centres of cities and whose means did not allow them a foothold in the country. Presumably having a site in mind, he suggested dividing up the twelve and a half acres into fifty gardens of about a quarter of an acre, which would be enough for fruit and vegetables. Each section was to be walled off for protection and the safety of the produce. The remaining part of the grounds were to be set up as a botanic garden cum flower garden of four acres, no doubt for the use of the subscribers' womenfolk. Subscribers to the botanical garden were to be allowed not to have an allotment and vice versa. The cost was to be £16.2.0d per annum if the quarter acre patch was managed by a hired labourer, and with a small 'sub' to the botanic garden.

Paxton, of course, designed many fully urban parks, starting with the still heavily Victorian Princes Park in Liverpool. He was working on this from 1842 to 1843. He was thereafter soon at work on Upton Park in Slough, and then Birkenhead (unique in that internal traffic was kept separated from external and 'through' traffic). The grandly named 'People's Park', Halifax, followed in 1856–7, and he worked on various Scottish projects at Dunfermline, Dundee and possibly in Glasgow.

One of the problems with parks (and Princes Park is a notable example) was that in big cities they offered such an attractive amenity that property prices in the immediate vicinity soon rose, to such an extent that the land was no longer available to the sort of public who were most expected to benefit. Thus there are parks which still retain much of their Victorian and philanthropic flavour but which are mostly quite ringed by vast merchants' houses rather than the tenements of the poor. However, by 1877 such problems were not too much noticed, and parks were being created all over the country. Finsbury Park was in formation, dahlias and roses were in full flood at the Crystal Palace. Liverpool and Birkenhead had six parks, of which five were new or just completed.

Once the land prices had risen the parks themselves became immensely valuable assets which were endangered by the same speculative pressures that had created that value. Soon property developers were nibbling at the edges of some of the 'weaker' parks, and in 1851 Colchester botanic garden was actually being auctioned for building land. In London, popular and attractive places like Victoria Park (designed by the author Joseph Newton, of Oxford Terrace, whom we have already met (p. 22)) were soon under threat from development at its margins. Unlike poor Colchester, this provoked considerable public concern. Here, incidentally, the park had been planted up with many rare trees and shrubs after the big Loddiges sale. Even better, the vast subtropical bedding schemes were displayed without railings, whereas in Hyde Park the lush foliage was kept firmly behind bars.

When they weren't being eyed hungrily by developers, parks were acting as a model for gardening taste (a role which they still, alas, play). By 1869 Burbidge could aver that

It is to our great public gardens that we must look for improved examples of garden decoration, and if their contents consisted chiefly of plants well arranged that would withstand our climate, that would be all the more desirable, inasmuch as these public examples are seen by thousands annually, and are copied as closely as possible in many private gardens throughout the country...

At Battersea, the park he had in mind when writing, the bedding, whether subtropical or hardy, had long been much admired. It was there that the curious practice of having what were called 'cocked-up flower-beds' took hold. These were in effect raised beds, with 'swept-up' grass sides. The fashion came to London via Paris. It was first used there for sub-tropical bedding, for it was thought that the inclined sides of the bed would absorb extra heat and so make the plants feel more at home. However, it caught on and was soon used indiscriminately, for all sorts of plants, all over the country.

23. Weeping willows, pagodas and punts on the lake at London's Victoria Park.

Battersea and Victoria parks were two of the most expensive to run, costing, in 1877, £7,824 and £8,613 respectively. By contrast, Kew, far more sumptuous, cost nearly £21,000, whereas Richmond cost £3,000, and Edinburgh botanic gardens less than £2,000. They were all good value for money. For instance: 'The East End has Victoria Park; and during the spring and summer months this garden is a most enjoyable one, plenty of bright colours being afforded by the parterre plants; and the herbaceous perennials, which are grouped very tastefully along the margin of the shrubbery borders, are also highly effective.'

The interest in planning public spaces in the midst of rapidly expanding cities was soon associated with an interest in town planning, and the creation of new and attractive cities was soon seen as another palliative to the problem of social unrest and unhappiness. It was the lack of planning of the structure of the old cities themselves that was an obstacle to progress, not just their lack of provision for the needy and the oppressed. Of course, cities had never before had to cope with so many humans or with such vast diversity of activity.

It was, in a way, natural that those concerned with garden and landscape design should take an interest in these problems. William Robinson travelled extensively, looking at what other countries were doing in this field, and in 1878 he published the widely read *Parks and Gardens of Paris* in an attempt to introduce the best ideas of the newly emparked French capital to the rapidly worsening British one. He wrote:

I think it is very clear that many quarters of London, beautiful in themselves, are greatly lowered in value owing to bad approaches. A good and simple system of broad tree planted roads, radiating from the centre to the suburbs, and connected by outer circular roads, would tend to make all parts of the town more equal in value, and would go far to prevent that terrible isolation of the poor in various parts of the city, the misery of which is at present a by-word throughout the world. . .

A most crying evil of this period of change when masses of workers are steadily deserting the country for the city, is that our towns are still built upon a plan worthy of the Dark Ages, and only barely justifiable where the breath of the meadow sweeps through the high street.

He points out that many people associate this sort of major planning with autocratic government, while he himself appears to regret that there has been no English Napoleon (which, in the light of the Howardian lectures which we meet below, is ironic). He remarks that it has been democratic France that has done the best and most economic re-vamping of a major capital, though, characteristically, he regrets that many Parisian parks have been designed by botanists, architects and engineers, not gardeners.

'But improvements,' he writes,

will probably never come through botanists, whose true and very sufficient field is the world, with the herbarium in which to store their treasures; nor through architects and engineers because their own work is different even in kind ... The only direct way onwards is through the trained and artistic gardener ... The art of garden design is yet in a very barbarous state, only a few monotonous notes are, as a rule, got out of it, and we shall not know its true capabilities till there is a school of young men trained for it from the beginning, and devoted to it heart and soul.

The urban squares in Paris were open to all the public, and of this Robinson heartily approved.

What bright and refreshing spots would these be in the midst of our huge brick and stone labyrinths ... and if the poor children who now grow up amidst the filth and impurities of the alleys and courts, were allowed to run about these playgrounds, so much healthier for the body and mind! We have them all ready, a word may open them. At present the gardens in our squares are painful mementoes of exclusiveness. They who need them least, monopolize them [a quote from *Guesses at Truth*, by another author].

Robinson then illustrated the plans of several of the London private gardens of which he approved, though, at least on paper, they all look awfully dull. He then quotes from a paper by a Mr Robert Mitchell (a resident in Paris) about the new squares:

These masses of vegetation widely distributed amongst the most populous neighbourhoods, cleanse the air by absorbing the miasmic exhalations, thus enabling everyone to breathe freely... Now, thank God, this dark picture [of the old city and its fevers and fervours, and of children passing their days in squalor] has become bright. Within a couple of steps of the poor man's house there are trees, flowers and gravel walks where his children can run about, and seats where their parents may sit together and talk. Family ties are strengthened, and the workman soon understands that there are calmer and more moral pleasures than those of the wine-shop . . . Some time ago, while walking through the Square du Temple, where hundreds of children were running and jumping and filling their lungs with the country air that has thus been brought into Paris, we could not help saying to ourselves that, strengthened and developed by continual exercise, these young-sters would one day form a true race of men, which would give the State excellent soldiers, good labourers for our farms, and strong artisans for our factories.

Many of the boys must have taken part in the First World War.

The French seem to have had no problem with vandalism, though many proposals for public parks in both London and Edinburgh foundered on the belief that they would never survive. Robinson was reduced to proposing naïvely that the 'exclusive' London squares, which all had an outer belt of privet and lilac to screen the interior, should have 'peeps' cut through them to provide those without keys with a view of the beauties within; a quick route to revolution. In Paris, the squares had proper play areas for children, often as an expansion from the main paths, shaded with trees, and with benches for nannies or mothers. In London, there was nothing comparable; often all the available space was devoted to elaborate parterres that made play impossible. He wanted avenues and boulevards for London, and was all for opening up what he saw as the richest city in the world, where property was both cheap and gimcrack (unlike Paris). 'Our narrow streets, and flimsy houses, and the want of anything like a generally recognized plan, are worthy only of a period when men first herded together within walls for security, not of the Victorian era.'

Of course, as soon as there were reasonable numbers of parks in British cities, their first attacker was, naturally, William Robinson, who disliked the design of their shrubberies, which he thought were done only on paper.

The ground plan of a garden has no business to look pretty, and flowing curves on paper are almost certain to be tame and ugly curves when carried out in walks and beds. Gardens should be designed and staked out on the ground they are to occupy, – not drawn on paper and then transferred to the ground. The main difference between real medieval building and modern imitations of it is that the old work was staked out on the ground from a rough sketch ... modern work fails in picturesque effect because it always looks like a built drawing. Our gardens have exactly the same fault...

In 1899, as a development of all the discussion about new sorts of city and town, the Garden City Association was formed to promote a slightly mythic fusion of countryside (and nostalgia for the Golden Age) with the inevitable needs of industrial society. Set up by E. H. Howard, a somewhat eccentric man whose book on the subject (*Garden Cities of Tomorrow*) created enormous public interest, the association became the focus for all conditions of men, from angry workers looking for better conditions, failed craftsmen and temperance workers, to wealthy philanthropists like Mr William Lever and Mr George Cadbury. Howard's ideal was a development of the allotment movement, and was to provide smallholdings cheap enough for small operatives from towns to lease and still make a profit. However, *Tomorrow: A Peaceful Path to Real Reform* proposed an idealized plan of a vast circular garden city, with central gardens containing a cluster of museums, libraries, concert halls, a town hall and so on. These were in turn to be ringed by a park, bordered by an immense Crystal Palace, used as an annular shopping street and winter gardens. Then were to come a ring of houses and gardens, then an outermost ring of factories (for jam, boots and bicycles). Beyond this again was to be a ring of allotments, then of farms. All were to be linked with radial and annular roads, and an outer railway serviced the industrial and productive areas.

Dotted among farms were to be various charitable and philanthropic institutions, orphanages and so on. Everything was to be owned by the municipality, and financed by rent and rates. However, the scheme didn't stop there, for he proposed suggestions for linking six such peripheral garden cities to 'Central City' by canal and 'tube'. The intervening areas of farm and forest were to be scattered with 'Homes for Waifs', epileptic farms, insane asylums (presumably for people for whom the garden city had been too much), convalescent homes, homes for inebriates, colleges for the blind and cemeteries.

In 1904 a company called 'First Garden City Limited' was established and bought a large estate at Letchworth which the association's magazine aimed at promoting. It rapidly became a big movement with international connections, holding a vast range of meetings, seminars and lectures. It all sounded wonderful, and Letchworth was intended to become a health-giving and rather nostalgic mix of small industries, smallholdings, cottars and craftsmen (presumably with gardens filled with old-fashioned flowers). In fact it developed a slightly more sinister tone, perhaps best exemplified by a speech of Rider Haggard's.

Whatever may be said against smallholdings, I am persuaded that they, in conjunction with such other remedies as I have referred to, will serve to keep upon the land that clan of English yeomen which is absolutely necessary to the stability of our Empire. We need the strong and steady and equal-minded man who can only be bred upon the land. For this purpose, the fair lands of England have been made our heritage; not for the purposes of pleasure or ostentation, but for the growing of the nation's food, and more than that, for the breeding of a healthy, industrious and contented people!

A little later he comments on 'The Nightmare of Our Towns':

The scarcity of work is a difficult factor to overcome ... But the Garden City will create a labour market marked by the absence of unfavourable conditions, and the inhabitants will be protected by the presence and existence of all that tends to make life pleasant and bright...

In modern towns, the environment of our less fortunate classes is horrible ... We have in Manchester thousands of children ... [who] knew not a single English flower by sight, knew no common birds except the sparrow, nor anything that is found in the country.

The absence of nature, this gloom coming from the crowding together of houses, the gloom also coming from the horrible impurity of the air, and other awful conditions, make an environment so powerful, especially when it is aided by the public-house, that the wonder is not that we have such a large number of unemployables, but that we have such a large proportion of people who can be trusted, and who will do work when they can get it...

The Association became very keen on German town planning examples, and many lectures were given by German technical attachés to the London embassy. Many illustrations were published of suggested model cottages (just as they had been in the early years of the nineteenth century), often in a minuscule Queen Anne style. However, the most popular ones were shown in the 'Cheap Cottages Exhibition'; there were numbers of photographs of prefabricated cottages erected by Messrs Krupps of Barnhof. The irony of it all...

Perhaps the leaders of the movement had followed a favourite Emerson quote too well: 'To live content with small means ... to listen to stars and birds, to babes and sages with an open heart ...'

CHAPTER
4

THE
NEW STYLE

B UT WHAT SORT OF STYLE WAS IT THAT SO
perfectly suited all these new markets? At first it was the
'gardenesque' in its parterre mode, one to which many
gardeners still subscribe with great fervour every summer. It
began to become 'the rage' in the early nineteenth century; by
1836, the thirty-three-year-old Paxton could write:

> Grouping, or arranging showy plants, en masse, has of late years
> become so general in all good gardens, that we are somewhat surprised
> some efficient person has not attempted to give practical instructions,
> so as to ensure a succession of beautiful flowering plants for this
> purpose. Although the system has become almost universal, it is, we
> conceive, but imperfectly understood...

The hints he goes on to give

> apply to flower gardens with small detached asymmetrical beds, whether
> formed upon grass (which is the newest style), or gravel: and as one
> or two shabby or declining beds spoil the whole effect, the earliest
> opportunity should be embraced to refit them... in fact, until the last
> few years, flower gardens were for the most part a mere secondary
> object, as far as regards management; ... the principal things in the

flower garden were such as annual lupins, thrift, double feverfew, bachelors buttons, honesty etc, with some bulbs, and these planted almost indiscriminately, without reference to height, colour, or duration; there were none of the petunias, dahlias, verbenas, calceolarias, eschscholtzias, and dozens of equally elegant plants that adorn so beautifully our borders and beds at the present time ...

... There are some who advocate beds with mixed plants ... still they never have that striking effect that the same beds would have if filled with suitable plants, arranged in groups, and in large flower gardens we think them decidedly bad.

This article, from *Paxton's Magazine of Botany*, is Janus-faced, looking backwards to the very beginning of the bedding system in the earliest nineteenth century (when simple mixtures of hardy flowers were fashionable), and forwards to the fullest heights of the Victorian infatuation. And of course Paxton was then intending to become that 'efficient person', though twenty years later he'd become so grand and so famous that he had rather little to do with the furtherance of garden design.

Paxton's ideas about layout were not original. The detached asymmetrical beds to which he refers in these early articles are just the sort already illustrated by Loudon, and to be found at Dropmore. This, probably the 'type location' of such things, with its tadpole shapes cut out of the lawns, had beds filled with a simple mixture of two or three species of flowers. Though Loudon's illustrators copied the plans, and should therefore have known, it isn't absolutely clear whether it was actually the *first* garden where such beds had been made (in general, new developments, whether of science or interior decoration, often happen in several places at once). For such an important development there were quite soon several claimants, especially once it was clear, that is, that the style was in fact going to become supreme. Everyone likes a touch of glory.

The new media provided the forum for the contenders. There were, by mid-century, two – Dropmore and Campden Hill. The gardener at Campden Hill was John Caie, who was beginning to write and talk about the new grouping system (that is, grouping

1. Cragside: royal ladies among industrial splendour and the latest rhododendrons.

2. Zonal pelargoniums gave handsome foliage as well as luxurious flowers.

3 – 6. Nasturtiums, tiger-lilies, dahlias and the tulip 'Prince Albert', all widely
grown garden flowers.

7, *Top:* Stone and gravel: the parterre at Trentham.
8. *Bottom:* Windy magnificence on the parterre at Eaton Hall.

9, 10. *Top:* Rustic work and tasteful climbers around the arbour at Shrublands.
Bottom: Nasturtiums and Italian cypresses in the view from the upper
terrace at Shrublands.

11. Calla lilies and ferns in this elegant Wardian case for the drawing-room window.

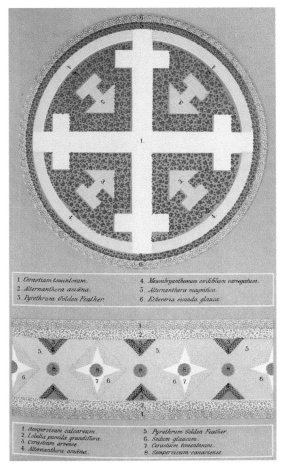

1. *Cerastium tomentosum.*
2. *Alternanthera amœna.*
3. *Pyrethrum Golden Feather.*
4. *Mesembryanthemum cordifolium variegatum.*
5. *Alternanthera magnifica.*
6. *Echeveria secunda glauca.*

1. *Sempervivum calcareum.*
2. *Lobelia pumila grandiflora.*
3. *Cerastium arvense.*
4. *Alternanthera amœna.*
5. *Pyrethrum Golden Feather.*
6. *Sedum glaucum.*
7. *Cerastium tomentosum.*
8. *Sempervivum canariense.*

12, 13. Carpet bedding ideas from the *Gardener's Chronicle* of the 1860s.

14. *Lapageria*, ferns and fruit used on a centrepiece for a dinner-table of 1863.

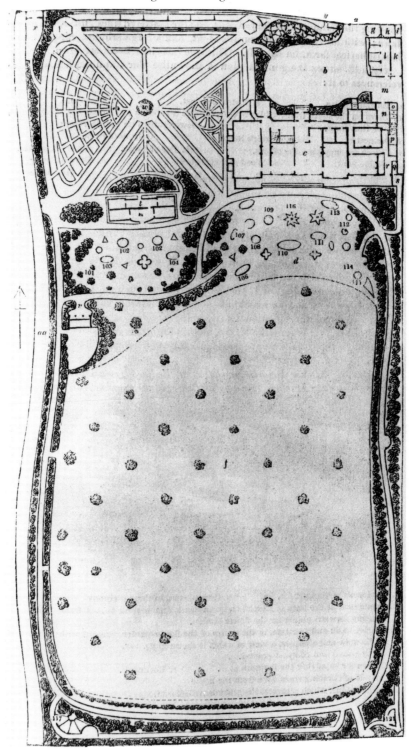

a quantity of plants of the same species by themselves in a single bed) from the late 1830s onwards. He enjoyed writing and talking to such an extent that he gave up gardening altogether some years later to devote his considerable energies (if rather lesser imagination) to writing and editing. Even by 1840 Caie had published a paper on the grouping system for flower-beds at Campden Hill (fifteen years after such things were first illustrated), claiming that that garden was the original location of the style. He was still, at the time, gardener to the Dowager Duchess of Bedford (the owner of Campden Hill), and the paper includes (usefully for anyone now wanting to copy an 1840s bedding scheme) a rare and rather good colour plate.

However, Caie had already been laying claim to the style for several years: a correspondent to another garden magazine describes

a vivid recollection of the evening of the 10th April 1837, on which Mr Caie, of Bedford Lodge, Cam[p]den Hill, read at the West Londoners Gardens Association, his admirable essay on the grouping system in the flower gardens, accompanied with a coloured plan, a draught of which, as well as the essay, appeared in the 'Gardeners Magazine' of that year [it didn't]. To that gentleman belongs the chief honour of giving an impetus to the grouping system; – but also to a leaning to aristocratic notions, and using only, and chiefly out-of-doors, tender plants...

(actually Paxton was their first advocate.) His admirer is so admiring that Caie is absolved from one of the soon-to-be-discovered problems of half-hardy bedding. Due to the generality of gardeners, 'and not any particular individual, do we owe the too usual baldness of our gardens during the winter months'.

The gardener at Dropmore (and his employer, Lady Grenville) seems to have been too modest to dispute Caie's claim in public, other than by a short note to the *Gardener's Chronicle*. William Robinson later republished this in his *English Flower Garden*. One of the contributors to that work mentions that

John Caie, who was gardener to the Duke of Bedford, and afterwards at Inverary Castle, is often said to have originated the system, but Mr Frost, writing from Dropmore, said: 'I helped fill the beds here in the spring of 1823, long before Mr Caie had charge of the Campden Hill gardens. It was Lady Grenville who began the bedding system in the first place, but she quite abhorred both ribbon and carpet bedding [Mr Frost is getting confused here, for neither sort of bedding was yet developed]. The Dowager Duchess of Bedford used to visit the gardens here, and much admired the garden, and when she went to Campden Hill to live, she sent Mr Caie here to see the place, and very probably to take notes of what he saw.'

Ah...
Certainly Lady Grenville was an imaginative gardener, and one of the first women of rank who became something of a garden star. She was, apparently, especially good at constructing rustic flower baskets out of garden and household detritus; these were said to be very beautiful if also very numerous. The Dowager Duchess of Bedford, on the other hand, does not seem to have played any role in the garden world, apart from employing John Caie. However, her house, Bedford Lodge, at Campden Hill, remained an important garden into the 1850s, by which time Dropmore seems to have declined. Various pictures of that date show Bedford Lodge to have had a curious geometrical flower garden with beds all edged with straight lines, though not in the least 'historical', all radiating as they did from a basin under a pretty canopy of trellis and climbers. Beside it there was also a slightly earlier lawn dotted with flower-beds — stars, ovals, triangles, flower-shapes and so on, some with central standard roses. It must have been this part of the garden that Mr Frost supposed copied from Dropmore by Mr Caie. There was even more evidence of copying, for the plans show that one set of paths had a fancy guilloche border, the basic design done in stone, enclosing small circular beds (planted for succession: early, middle and late flowers — bulbs, annuals and perennials, but with their colours not related, though there was only one colour for each bed at any one time). There had once been exactly comparable beds at Dropmore.

Wherever it started, the grouping or bedding 'system' was a new development. The old method of planting garden flowers was in a mixture, and flowers had been planted that way certainly since the seventeenth century. It was once believed that to have two flowers of the same sort next to one another was a grave error of taste, and it seems likely that such planting ideas had an even more ancient past. The idea of 'grouping' flowers, so that only one sort was to be seen in each bed, was as much a major departure from the conventions of history as was the passion for informal landscape gardens of the previous century. The mixed mode of bedding survived in rather specialized areas of gardening until the end of the nineteenth century.

Paxton, Caie and Ferris hammered away at the 'grouping system' idea for the next few years. By 1838 Paxton was publishing flower-garden plans of quite remarkable complexity. Following an extraordinary double crown design, he wrote:

The great number of flower beds which form the central part of the garden, will furnish the means of grouping some of the most ornamental border plants; and by a judicious selection of sorts, so as to have an interesting combination as well as variation of colours, such a system will produce a most engaging effect. In modern flower-gardens, the old practice of having a variety of plants in one large bed, and arranging them according to their height and colour, has been entirely superseded, and the system of grouping plants of one sort in small beds substituted for it. That the latter possesses many advantages over the former, although it is not so extensively adopted as it deserves to be, needs little argument to prove; and we shall now enter briefly into the mode of effecting it . . .

With the breathtaking aplomb of a gardener working for a fabulously rich employer, he goes on:

We purpose banishing entirely from the flower-garden all such plants as are perfectly hardy, or, in other words, those which are generally termed hardy herbaceous plants, and supplying their place with the more showy and favourite kinds which require protection during the winter. We would not, however, exclude those sorts which are

25. Paxton's grand ideas for a flower garden.

ornamental, and especially the dwarfer ones, but only those tall, strag-
gling, uninteresting, or rather less interesting species, which are much
better adapted to the borders of shrubberies... A number of garden
frames, or pits, are essential...

He thereby dismissed centuries of work, and an entire garden
flora, much of which was to vanish irretrievably.

Of course, the new system was a magnificent fulfilment of the
new passion for 'artificiality', but it fulfilled many more aims of
the age. For a start, it was showy and colourful, in contrast to
the chaste understatement of the gardens of Georgian Britain. It
also depended on new technologies in the production of glass, of
glasshouses, and of the methods by which the latter were heated.
Although it depended therefore on the ability of the garden
owner to purchase either the technology itself, or the plants from
nurseries who had already done so, it meant that relative wealth
could be shown by all classes of person. The lawyer, the shop-
keeper, and even the clerk could have a tadpole bed or two on
the front lawn of his second or third rate house, and so dem-
onstrate his advanced tastes as well as the depth of his pocket.

By 1830, with a rush of books and articles on suburban houses
and gardens, all designed for the new middle-class market, the
new sort of bedding plan exemplified by Dropmore was catching
on. For instance, in the *Gardener's Magazine* of 1835 there is a long
article by a Mr T. Rutger called 'A Series of Designs for laying
out Suburban Gardens and Grounds, from One Perch to several
Acres in extent', in which almost every plan is for the front garden
of a semi-detached house. Some are for grand 'semis', with either
one large entrance to allow carriages to both front doors or two
smaller private ones not allowing any carriages at all. The garden
designs soon became so standardized that the ones he illustrated
in his articles could be from any time during the following fifty
years. All had very Loudonesque 'angel' beds, small lawns, vases
and isolated bushes, and an outer boundary of shrubs.

It is not fanciful to suggest that the bedding system also
demonstrated a new attitude to real-life nature, rather than the
fake 'garden' nature of the followers of the picturesque. In the

old way of putting flowers together, long before any notion of 'landscaping' had evolved, account had been taken of each individual flower so that it would look attractive beside its neighbours and complement them in terms of scale and colour. For such schemes to work, attention needed to be paid to each plant. In the early Victorian bedding or grouping system, plants' individualities were of no importance, each individual merely yielding the colour of its flowers to the general show. Consequently, the myriad possibilities of the gardens' plants were not considered, and an interest in that sort of variation therefore evaporated. The obsession with 'show', with plants merely as a 'blaze of colour', was all. The garden flora, as we shall see, could therefore become reduced to almost a handful of genera which were capable of providing varieties with an infinite variation of basic colours and which were tolerably well adapted to the whole bedding system. This is in a way comparable to today's nostrums about 'colour the year round', and the increasingly few genera commonly being grown to supply that rather debased need.

Though the idea of having amusing and colourful flowerbeds cut from the lawn swept through nearly all gardens almost instantaneously, the 'grouping system' of using one type of plant in each bed met with some resistance. Inevitably some gardeners found it either too advanced or only capable of rather crude effects. Those in the first group kept the old 'mixed' style going well into mid-century but kept the mix to just two or three different flowers. Almost everyone avoided the even older planting methods, which had received the opprobrium of the word 'promiscuous'. An example of the mixed style can still occasionally be found planted out on traffic islands or around the public conveniences of seaside towns. It seems first to have been described in the *Cottage Gardener* of 1850 by a writer who admired a hardy species of verbena: 'I shall recommend a way of using it in a mixed flower garden, which, if I mistake not, will ensure of it being retained as a permanent plant ... I mean the mixed style of planting single beds...' *Verbena venosa* (still easy to obtain as seed) was mixed with 'Old Scarlet' geranium, to give what parkkeepers still call 'the shot silk effect'. It is by no means as spectacular as that fabric, though with a haze of small violet flowers above the more solid mass of scarlet ones it is certainly quite interesting. Another pleasant mixed bedding scheme of the same date was designed by Donald Beaton and used the lovely *Felicia amelloides* (popular from 1845) mixed with about a third of mid-blue lobelia (try using the double-flowered 'Kathleen Mallard').

In an attempt to tighten the grip of the rival grouping system, various authors began to promulgate 'rules' (it is astonishing how many gardeners turn out to be passionate authoritarians). Caie started it off in 1837: his *On the Proper Arrangement of Plants, both as to their height and the colour of their Flowers, being indispensably necessary in a Flower-Garden* suggested that

... our ideas should be greatly expanded and diversified, before we can produce the effects most desirable in flower-gardens, namely, harmony and variety; without which the plants will appear quite as irregular to the cultivated eye as they were previously to their being removed from their natural situations. As long as gardeners acted without any fixed principles to guide them, it is no wonder that individuals, ignorant of the art of gardening, succeeded as well in making flower-gardens as those who were then called practical men.

It plainly did not occur to him that the non-practical people might actually have had 'taste' and the practical ones might have lacked it (many certainly did).

Another rule-maker turned out to be Donald Beaton, who by 1851 had so formalized the whole thing that he thought that every parterre had to contain different heights of plants in different shades, but only in three shades and three heights. This gave only nine beds, or groups of nine, still with one sort of plant in one bed. By the same date, too, many grand nurseries were beginning to employ parterre designers for their grandest customers; Messrs Standish and Noble of Bagshot, for instance, published their artist's plans for the garden of Miss Boulton at Haseley Park. These are rather fun; they used a rather butterfly-like symmetry done in Tudorbethan strap-work, like some modern stencil designs. The planting, still with a single variety in each bed, made

26. A pair of compasses and a ruler made planning flower-beds easy.

use of *Gazania, Tropaeolum canariense,* pink geraniums, *Verbena* 'Elizabeth', *Cuphea, Nemophila, Phlox drummondii,* dahlias, escholtzias and so on. For 1854, it was rather good.

Naturally, once the grouping system had clearly triumphed over the mixed one, and once it had developed its own flowers, elaboration could begin. However sumptuous the effects that could be created with single sorts of plant in each bed (whether contrasting or harmonizing colours were used), it was only a short progression to using one sort of plant to make a margin around a ground colour of another, or to start playing around with different areas of flat colour within a bed.

121

The first models for these new sorts of complexity were probably found in the sort of tiny bouquets or nosegays sold by flower-
girls on almost every street corner (posies to protect the nose
from noxious smells were still as important in Victorian cities as
they had been in sixteenth-century ones). A writer in 1854 was
astonished that these were available every day of the week, even
in the depths of winter, and that

A good nosegay [could be had], with six or seven camellia flowers
in it, and Geraniums, Pinks, Picotees, Violets and Azaleas, with
Mignonette, and Sweet scented leaves, all made up in circles, and
wrapped in paper, the size not less then ten inches in diameter, and all
for one shilling that very day!
I saw one nosegay quite new in design, and most beautiful and telling
a combination, which one might imitate in a circular bed of four or
five feet in diameter. First, get nine white Camellias, one in the centre
of the circle, then two on the right and two on the left of the centre,
in a line ... then two in front and two at the back ... Now get four
azure blue flowers, or four little bunches of the same blue, in Cinerarias,
and place them up against the four angles formed by the white Camellias
... then scarlet Geraniums, [and] you may fringe it with Mignonette.

Of course, such a bedding scheme would easily have been worked
out in the contemporary flora of geraniums, calceolarias, lobelias
and so on.

Such schemes, even tiny ones for front gardens, needed vast
nurseries to service the demand for plants. Even a smallish firm
like the still extant Scotts of Merriott sent out, in 1854, 'Many
thousands of above ... one hundred sorts of Verbena, fifty sorts
of Geranium, one hundred sorts of Fuchsia, etc. etc.' In private
gardens the situation was just the same; Donald Beaton, at Shrubland Park, overwintered each year well over 5,000 young 'Punch'
geranium cuttings, and several other varieties on top of that.

As in the posy described above, some of the edgings used
in flower-beds were thoroughly imaginative, especial use being
made of some of the interesting variegated plants coming into
vogue, like variegated daisies, London pride, and some of the
variegated grasses. Most popular, by 1850, was the variegated

alyssum (*A. caucasica*), still available, which must have been quite spectacular. 'The Variegated Sweet Alyssum is, indeed, the richest edging to a scarlet, or blue or yellow bed, of all plants we possess...' though in order not to be caught out, the writer continued '... but some tastes might prefer MANGLE'S VARI-EGATED GERANIUM before it; but as I keep strictly to white flowers at present, that geranium cannot be admitted, on account of its purplish flower'.

There do seem to have been 'white gardens' in the 1850s though of course white flowers were most often combined with other things. However, an all-white garden of the period could have had white petunias, clarkias, even verbenas (some writers thought that white verbenas were terribly boring, and, like all colours of *Verbena*, they suffered from mildew; dusted every fortnight with flowers of sulphur, the overall effect must have been spoilt), the now vanished white *Salvia patens* and so on. Indeed, white was thought to be 'the eye of the garden'.

Even Jackman's new clematis, hailed in the 1850s as 'The latest new sensation in bedding out' was brought into use. The plants had been a sensation as soon as they appeared; Robert Fortune had imported *Clematis lanuginosa* from China in the late 1840s, and Mr Jackman decided to cross it with *C. Viticella* 'Atro-rubens' and *C. Hendersonii*, a decision that ensured his immortality. He was at once swamped with superb seedlings. The plants were at first grown up poles and strings, like a hop garden, but a storm broke them all down and, as in all busy nurseries, they were left as they were. The plants sprouted and flowered all along the stems. So all subsequent seedlings were pegged down to the ground to test their abilities as bedding plants. The idea caught on, and soon every clematis bed, a sheet of mauve or silvery lilac, was edged with silver or variegated foliage. They must have looked wonderful.

Blue and white was always a popular combination, especially for edgings; the blue and white of lobelia and alyssum still seen in almost every public park was first carried out at Kew in the mid-century and was instantly copied throughout the country. At Kew the flower-beds were mostly chaste circles, and old-

fashioned, having been widely popular since the early years of
the century. However, many gardeners attempted a wider range
of shapes. One, coyly calling herself 'Incognita', writes of her
Maltese cross bed that the centre was filled with *Oenothera macro-
carpa* while the arms were filled with alternate red and blue
flowers, though one arm was, for some reason, filled with fuchsias
(perhaps because the flowers themselves consisted of those
colours), and edged with alternate white and blue campanulas. It
must have looked most strange. However, 'Incognita' was doing
something entirely typical of the 1850s, which was to have an
edging around a simple centre usually consisting of a mix of just
two types of flower. Another correspondent of 1851 complained
to an editor because she'd tried snake-shaped beds but didn't
like them, and asked if butterflies would do better (she plainly
envisaged some nice colourful wings).

Of course beds were (and are) very easily made – it was simply
a matter of asking the gardener to cut some holes out of the lawn,
or of marking out some spaces and filling the interstices with
gravel to make the paths. More difficult was deciding whether to
have a more or less random arrangement of tadpoles, snakes,
butterflies and so on, or some more clearly organized and 'geometrical' arrangement. Even by 1837 this problem alarmed gardeners. In that year C. F. Ferris published *The Parterre: or, the
whole art of forming Flower-Gardens*, filled with various plans in a
number of modes. Of one, in the 'French' style, the author wrote
airily: 'We do not condemn this kind of parterre: far from it, we
should like to see one in the grounds of every extensive residence,
where, in spite of all that could be said against it, it would delight
by its contrast with the modern English parterre, and in recalling
the ideas of former times.'

Then, as now, parterres offered any gardener a major design
problem and it is one still seen today where gardeners have tried
to recreate knot gardens or formal herb gardens. If they're simply
placed out of context on a lawn, or beside a wall, the eye is very
easily distracted away from their complexity. In his review of
Ferris's book, Loudon picked upon this difficulty; Ferris did not
point out that if there was no walled enclosure specifically for

them, old parterres were surrounded with several rows of
hedging, each higher than the last (carried out in box, then yew,
then hornbeam). They were thus able first to enclose the eye's
attention, then delight it.

English parterres, with their messy tadpoles and stars, were
visually so weak anyway that the eye was unsatisfied whether they
were hedged and walled or not. Ferris's book, and Loudon's
strictures, had little effect, and fanciful English parterres were
soon general. While there was a historical element in some geometrical or French parterres (see below), it was perfectly easy to
design an 'English' one entirely free of any such association.
Many writers published parterre plans that can have taken only
a few minutes' work with a pair of compasses, and a few further
minutes' thought deciding what colour to put in each bed. Many
ended up looking like crude colouring patterns in children's
painting books. One of Caie's had sixty-six beds, all in concentric
rings. In this extravaganza not one plant was repeated, and only
those in the central disc of twelve beds had a two-sided colour
symmetry. No wonder Ferris thought there were few good parterres to be seen. Compass parterres existed even by 1852: 'A
flower garden should be made up of some geometrical form,
either by means of box-edging or gravel paths ... or cut on the
smooth lawn, when the grass must unquestionably predominate,
because, if limited to the width of a path, it would soon be
trodden bare and spoiled.' The writer gave diagrams for each
type, mostly drawn with a compass, and then explains how to fill
the flower-beds with red, yellow, blue and white, already the
conventional sequence. The beds were to be filled in winter with
small evergreens and pots of bulbs.

The red, blue and yellow theme, however hackneyed, was easy
to remember and caught hold of the popular imagination. It was
to be found everywhere, and survives into many present-day
bedding schemes, even though few nowadays use the old half-
hardy plants. Perhaps one of the great disappointments of the
Crystal Palace, when translated to Sydenham, was that however
innovative the astonishing building was in itself, Paxton did
not advance actual gardening when he used vast amounts of

the 'old' yellow calceolaria, conventional geraniums and so on.

Other elements at Sydenham were equally standard: the 'grouping system' was used for almost all beds, and the edgings used in them were even found in bands of colour wrapped like a scarf around the margins of shrubberies of rhododendrons and other evergreens (this became wildly popular). Elsewhere, calceolarias were teamed with the famous 'Tom Thumb' geranium, and where any other plant was grown, especially if it wanted to grow too tall, it was kept trimmed or pegged down to give the right height. This seems to be a new practice, and one which soon became widespread. Plants like the noble *Salvia patens*, or the more vigorous verbenas, were pegged. Pegging worked poorly for salvias, but some plants like heliotropes coped perfectly well. For geraniums, which were absolutely essential for all bedding schemes, but which, in most bedding types, had completely inflexible stems, it didn't work at all. Gardeners were reduced to using varieties of the same height, or to excavating beds to various depths to cope with any disparity between varieties.

Many of the beds at Sydenham were still of the now deeply conventional circular shape, as 'no other figure is so graceful'. But it was immediately apparent to every Victorian gardener that, whatever the shape of the beds, there were endless possibilities for elaboration once the idea of using several colours of flowers 'grouped' in one bed became accepted. More exciting, there were now no boundaries to taste, and, for many people, little boundary to expense. Labour was cheap; glasshouses and half-hardy bedding plants were getting cheaper by the month.

For those who hated the amorphous 'English' parterre, yet fancied historically geometrical flower-beds, it was natural to want to match the house's architectural style, whether Italianate, Old English, or castellated in either Scottish, French or German styles, to parterres of the sort that the originals would have had. Garden books of suitable period and provenance were raided, and parterres began to appear in which the form of the beds, if not the manner and flora of the planting, was based on period plans. The effects were variable. Some resulted in lovely and entirely Victorian flower gardens.

In the hands of educated (and rich) patrons, and usually towards the end of the century, some quite astonishingly lovely mock-period gardens were made, some of which still exist, though most of the loveliest only exist as fading photographs. One of these, made by Andrew Pettigrew in the 1890s, is the vast 'Jacobethan' parterre at Hewell Grange (a house of the same sort). Here, four hedged parterres enclosed an elaborate circular fountain and contained trellis- or box-edged flower-beds planted up with old-fashioned flowers. Another, and much more restrained, example is the wonderfully elegant four-square parterre surrounding a handsome sundial at Great Forsters (where the house is both handsome and ancient).

Other patrons, or their gardeners, were enthralled by the possible developments of planting up relatively simple bed shapes, but turning them into panels or ribbons or carpets in which both colour and imagination rioted. Everyone everywhere lost their heads. 'Bedding' was now absolutely the rage, from the humblest plot of ground to the very grandest. The gardens at Osborne and Windsor sported Italianate beds, minor country gentlemen in the

27. A winter/spring bedding proposal of Hibberd's, using potted plants.

Midlands vied with each other to have parterres in the best French or Dutch manner, factory managers in Paisley and Falkirk had patches of violas and pinks set out in stars and moons on their sooty front lawns.

While a few voices sent up plaints of caution, like a commentator writing on 'The Beautiful and the Expensive not Identical' who said, 'But no love for the system can make me blind to the facts, that the mode in which it is generally carried out has made next to a wilderness of many a garden until June, and not July, has begun to wane; and that many gardens belonging to the middle classes have lost their distinctive charm because the owners, forsooth, must copy the great man of the neighbourhood', no one cared.

Even the great botanical gardens followed suit. By 1850 Kew Gardens had flower-beds in the latest fashion to amuse the public. One Jeremiah wrote of this:

Now this is a very harmless and enjoyable way of amusing the public; and yet there are those in the high places of gardening who sneer at all the modern improvements in arranging flower-gardens, whether public or private; and who, assert that an unskillful *race of degenerate gardeners* have brought about such a state of things, substituting yards of this, that, and the other kind of scarlet verbenas, and scarlet geraniums, with 'patches' of petunias etc. etc. for hollyhocks, gilliflowers and herbaceous plants, which are all most beautiful in their way. So they are, sure enough, but a gardener of these days, who could produce nothing better than these good things might as well sing 'Bundle and Go', and be off at once to New Zealand . . .

All Britain burst into a blaze of colour, but before we deal further with the developments which the bedding system soon undertook and at some of the splendid achievements it created it is important to look at Victorian ideas on colour, many of which were much at variance with those that most modern gardeners now hold.

With advances in optical sciences, and also in the arts of printing, information about how colours were constructed became much more widely disseminated. As it was also still widely believed that there were absolute rules concerning beauty, it was felt that now that colours had become amenable to science, then so should the mixing of them. Gardeners became deeply interested in colour theory, whether emanating from scientists or from artists.

An early publication called *Two Letters to an Amateur, or Young Artists, on Pictorial Colours and Effect*, by Robert Hendrie (1842) suggested that

A pleasing arrangement of colour is necessary in order to gratify the eye, and for this purpose a simultaneous presentation of the three primitive colours RED, YELLOW, and BLUE, either in a simple form, or any two in a compound, and the third in a simple form, is required... Any one primitive colour balanced by its opposite secondary, or the compound into which it does not enter, will be accepted by the eye with pleasure, as green balanced by red, violet by yellow, or blue by orange.

A still greater degree of pleasure is afforded if the secondary colours are combined with the primitive, and are introduced in the order in which they are naturally presented to us by the rainbow.

The possibilities that this suggested were enthusiastically taken up by some gardeners, though the majority never got much past using red, yellow and blue.

The article prompted correspondence in the *Gardener's Chronicle* of the same year about how to start looking for plants to fit the theories. It also sparked off a controversy that was to last into the 1880s, by which time subtlety at last prevailed. For instance, a writer to the *Cottage Gardener* of 1850 opined:

There is no doubt that arranging flowers according to their contrast is more pleasing to the eye than placing them according to their harmonies. Consequently, a blue flower should be placed next to an orange flower, a yellow near a violet...

Another went on:

One of the most beautiful bouquets I ever saw was comprised of a mass of scarlet geraniums interspersed with fairy white roses, and surrounded by half blown double white camellias. A very pretty bouquet for mourning may be formed of white flowers surrounded by double violets. No bouquet is good without a rich green and a dead white.

In this period, then, there was a general passion for deep and intense colours, strongly contrasted. To help the aspiring bedder, a colour wheel plan was published: violet/lavender/blue/sea green/green/olive green/yellow/apricot/orange/scarlet/red/lilac/violet. Readers could choose neighbours for harmony, opposites for contrast (more respondents liked contrast).

By 1853, McIntosh's *The Book of the Garden* propounded that 'there has been an improvement of late years in the arrangement of both form and colour in our first-rate flower-gardens; the first step to which was, grouping the plants in masses ...' McIntosh was, as we might expect, a considerable admirer of the three primary colours. These he elaborates into primary harmonies, which are combinations of orange and blue, purple and yellow, green and red. There are also tertiary colours – olive (green mixed with purple), citron (green and orange), russet (orange and purple) – as well as secondary harmonies: olive mixed with orange, citron and purple, russet and green.

Finally McIntosh can no longer resist giving a few rules:

As a practical rule in planting parterres, the most intense colours should be placed in the centre, gradually softening down towards the margin of the bed or the sides of the garden.

He goes on with page on page of possible colour combinations.

Contrast of colour – The rule in this case is to put one of the primitive colours – red, blue, or yellow – next another of these colours, or some other colour formed by compounding the other two. In bedding plants, wherever a handsome plant of the colour required cannot be obtained for any of the particular beds, white, or some neutral tint, should be employed as a substitute.

Nowhere in any of this, or for that matter, in any of the other gardeners' writings on colour, is there any suggestion that flowers may contain several colours, let alone veinings, tones or washes of one colour over another. That would have made it all too difficult to theorize.

None of the mid-century garden writers has much to contribute to the debate, and the grip of beds in the familiar scarlet, yellow and blue simply tightened. The most interesting comments on colour at this period come, not surprisingly, from interior decorators, artists and architects. The triumvirate's grip, however much it was shrugged off by those with a sophisticated eye, remained imposed upon the less educated for the entire century, and even now 'Parks Departments' displays show it with sometimes only the slightest modifications.

The architect and garden designer Nesfield, who'd already been playing around with the seventeenth-century idea of filling parterres with coloured earths and sands (producing some exquisitely subtle colour schemes), waited until 1862 to publish, in the *Gardener's Chronicle*, some really fine colour combinations that he thought would be good in the flower garden. The paper is quite long, but some of the nicest combinations include a subtle scheme in buff, olive, grey, and one or two soft greens. It is rather 'Robert Adam' in style.

The same magazine also ran an article by Mr Crace, whose firm had become one of the most famous interior decorators in Regency Britain. Speaking at the Society of Artists on the colours used at the International Exhibition, he said:

Avoid blazing contrasts of colours, such as bright red next bright green; or bright blue next bright yellow; such contrasts are not harmonious ... Nothing is so charming and so refreshing to the eye as an harmonious arrangement of colours ...

He went on to suggest some wonderful-sounding colour combinations, some of which would look quite marvellous in a garden of the period as well as stretching the gardener's imagination for suitable plants. Some of the combinations were: black and warm brown, violet and pale green, violet and light rose colour, deep

28. Subtle colours of gravel and sand were used for this parterre, commissioned by the Royal Horticultural Society.

blue and golden brown, chocolate and bright blue, deep red and grey, maroon and warm cream, deep blue and pink, chocolate and pea green, maroon and deep blue, claret and buff, black and warm green. Lovely.

Following on from some of these more sophisticated colour ideas, gardeners, men and women, began to take a much more exciting look at the plants in the garden (there was, in any case, a reaction against the botanical poverty of the high Victorian bedding schemes, so the range of possibilities was suddenly very much wider). For instance, Miss F. J. Hope, a suburban Edinburgh spinster, well bred and of forceful and determined character, began a series on flower arranging in the *Gardener's Chronicle*. She planned this to suit anything from small flower glasses three inches high to tall ones three feet high. She liked to have the bases covered with some sort of creeper – bryony especially (she seemed to like poisonous plants). Some of her schemes were central to ordinary Victorian thinking; red or white paeony with, say, the lemon yellow flowers of *Hemerocallis flava*. More fun, she liked *Delphinium formosum* (now *D. cheilanthum*, in shades of blue) with the greeny-pink and thread-like petals of *Tellima grandiflora*, or the creamy-white spires of *Aruncus sylvester* with the cold yellow *Aconitum vulparia* and the cream variegated leaves of gardeners' garters (*Phalaris arundinacea* 'Elegantissima').

Other ideas of Miss Hope's on which modern gardeners could base a spectacular herbaceous border include mixing scarlet and black *Papaver orientalis* with straw-coloured irises; the creamy *Aruncus* with the pastel blue leaves and arching grey flower stalks of *Avena* 'Sterilis'; dark blue and straw-coloured irises with oriental poppy buds; Aaron's rod (the native *Verbascum thapsus*) with *Valeriana pyrenaica* in red and pink; or roses like the ravishing 'Coupe d'Hebe' with the gorgeous and ancient *Lilium candidum*, anise-scented leaves of myrrh (she meant *Myrrhis odorata*, not the biblical myrrh) and a few passion flower trails. More sumptuous still, she liked the blazing and waxy scarlet flowers of *Lilium chalcedonicum* with the purplish black spikes of *Veratrum nigrum*, or some of the new peachy yellow flowers of the contemporary hybrids *Gladiolus* × *brenchleyensis* with deep blue *Agapanthus umbellatus*.

Miss Hope carried her ideas for putting plants together out into the garden, and published some elegant bedding plans. Some of these schemes had edgings of rosy *Heuchera* leaves; a bed of the lovely double 'Old Bloody Warrior' wallflower was edged with the cream-white froth of double meadowsweet; a bed of China roses with pale autumn crocuses was finished with heucheras and Mangle's geranium.

Naturally, everyone soon wanted to play around with colour. Keeping with the geometric, *The English Flower Garden* of 1883 illustrated an extraordinary 'panel' bed, a marvellous Gothic fabric design carried out both in flowers and, by now, in foliage. The flora was fairly standardized but the final effect must have been gorgeous. *Cerastium tomentosum* (the formidable snow-in-summer) and *Stellaria aurea* supplied silver and gold, with lobelias supplying the azure blue ground colour.

The unidentified writer suggests that the most sumptuous effects are actually obtained by utilizing harmony rather than contrast, and also suggested that if readers, planning a flower garden, felt that they knew nothing about colour, then it was worth taking a look at wallflowers, auriculas, polyanthus, alstroemerias and Spanish irises for ideas on how to combine them with the greatest elegance (still a brilliant idea for today's plantings). In long borders, he (or quite probably she) suggests keeping colour design constant through the seasons, though of course using different species – perhaps red wallflowers, followed by red oriental poppies, and lastly vast clumps of red hot pokers. The writer's other colour notes have a rather painterly ring, suggesting good nostrums like 'purple and lilac do well together, with cold white and silver foliage, but to add heat, use soft yellow and warm white'. Of white flowers: don't dot them around, and they all look best in broad masses. Of the colour blue: all are difficult to use well (entirely true), but try using them with warm white or palest yellow; they're sometimes best in beds set in grass.

A clue to the author's identity can be found in the passage that suggests a progression in colours along the length of one of the new mixed borders:

... start with strong blue; then rose colour, crimson, and strongest scarlet, leading to orange and bright yellow. A paler yellow followed by white would distantly connect the warm colours with the lilacs and purples, and a colder white would combine them pleasantly with low-growing plants with cool coloured leaves...

It may have been early work by Gertrude Jekyll. However, though her final work was with herbaceous borders, at this date she still needed to acknowledge the bedding systems: she goes on to suggest that silvery-leaved plants are valuable as edgings, as well as sumptuous carpets to purple flowers. And of bedding schemes in general, she writes:

Colour in Bedding out – we must here put out of mind nearly all the higher sense of enjoyment that we have in flowers ... and must regard them merely as so much colouring matter, to fill such and such spaces for a few months ... The introduction of the bedding system changed all this [plants being grown for their own sakes; not as ensembles], and showed the possibility of arranging plants so as to produce a preconceived colour effect ... But however useful the bedding system may have been in directing the attention to a brand of garden design previously neglected, it has many drawbacks...

America followed the discussions of European gardeners with great interest, importing colour schemes and prejudices along with the plants. By the late 1890s these were widely disseminated, including the still current dislike of the colour magenta, which was thought to be so discordant that it should never be allowed into the garden in any form. White flowers were popular there too.

At the end of the Victorian period a slightly unnatural sort of alliance developed between the shattered remnants of the old guard, still cherishing their old-fashioned gardens with their promiscuous and probably rather untidy mix of flowers, and the advance guard, their refined sensibilities outraged with the vulgar and brilliant show of most contemporary bedding schemes. So the gaudy and glorious high Victorian garden is sandwiched in between the often provincial and the quite often precious. More surprising is the quite considerable debt that the next sort of garden, especially those popularized by Miss Jekyll, in fact owed to the Victorian infatuation.

However, to return to the development of bedding itself ... Within the confines of the new garden ideas current from 1830 or so, gardeners experimented in all sorts of ways, some novel, some strange. For instance, once the half-hardy flora from South America and Africa advocated by Paxton in 1838 had really caught hold throughout Europe, it was an entirely natural progression to try some of the vast numbers of species from even warmer climates, which were most usually grown in the warmest glass-houses. This idea seems first to have taken root in Europe, perhaps where the more severe and longer winters of the Continent affected glasshouses more severely than they do in Britain (the growth of algal jelly on the glass being one of the most important difficulties). This led to plants being set out of doors in summer while the glass of the 'stoves' was being cleaned up for the succeeding winter. 'Subtropical' bedding, as it became known, seems to have first been noticed in 1852.

One thing struck me in the gardening of Germany, which is the love of fine foliage; and whole parterres and clumps are planted solely to exhibit specimens of foliage. I think much might be done in this country with the same object ... Among the different plants ... the *Ficus elastica* appears to be the favourite; the *Canna indica, C. discolor* and especially the New Zealand flax ... There is a large *Caladium* much used in these parterres ... and *Maranta zebrina* from the stove appears to stand out for the summer ...

Soon every owner of a palm, a cycad, some aloes or cactuses, philodendrons and so on pushed them into the centre of the bedding schemes. Trials were done in the public gardens of Paris to see which tropical plants would 'do' well, and soon after, such things appeared in Britain.

By 1861 William Robinson, however much he came to hate all

29. Sub-tropical bedding produced some surprises.

forms of bedding, thoroughly approved. He wrote that tropical bedding was first seen in Paris using cannas, caladiums, 'either in distinct round or oval clumps, or in the tall centres of the flower borders...' In the Paris trials, *C. indica* won, and remains widely popular. The castor oil plant also turned out to be a winner. By 1861, too:

> The practice which embellishes so much of the St Petersburgh gardens during their short summer, of planting out green and hothouse flowering trees and shrubs in single specimens, is also beginning to be tried here with success. They are planted out in May without their pots, and two or three weeks before taking them in in autumn, they are prepared for potting by cutting round their roots.

The British at once copied and excelled. Soon Robinson reported that Paris had been trying to compete with the rarity of species found in English gardens, but had given up – it was too expensive.

Though early bedding schemes had been designed to be of much the same height, often with plants being clipped, pinned, or even sunk in pits so that they would give an even 'carpet' of colour, the idea of picturesque bedding grew up, advocated mainly by David Thomson, the gardener to the Dukes of Buccleuch at Dalkeith and Drumlanrig. In this, totally at variance as it was with the picturesque of the early years of the century, the bedding was deliberately contrived to have a vertical element, usually central, often with subsidiary verticals at the edge or in the corners of the beds. Naturally, subtropical plants were often used. 'Picturesque' may not have entirely described the final effect – which survives still in the use of canna lilies, or a standard fuchsia plant, as the central 'dot' plant in a bed of colourful *Begonia semperflorens*, all edged with alyssum and lobelia.

Though Thomson claimed the development as his, something similar had already been seen by William Robinson, as a young garden correspondent, in Paris. In 1861 he wrote to the *Gardener's Chronicle*:

> In general design, straight walks, terraces, steps and parterres are gone quite out of fashion [I wonder how many headaches this caused

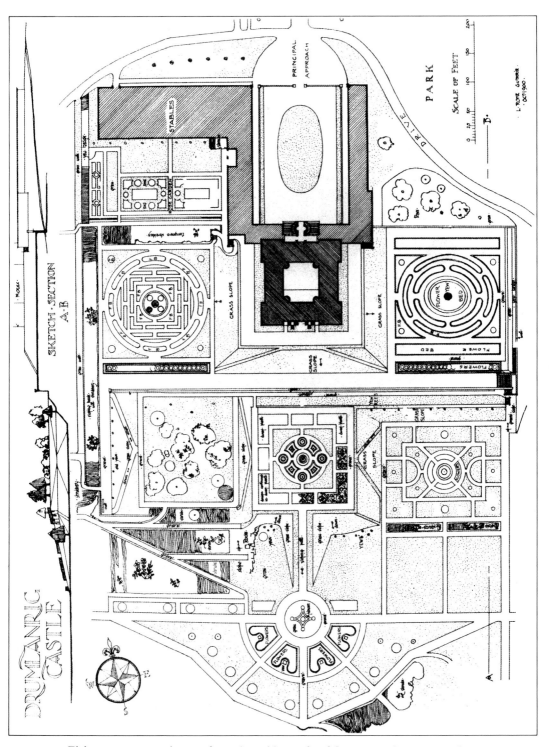

30. Elaborate parterres, the grandest using white sand and flowers, on the seventeenth-century terracing at Drumlanrig.

in gardens which had just been expensively got up in a geometrical way – for he was quite wrong], and in Paris appear only to be maintained in the Tuileries and Luxembourg; curved lines, irregular clumps, borders or beds being everywhere substituted. In some places this irregularity may have been carried too far, or too much may have been attempted for the limited space; but in general the sight struck us as remarkably good ... and in the Champs Elysees, the arrangement of the raised clumps and slightly hollowed intervening lawns is such as to give variety and an appearance of extent. Some persons object to the clumps being too much raised, but in the Champs Elysees ... it gave the means of shutting out in great measure the cafés chantants.

Contemporaries, even a more mature Robinson, approved, finding that it did much to reduce the glare of the less harmonious colour schemes, especially if it was done in the big central bed of a group. Contemporaries, too, thought 'picturesque' beds looked best if they were given outlines using a long wagon rope and curling it into shapes on the lawn (modern garden magazines suggest using a plastic hosepipe to make 'island' beds).

More widespread was the development of 'ribbon bedding'. This was an entirely natural progression from the idea of contrasting margins, and meant that effectively the whole bed consisted of contrasting margins or bands of colour. It was foreshadowed in the 1840s, for instance, by this planting scheme of 1842 from the *Gardener's Chronicle*: 'Many of our Correspondents are desirous of knowing what plants are best adapted for a circular or oval bed upon a lawn ...' The writer suggests:

In the centre ... a patch of purple *Phlox paniculata* should be planted, around which should succeed a circle of the white variety of the same plant. Then follows a ring of *Coreopsis tinctoria*, after which may come one of *Penstemon gentianoides*, and *P. gentianoides* 'Coccineum', but most of the latter. Next plant a circle of *Phlox omniflora*, surrounded by one of the tallest sorts of pink verbena; then another of the dwarfer kinds of scarlet verbena: the outside of the whole bed being planted with *Lobelia azurea* ...

By 1862 even Kew Gardens had an example that was typical

of the whole phenomenon, and it drew all London by its magnificence.

It is however in four beds forming a necessary accompaniment of this central mass in which by far the prettiest mixture is to be found. These are about forty-five feet in length and a trifle more than eight feet in width . . . Along the centre forming a chain is a series of diamonds measuring four feet in the side, made with *Perilla* [a bedding plant, now rare, with deep brownish-red leaves]; inside the diamond is 'Flower of the Day' geranium, from which the flowers are kept constantly cropped [the plant had yellowish-green leaves]; outside, the angles are occupied with 'Lord Raglan' verbena, and round the whole is an edging made of variegated *Alyssum* and *Lobelia speciosa* planted alternately, the white and the blue associating well together and forming an agreeable and pretty contrast.

Elsewhere in the same garden and at the same date, variegated balm (*Melissa officinalis*) was used as an edging and kept pinched out to stop it sprawling,

. . . and in front of the old museum in what have been popularly named by the daily press a 'Coventry ribbon' is a long bed containing lines of equal width (about fifteen inches) of the following plants, viz., in the centre *Perilla*; on each side of that *Cineraria maritima* [silver, almost white, leaves] surrounded by an edging of 'Purple King' and 'Robinson's Defiance', the two last forming a charming mixture of scarlet and purple. This ribbon being quite thirty yards in length . . . is even better this year than last . . .

Three years earlier, Shirley Hibberd had been using the ribbon system not only in his flower borders but also in large containers. So enamoured was he by it that even his winter bedding (of fancy beets and coloured cabbages) was 'ribboned'. The summer colours were purple, cerise, pale yellow, crimson. The beds were edged with white tiles.

Later, in the late 1860s and 70s, ribbon borders were in common use alongside walks and paths to give a continuous dazzle that must, in some instances, have given many walkers a headache.

141

They were also wrapped around shrubberies, to form a sort of doily of colour around the fashionable planting of evergreens.

Then there was 'carpet bedding', a phrase now commonly used incorrectly, being often applied to any sort of bedding. Originally it was used only for a specialized sort consisting only of foliage plants, or of some of the more usual bedding plants with their flowers continually suppressed. Carpet bedding, making use of all the shades of green, bronze, yellow, russet, purple, glaucous blue and silver, meant that the palette of colours was extremely subtle and could at least begin to approach the washed-out colours of faded Persian carpets.

There were other advantages than those merely to the eyes. The conventional bedding flora was quite often ruined by continued rain, and a poor summer could rot every garden in the country. Foliage was not so affected by the weather. It was also possible to use it in cold areas, so it worked as well in Caithness (where geraniums and lobelias refused to grow and flower outdoors) as it did in Cornwall. It also taxed gardeners' minds a little more than the conventional combination of verbenas, calceolarias and geraniums; some interesting plants were made use of, splitting into two separate divisions depending on whether the plants were winter hardy or not. It seems to us today that it might also have been less labour intensive; that was not the case, for almost every plant needed to be manipulated in some way, for example having its flowers regularly nipped out, or the stems kept trimmed so that they didn't swamp the design. As with flower bedding, there were some spectacular examples. In 1871, for instance, a big carpet scheme at Mr Cannell's Woolwich Fuchsia Nursery was thirty-four feet long and eleven wide. It contained 2,900 plants to a value of £60. Many visitors thought it the finest they'd ever seen. The redoubtable Miss Hope published her perennial carpet schemes which required little in the way of replacement: she used edgings of *Heuchera* leaves, and sedums and houseleeks for a base planting, adding a few geraniums in summer. She also used much more unconventional plants, like the exciting but invasive variegated bishopweed and the nice variegated cress that she found in a nursery in Berwickshire (both are still worth having).

Towards the end of the century this sort of perennial carpet bedding began to evolve into what is now called 'ground cover bedding'. Miss Hope seems to have been the first to publish plantings that approach the idea. In *Gardens and Woodlands* (1881) she says that the mania for proper geometrical bedding is on the wane. It is surprising that her own ideas didn't prolong its life; one bed she had centred on a yellow-leafed holly, with an outside edging of *Euonymus radicans* 'Variegata' and a groundwork of *Aster ericoides* and the now rare and almost impossible to grow double sweet william 'King Willie'!

A purer carpet bedding combination still, and most exotic for the grey suburbs of Trinity, she had *Yucca gloriosa* set in a groundwork of purple-leaved *Ajuga*, all dotted with the rosy leaves and flower heads of *Sedum spectabile* and edged with a variegated ivy. That sounds a little too much.

William Robinson, at the end of a tirade against bedding in all its forms (one of many), in which he says appreciation of beauty of form is far more intellectual and advanced than appreciation of colour (a typically one-sided statement), goes on to suggest sweet woodruff and other carpeters as underplanting for a shrubbery. He describes 'Mr Brockbank's border', which is a sort of permanent bedding with an otherwise conventional guilloche pattern. However, other borders in the same garden had no fixed lines at all and begin to resemble some designed by a Mr F. Miles, who, it appears, was the first to see the merits of natural carpeting beds. From the plan of his most important border, it looks as if it would have been an excellent mixed planting of today, complete with irregular drifts of bulbs and shade plants. It therefore begins to approach the waved patches of 'bedding' that Gertrude Jekyll eventually proposed for some of her marvellous herbaceous beds.

All these sorts of bedding, aspects of the gaudy infatuation, provoked strong reactions from the small minority of gardeners immune to the excitements offered. As with all gardening styles, widely adopted, many must have been dull, unimaginative, even ugly. In the hands of a good gardener, with a good eye, the effects of a high Victorian garden must have been quite magnificent. But what did these gardens actually look like? We know how some of them appeared from photographs which survive in large numbers; for the early gardens of the period, though, there is no record. For the gardens of Campden Hill all we have are Caie's planting lists, published in 1850, and a handful of woodcuts. However, the lists themselves are instructive, giving colour (at least in part) to the plans and views.

The February/March bedding lists include *Helleborus niger*, *Crocus reticulatus*, *Galanthus plicatus*, *Narcissus minor*, *Erythronium dens-canis* (usually violet pink, but here some were in white), *Corydalis tuberosa* and *Erythronium lanceolata*. The colour triumvirate is present, though in the softened colours of spring. In April/May he used *Anemone appennina* (probably then in sky blue only), *Arabis praecox* (he probably meant a white *A. caucasica*), *Cheiranthus alpina* (now *Erysimum*, and in brilliant yellow), *Aubretia* in purple, *Alyssum saxatile*, *Iberis saxatile*, *Tulipa oculis-solis* (red and black), *Polemonium mexicanum* (blue, he says, though it is not clear which species he meant) and *Vesicaria utriculatum* (light yellow). Sometimes, for the same season, he used hardy annuals like *Silene pendula* (pale pink), *Nemophila* in white and blue, the still popular *Eschscholtzia*, the now rare *Collinsia grandiflora* (bluish purple), *Clarkia* in white and rosy purple and, lastly, *Erysimum peroffskianum*. For the gaudy season from May to November Caie used the usual range of things like the geranium 'Lucea rosea' (rose), the verbenas 'Princess Royal' (white), 'Heloise' (dark lilac), 'White Perfection', 'Duc d'Aumale' (bluish lilac), 'Robinson's Defiant' (scarlet), 'Mont Blanc' (white), and 'Walton's Emma' (purple). For bright yellow he used the inevitable *Calceolaria viscosissima*.

The later part of the period is captured in Trigg's *The Formal Garden in England and Scotland*. This contains, as well as Trigg's wonderful architectural drawings and plans of old or at least partly old gardens and garden detailing, some marvellous photographs of all sorts of gardens, from the most grandly Italianate of all to town and country cottage gardens. Some are photographed still at the height of their glory, others are clearly on the slide to dereliction and extinction.

For instance, Longford Castle still had very elaborate parterres, with many of the beds edged with echeverias. There were Chinese barrel seats along the main walk, and solid masses of echeverias and sedums around statue bases and urns. The terrace walls were built of fake Roman roof tiles, but finished with stone tops and balls. There were also vast amounts of gravel, with almost no grass to walk on at all, even though the beds had narrow edges of it, and inner bands of alternate blue and white lobelias and alyssums. The final effect was of slightly tattered richness, for the walks needed weeding, and the echeverias were planted with slightly less than perfect regularity.

Another example, also lacking maintenance, but this time with charm, were the gardens at Catherine's Court in Somerset. Here fine stone statuary was set amid rather narrow formal beds planted with fancy variegated geraniums, dahlias, nicotianas and so on. Everything is rather rampant and only the Irish yews as obelisks give green vertical axes. It must have been a delightful place in which to wander.

And so on . . . Broughton Castle with its attractive rose garden, rustic chairs, and a desert-full of gravel; Bowood, whole then, but with the parterres empty for winter, leaving only the grass cut-outs and a few standard roses; or Wilton, with its already overgrown parterre, simply planned with an apse end, relaxed in feel, with Chinese ceramic seats and masses of wire 'baskets' holding ramshackle masses of flowers. And on, through Hatfield and Kellie and Earlshall, Arley, Thoresby and Eaton Hall, Melchett Court, Compton Place . . . Gardens waiting for the next revolution certainly, but none of the photographs give any idea of the astonishing richness of the Victorian garden flora.

THE
VICTORIAN FLORA

THE VICTORIAN FLORA WAS UNIQUE. IT WAS unique in its richness, as well as its newness. The most amazing welter of extraordinary plants poured into Britain from all over the world – orchids, waterlilies, and calceolarias (many from the jungles and prairies of South America), exquisite alpine plants from the mountains of Africa or Northern India, and wonderful garden plants that had already been cultivated for centuries in China and, especially, Japan.

The speed of introduction was entirely new, too, though occasional new garden plants had been arriving at least since Roman times. There was a major burst of new introductions with the discovery of the Americas in the fifteenth century, and minor bursts following the development of trade links with the Near East in the sixteenth century and with China and India in the seventeenth. Throughout the eighteenth century, as European explorers, merchants and collectors began to move inland from the coasts of America on which they had established themselves, the interest in new garden plants grew. However, during all these centuries introductions were mostly restricted to plants with the toughest imaginable seeds; the technology of seed transportation was extremely primitive and even deleterious (seeds were often stored in honey, in wax, or in sealed barrels of soil). Seeds that survived their bizarre journeys were then germinated into the

31. Cast iron and orchids, a very Victorian combination.

ignorant gardening world of the day. Only rarely did living plants survive the crossing of an ocean, with rats, seawater and ignorant sailors making sure that the journey was almost always fatal.

With the discovery in the late eighteenth century that most seeds lasted perfectly well if dried off and stored in simple packets of brown paper, and with the early nineteenth-century invention of the Wardian case, which ensured a safe journey for entire young plants, the scene was set for a monstrous invasion of plants from every exotic area in the world.

All this would have been in vain, of course, had there not also been thousands upon thousands of avid gardeners wanting to grow all this new material, as well as hundreds of nurseries, metropolitan and provincial, happy to grow on, propagate, advertise, overwinter, show, and sell it. For the whole of the Victorian period, it was not in the least surprising to find some obscure nursery in Musselburgh or Finchley almost as well stocked with some of the latest plants from Brazil or Java as the great nurseries like Veitch or Jackman or Waterer's. Thousands of amateurs made astonishing collections of all sorts of novelties – orchids, cactuses, new varieties of oriental chrysanthemums, florists' tulips, citrus varieties – bankrupting themselves frequently enough to make auctions of their abandoned plants one of the features of the social calendar, almost as if Sotheby's or Christie's were to auction a neighbour's house plants.

Meanwhile, in the jungles and deserts worldwide, all sorts and conditions of men collected plants from the wild and sent seeds or plants home to friends, employers, or the great botanic gardens. They varied from colonial officials, to merchants hunting for new markets and new merchandise, to failed gardeners emigrating to new countries in the hope of work and advancement. Some of the professional plant collectors became garden stars in their own right, and published memoirs of their exciting travels (others perished in sometimes terrible circumstances, some even with rare flowers still stuffed in a crushed vasculum).

Such was the impact of the floral deluge that the Victorian flora developed its own power to affect the progress of garden design. This was entirely new. All previous garden styles, from the knot gardens of medieval Europe to the landscapes of eighteenth-century England, had progressed according to the dictates of fashionable gardeners and their advisers. The plants had occupied an entirely secondary place. Now, much of the enthusiasm for the new-fangled parterres advocated by Paxton in the 1830s, which were found in almost every garden in the country twenty years later, was based on the brilliance of the flowers of plants like the verbenas, the calceolarias, the showier geraniums and so on. Most of the basic species of these enormously important genera arrived on these shores only in the early years of the nineteenth century. They made all sorts of new gardening possible. Those taken up enough to dominate the whole Victorian period were subtropical weeds that, seasonless, flowered for the entire time that the plant was growing. In Europe, therefore, these were in brilliant flower right up to the first frosts of October or November. For most gardeners this was an enormously exciting phenomenon, for the old garden flora was virtually over by the end of August and the gardens half dead; now they could have colour until they themselves no longer wanted to be outdoors.

While some of the old flowers had been brilliantly colourful (like the cross-of-Jerusalem – *Lychnis chalcedonica*), most were in flower for just a few weeks, so the old mixed borders were a continual sequence of different colours, some of great softness and subtlety, but evanescent. Except for brief seasons, like the flush of bulbs in early spring, this made planning colour schemes difficult (though it was certainly done in late Georgian gardens). Plant height was always a problem; the weedy nature of many of the new South American and Australian introductions ensured that they were either naturally low-growing, or could be clipped or pegged to the ground so that they remained low. Thus, the new plants could be treated as areas of brilliant colour, constant for the whole growing season, as rich in effect as any gardener could desire (and as we shall see in Chapter 10, too rich for some). Even the later developments of the new parterres, like the so-called picturesque bedding, subtropical bedding, and even the subtle splendours of carpet bedding, were based mostly on plants which were all Victorian introductions.

In spite of the richness of the Victorian garden flora, taken as a whole, the number of genera developed by breeders and nurserymen and which became the key genera for the entire period were surprisingly few. Verbenas, calceolarias, geraniums and lobelias constitute the four main genera (only the last two are much used for bedding today), with a secondary group of petunias, dahlias, ferns, chrysanthemums, camellias, rhododendrons, roses and azaleas; beyond these were vast ranks of marvellous, but almost unexploited, vegetation.

There was, however, a quite astonishing burst of activity on the part of plant breeders. The old florists had been working away on their traditional genera for several centuries, and so the idea of breeding plants was widely disseminated, as were the techniques for doing it. Now, the wild enthusiasm for the new, especially for new species, poured over into a widespread passion for new varieties of plants. Consequently, almost as soon as new species appeared in commerce, often only a season or two after

149

they had first flowered, hybrids were being hailed in the gardening press, being advertised by raisers or nurserymen (often at remarkably high prices), and even being auctioned at salerooms up and down the country. Correspondingly, last season's varieties were sold off cheaply and soon vanished from view.

The enthusiasm for breeding was not in the least confined to new genera. The notion spread into many genera that had been in the garden for centuries. Sometimes the new passion simply took old garden flowers in remarkable new directions, as we shall see with hollyhocks, say, or roses. More often, newly introduced species were hybridized with those familiar here for hundreds of years, to produce entirely new groups of plants. The pansy, the gladiolus and Malmaison carnations are all important examples (the first really exciting pansies used to sell for 5s. or 6s. each, the wages of a gardener for a week or more).

While most of this multi-layered flora was based on wealth (all flower gardening, and even some kitchen gardening is, after all, only conspicuous consumption), it did represent a sort of wealth of its own, as part of the whole culture and aspirations of an age. Rather little of it is left. The underlying economic wealth has gone, and the fleets of gardeners, the myriad conservatories, frames and stove houses, the tens of thousands of miles of box hedging, the terraces on which to stand the tubs of agapanthus, canna and hedychium, vanished. What is left of all this marvellous wealth?

There are almost no early pansies left, and only a few violas. A few of Mr Chater's hollyhocks are still available, a few Sutton's strains (like the apricot foxglove) are in circulation in the gardens of keen amateurs, some of Perry's chrysanthemums are being collected, and a handful of bedding geraniums are still in commerce. Only a fraction of the 'old roses' survive, and almost all the double wallflowers, double antirrhinums, bedding verbenas, and so on are gone for good. Some of the shrubs have fared better, and it is not difficult to find plenty of fine Victorian lilacs, rhododendrons and camellias.

Of course, if you ask most people what plants they associate with the Victorian period, many will think of aspidistras, spotted laurels, monkey-puzzle trees, other trees like *Wellingtonia*, perhaps the ivy found carved on almost every Victorian tombstone, perhaps even, more remarkably, the gigantic waterlily named for the period *Victoria regia*. Certainly all these were important, though some were introduced so late in the period that they have scarcely gone out of fashion. For instance, the spotted laurel (*Aucuba japonica*) first appeared from Japan in 1783, though it was fifty years before it became widely grown. Plants are either male or female, and as only one plant had arrived in Europe, the scarlet berries, one of the delights of the plant when associated with an attractively variegated leaf, had to wait until the other sex arrived. By 1838 they were used as screens to give privacy to urban gardens, often planted below standard holly trees. Once breeding could begin, new and more heavily speckled variants began to appear in the late 1860s, making the plants popular all over again. New sorts were soon planted in shrubberies (where they can still often be found), pruned into fancy shapes for tubs, and dwarf sorts were used in winter bedding schemes. In the 1840s and 1850s many were used as balcony plants, for which they are still especially useful. They became so popular, and so associated with unimaginative park planting, that they, like the aspidistra, must have been burnt by the thousands during the upheavals of this century. They are now making an entirely justified comeback, being both decorative and easy to grow.

On the other hand, there may now be hope, at least in Britain, for the aspidistra – though that is perhaps not too important while every courtyard and patio in southern Europe is still packed with them. However, the aspidistra is quite a late introduction, appearing first in France in the 1850s and still being described here in 1861 as 'a little-known plant'. One article goes on that '*Aspidistra elatior* is strongly recommended for the decoration of sitting rooms. It is capable ... of living there for any length of time without suffering in the smallest degree ... ' Certainly the conditions in Victorian drawing-rooms, halls, and even parlours, were quite dreadful. Sadly the plant's tolerance of all this, its cast-iron invincibility, led ultimately to its downfall. A shame, for a well-grown plant, glossy-leaved and perhaps with some of its odd purple velvet flowers (at ground level to allow snails to cross-pollinate them), has undeniable charm.

Of the trees, both *Wellingtonia* and the monkey-puzzle date almost any piece of planting where they are at all mature. In spite of its Regency name, *Wellingtonia* is a high Victorian plant, first discovered in the Californian Sierra Nevada by William Lobb of the vastly important nursery of Messrs Veitch. Lobb first sent home a little seed, some dried branches and some drawings of mature trees. Every gardener was immediately excited. In 1854 the *Cottage Gardener's Magazine* announced that 'the plant of the year is *Wellingtonia gigantea*', though it was hardly a cottager's plant. The nursery itself announced proudly that 'Messrs Veitch of Exeter and Chelsea, have much pleasure in stating that their seeds of the above magnificent Tree are vegetating satisfactorily. They therefore hope to be able to send out well-established seedling plants during the ensuing summer and autumn ... ' The price would not have suited cottagers either. However, *Wellingtonia* at once became *the* tree for country house gardens, and places like Biddulph soon had avenues of it wherever they could be squeezed in. The fad for the tree lasted throughout the period, and many remain, gradually darkening the gardens in which they continue to grow. The first to get chopped down were owned by Robinson, who cut down the ones at Gravetye Manor in 1911.

On the other hand, the monkey-puzzle (*Araucaria*) was introduced in the previous century, arriving in 1796. It was first planted in the grounds of Castle Kennedy, the seat of the Earls of Stair, and, as might be expected, in the less grand gardens of Dropmore. At Castle Kennedy the vast expanse of early eighteenth-century formal avenues, once planted with suitably native species, was replanted with this remarkable tree in exactly the same pattern, with rather odd-looking effect. However, by 1847 Dropmore was claiming to have the largest specimen in the British Isles. Commercial quantities of seed soon reached Europe, and by the 1840s German nurseries were exporting young plants to the gardeners of Britain. By 1861, a Mr C. J. Stevens, who had an influential auction room at King Street, Covent Garden, was auctioning a consignment of ten bushels of seed imported direct from Chile. The tree grew fast on the west coast of Scotland, and by 1872 there were even hopes that it would become a timber crop in suitable parts of the country. Its eventual fate was less grand.

Young *Araucaria* plants have a remarkably formal arrangement of new branches, and this appealed to the Victorian sense of organization and tidiness. Thus they were used as centrepieces for bedding schemes, both in summer and, more often, in winter (when they were combined with small potted ivies, aucubas and other hardy evergreens). It is from such a use that many present-day full-grown trees spring, for such plants were commonly left in the ground instead of being lifted as they should have been. Eventually the plants simply got too large to move, and after a longer period still they overtopped the humble front gardens where they were so often planted.

Among the more exotic plants, the vast waterlily was, of course, never particularly popular, requiring large pools in which to grow, and a high temperature. Nevertheless, it caught the popular imagination (as it still does), and pictures of its large flowers appeared frequently in the magazines, American as well as European, of the time. As a status plant it has never been equalled. It was first discovered in the Amazon valley by Sir Richard Schomburgh in 1837. It took ten years for the first seeds to be germinated, for which honour Kew Gardens took the palm. However, the flowers were first seen at Chatsworth, where it flowered the following year (1848) in the vast conservatories designed by that estate's gardener, Joseph Paxton. Though some slight attempts were made to popularize it, and a London nursery-eryman got it to flower outdoors at Chelsea by putting hot water pipes through a large tank, it not surprisingly did not catch on.

However enamoured the Victorians may have been of the new and the exotic, one of the central plants of the Victorian period flora was in fact a native, and one which had played a role in human society since very ancient times indeed. The common ivy, which eighteenth-century gardeners had used to give romance and spurious age to their newly built ruins and grottoes, had become, by the Victorian period, associated with rustic charm and cosiness. 'Rosa' describes, in 1849, a village woman's cottage that she thinks should be the model for all; it was so covered ' ... in this British evergreen as to look like an ivy bush pierced with two lattices and a doorway. It is the results of her own exertions and her own taste, and forms one of the most beautiful objects – the very perfection of a snuggery – with which the eye can be refreshed.'

The plant's attractively marbled leaves were also used in the posies that were so popular all over Europe at this time, and in the emerging art of flower arrangement. Rules for such things were being propounded as early as 1850, when vases and vegetation had to be matched, for 'in every case, whether the vase be an upright Etruscan or of tazza form, it should be very considerably concealed by the flowers ... as in the case of the vase being of flat form, by green leaves of the ivy or rose clustering round it. Dark leaves, such as these and of the camellia, always contrast better with the flowers in bouquets ... ' Bouquets were evanescent, even when ringed in ivy, for

the greatest enemy to endurance of a bouquet is the extreme dryness of the air in our sitting-rooms. The flowers will retain their beauty treble the time if a bell-glass be turned over them, so as to check the excessive evaporation of their leaves and petals. A very elegant mode of effecting this is afforded by a small table, having for its top a marble slab slightly hollowed in the middle to contain a little water, in which the edge of the bell-jar rests.... The vitiated air, or, in other words, the large quantity of carbonic acid and carburetted hydrogen gases produced by the combustion of the wax or gas, and the breathing of visitors in well-lighted and crowded assemblies, is also very injurious to the healthy growth of plants. Consequently, on such occasions, bouquets are more than ordinarily in need of glass shades.

Outdoors, in less nasty conditions, ivies were also used to drape outdoor baskets, hanging or supported, to soften the raw rustic look and the usually inexpert construction of these popular garden accessories.

32. A plate-glass Wardian case for the drawing-room; plants needed protection.

Though its eighteenth-century usage lived on, ivy being an essential veil for the bizarre pieces of rockwork so necessary for the gardens of suburban homes of taste (see p. 189), and being combined with the gayest of alpines around the mouths of miniature caves, new demands were soon made of it. On the one hand it was used as an evergreen bedding plant, in winter as well as summer (for the latter use it was carefully pegged to the ground to give a dark green outer band to over-brilliant bedding schemes); on the other, it moved indoors. Both Irish ivy and some of the new variegated sorts were popular plants for Wardian cases, and also for trailing over metalwork arches to frame sofas or tables (in which case the arch could support hanging baskets planted up with creeping Jenny, *Sedum sieboldii*, tradescantias or *Saxifraga sarmentosa*).

By 1850 or so, ivy (thought of as cheerful, as were all Victorian evergreens) was being used to make cemeteries more pleasing places in winter. It became a popular decoration for tombstones, and was rapidly associated with mourning and remembrance. By 1875 there were shaped planting tins available that could be slipped behind picture frames so that the ivy fronds could be twined around the picture frame itself. This was thought to be especially suitable for pictures of 'departed' friends. The plants must have been remarkably difficult to water without ruining the wallpaper. Incidentally, another reason for ivy's popularity was the fact that it was impervious to all but the very worst of urban smogs, though soot-smeared ivy leaves must be one of the worst of all possible garden sights.

Whatever you may feel about these remnants of a lost age whenever you see them still in existence, they have at least survived. For the flowers absolutely central to the whole of the Victorian era, few gardeners will feel anything but a mild sadness for so many plants that were so much admired but which vanished so quickly. In 1836 petunias, dahlias, verbenas, calceolarias, eschscholtzias, and dozens of equally elegant plants were absolutely new. The verbena, for instance, had only been in the country since 1826. A Mr Pousette found the first one, at Buenos Aires in that year. The Brazilian name was 'melindres' (hence its first Latin one of *Verbena melindres*), and the plant had good rosy pink flowers, which were seen the following summer at Bignor Park. Other species were soon found. The redoubtable Mr Tweedie sent home the next two, one of which, *V. tweedieana*, bore his own name. Tweedie, an only moderately successful gardener though foreman at Dalkeith in youth, then at the Royal Botanic Gardens in Edinburgh, later worked at Castle Hill in Ayr. After a move to Eglinton he took the surprising decision, at the age of fifty, to leave for Buenos Aires in 1825. There his career took off. He did some important garden designs, and a great deal of collecting throughout Brazil. His introductions of verbenas ultimately went on to produce all the subsequent bedding sorts. He is also remembered for introducing various *Bignonia* species and many cacti, though nowadays the most famous of his plants is the formidable pampas grass. As an ultimate honour, his journals were published by Hooker in the prestigious *Journal of Botany*.

Gardeners were quick to spot the potential of Tweedie's verbenas. By 1838 Paxton was suggesting that the species should be crossed by nurserymen as there were already some interesting hybrids around. Tweedie must have kept his Scottish connections, for commercial quantities of many of them were available only from a now-vanished nursery at Musselburgh, near Edinburgh. By 1842 named varieties were on the market, including a handsome white one called 'The Queen', scented, and costing seven shillings and sixpence. All had immediate impact, being planted in huge quantities by rich and fashionable gardeners. By 1849 the verbena was fast becoming a florists' flower, with show classes devoted to it even among the Cottage Garden Societies. As with any florists' group, all sorts of new traits were soon developed, and streaked flowers, or those now most often found in seed packets – ones with white eyes – were soon the rage. Colours ranged from purest white, through an infinite number of pinks, rose and scarlets, to lilacs so deep as to seem almost black.

Reaction was fast, however. First, gardeners found that some of the plants had disadvantages. Verbenas suffered terribly from mildew, and had to be dusted every fortnight with flowers of sulphur – an enormous job if the bedding was at all extensive, and the yellow powder, liberally distributed, must have been extremely unsightly (we find greenfly a much worse problem). Soon, in spite of all the new colours, and even new statures, from the minute 'Boule de Feu', to the immense and vigorous 'Robinson's Defiance', posh gardeners were beginning to get bored. Some suggested planting three close shades of verbena in one bed to give a richer effect (which must have looked startlingly good in skilled hands). Others stopped growing them altogether.

However, there was no stopping the verbena among the less garden-conscious classes. For these, often without their own means of producing the requisite number of plants needed, the big commercial nurseries started propagating vast quantities of plants. John Scott of Merriott (a firm which still exists, though it is now well known for its fruit trees and roses), stocked 100 varieties of verbena, and took thousands of cuttings of each every season. In the same year, 1861, other nurseries were selling rooted verbena at two shillings and six pence for a dozen. Another had 80,000 verbenas for sale to suburban Londoners.

The verbena was seen, even by contemporaries, as being central to the whole bedding movement. William Thomson, head gardener at Dalkeith Palace, commented: 'Looking at Verbenas, I cannot help recording my conviction that the present principle of arranging plants in masses owes them very much ... [its introduction] had a very considerable share in the advent of the grouping style, and helped to establish it.'

Verbenas followed bedding through its ribbon phase, as at Kew in 1862, and then into decline by 1884, when plants were sold as part of mixed lots of bedding plants, either imported from Holland and sold at '100 for 5/- carriage paid', or as ten-shilling collections containing 120 plants, with thirty-six geraniums in four varieties, eighty-four verbenas in a dozen varieties, and so on. It is difficult to know how such assortments can ever have yielded an attractive scheme.

Another genus, the calceolaria, had a comparable history to the verbena. Though the first available species were *C. pinnata* in 1773 and *C. fothergilla* in 1777, nothing much more happened until 1822, when four new sorts suddenly arrived. Discovered in the 1820s in Chile and Peru, they were first taken up in Scotland, where they were collected by a Dr Graham. He produced some fascinating hybrids, and his collection was bought by Mr Young, nurseryman at Epsom, in 1831. With a foothold in the south, they were soon the rage. Blotched and spotted ones were popular between 1834 and 1840, and William Lobb was still sending new species to Britain. By 1850 there were 'numberless' hybrids of greater beauty still, and by 1860 or so there was such a vast variety that some were already thought of as old-fashioned.

As with verbenas, native pests and diseases soon caught up. By 1857 there were warnings that garden calceolarias could collapse with mildew (they do still), but they were also equally easily devastated by over-zealous cultivation as well as by the awful triumvirate of red spider, greenfly and thrips.

The plant group that has survived the best is the one that holds most interest for gardeners today. It is the third in the other great trio; that of bedding plants. Almost everyone, even if they only have a windowsill, will grow a geranium or two, and although quite a few of these will be modern varieties, it is surprising how many of those that once played a crucial part in bedding schemes

33. Scented-leaf geraniums, trailing forms and others, perch on every ledge.

all over the warmer parts of Victorian Britain are still popular.
(Scotland's summers were often too cool for them to grow properly, though a number bear Scottish names.)

All the species had come from the drier parts of South Africa, and although many bulb species had come from that country in the seventeenth century, only one geranium species had followed them (*Pelargonium triste*; it too has bulb-like tubers). One or two more followed in the eighteenth century, but suddenly quantities began to arrive in the new Regency glasshouses. Hybridization at once began (some of the most charming early ones having the first introduction as one parent – though all of these lovely striped-flower and heavily perfumed hybrids have vanished). Soon almost all the geranium groups now known were in existence: zonals, regals, ivy-leaved and so on. Naturally they were taken up as bedding plants by the advanced gardeners of the day.

By 1838 grand gardens had several varieties of scarlet-flowered zonals (one called 'Frogmore'), some with variegated leaves, and ivy-leaved sorts were even making an appearance in fashionable rustic baskets. By the 1840s there were prize lists for new varieties at many local flower shows, though decent new sorts were expensive at two shillings each. This seems to have acted as a spur to growers, breeders and collectors alike, and the genus spawned the first of the new florists' clubs, the Pelargonium Society, which was set up on 18 June 1842. Once it had accumulated generous funds to support the grand prizes for newly bred varieties, the whole thing took off.

By 1852 geraniums were used for every aspect of bedding. Those that had attractively coloured leaves were used for their foliage alone (leaf colour often clashed nastily with flower colour, so the latter were pinched out as they formed; pinching out even a small area of bedding must have been a back-breaking task). Some of the leaf designs were exceptionally subtle and matched the more interesting mid-Victorian period colour sense almost exactly; like 'Lass o' Gowrie', in which a white margin surrounds a jade green leaf with a reddish 'zone', or the lovely 'Crystal Palace Gem', with a green zone on a yellow leaf and soft pink flowers.

Whole new groups appeared, based on different selections of underlying species. Some, like the Uniques, which started out with the old 'Purple Unique' or the white one (which cost fifteen shillings for a single plant when it first appeared), turned out to be completely unsuitable for bedding. The only way that stiff and leggy plants like the Uniques could be bent towards that end was by pegging down each shoot as it appeared. As they were also brittle, this didn't work. The group has virtually vanished, though 'Scarlet Unique' and a few others remain; the flowers are lovely.

However, geranium flowers, with their attractive markings or with brilliant colour, found yet another use as a proper florists' cut flower, used for making posies or decorating tables. Numbers were as prodigious as for verbenas. Scotts of Merriott, while propagating verbenas, also kept going fifty sorts of the latest geranium, and at the vast private garden of Shrubland, the gardener and writer Donald Beaton regularly overwintered 5,000 geranium 'Punch' cuttings and several other varieties as well.

With such an important group, it is not surprising that charming legends grew up around the most successful varieties, like the one called 'Tom Thumb', the most widely used of all the bedding geraniums. The story first saw print in 1861 – 'General Tom Thumb, the history of which is more like romance than reality (in being saved from a dust-bin, where, after the tender mercies of a nursery of children, it was cast to die the death of an unproved seedling) led the way to improvement'. The plant was supposed to have been rescued by a sharp-eyed nurseryman, whose fortune it made, being the first with a tricolour leaf. Bedding geraniums were quickly taken up in America too, and by 1849 red-flowered and variegated sorts, as well as ivy-leaved ones, were available. Of course, of the 'true' geraniums, plants belonging to the genus *Geranium*, not to *Pelargonium*, not much can be said here. They all belong to the later phases of Victorian gardening, when William Robinson's campaigns on behalf of the herbaceous flora began to gain ground.

Outside the main trio of bedding genera lurked (and still lurk), other good plants. Two, lobelias and petunias, share the same history as verbenas and calceolarias. Lobelias began to arrive from South Africa in the 1800s and were first used as greenhouse and conservatory plants, their trailing habit and pretty blue flowers suiting them to the front rows of the plant shelves. They were in use for bedding in continental Europe by 1830 (in one published scheme they were combined, alarmingly, with purple-leafed amaranthuses and scarlet-flowered celosias). Various species were introduced, though the most common garden plants had pale blue flowers. By the 1840s colour variants, perhaps hybrids, began to become popular. Ten years later lobelias were used everywhere: to hang round the edges of the vast urns at the Sydenham Crystal Palace, to edge beds at Kew, or to fill in the blue or white parts of panel beds, coats-of-arms beds, ribbon beds, and the rest. They're still popular wherever bedding is carried out, though some of the nicer colour strains seem to have gone (there were quite large numbers of good greyish heliotrope colours and very smoky blues). They're still sometimes found as chance variants from seed-packet plants, though most gardeners throw them away. As the plants are perfectly perennial in a cool greenhouse, they can easily be overwintered and increased.

The petunia has been a lot more successful in the survival stakes and is still undergoing developments. Whites and purples were widely used in suburban gardens in the late 1830s and were even found in cottagers' gardens twenty years later. They were almost vanquished by the geranium in the 1860s and 1870s, as geranium breeding produced more and more colourful types.

Even more successful has been the dahlia, which today still occupies pride of place at most flower shows and is still being developed in new and interesting ways, though it has become associated with a sort of gardening that not all gardeners espouse. The first hybrids of note were introduced from France in 1815, and dahlia mania soon ensued. By the 1850s they had already almost taken over every September flower show, where the extra-ordinary blooms were frequently doctored (and still are), to give them perfect shape. There were endless debates about the merits of the different groups, with rival factions proclaiming the death of the double dahlia, of the anemone-flowered sorts, of the singles, and so on. The roots that were not needed for showing the following summer were actually cooked and eaten (they were highly esteemed), and even in the 1850s the leaves were being put in salads.

In the garden, dahlias had various uses. Their often subtle colours enlivened the kitchen garden, where their brittle stems were frequently tied to the espalier rails that also supported apples, pears and greengages. In the flower garden it was common to use them to disguise the bare shanks of taller herbaceous plants, especially hollyhocks (the colour range is complementary too). A writer in 1842 enthused about a garden she'd just visited: 'Here ... the foreground was a mass of dahlias, American marigolds, mallows, asters and mignonette. It was the most gorgeous mass of colouring we ever beheld.' Indeed.

In the same year, the York Grand Floricultural and Horticultural Society held one of its first Grand Exhibitions, offering a first prize for dahlias of £100, in those days a quite vast sum of money, 'for the best stand of twenty four blooms ... of different sorts'. There were certainly plenty of new varieties around. The garden magazines all ran masses of advertisements for new dahlias, often with prize lists of the main shows so that future exhibitors could decide which sorts to try next season. So even organizations like the Newby Wiske Cottagers, the Salt-hill Dahlia Society, the Winchester Polyanthus Society, the Hammersmith or the Ipswich Cucumber Society (whose 'First Grand Show' was 'open to all England') played their part by having a dahlia section to promote the breeding and commercialization of new flowers.

Dahlias were even 'hyped'. Some methods were quite ingenious, though I doubt that such stratagems would work today for any garden plant at all. One advert ran 'Appleby's Queen of the Lilacs – By an unforeseen event, the whole remaining stock of GROUND ROOTS of the above Dahlia are destroyed. Fortunately, however, some fine healthy POT ROOTS are saved, a few of which will be supplied to the first applicants at fifty shillings each ... ' By the 1860s there were more than 100 varieties being regularly shown, and perhaps five or six times that number actually in commerce. Only a few seem to remain.

A plant associated with one of the major 'aesthetic' vogues of the Victorian period is now in almost every garden. The chrysanthemum, though a garden plant in China and Japan since

34. An early form of chrysanthemum, one of the great prizes of Victorian gardens.

ancient times, first arrived in Europe in 1689 (these first plants were from Japan). Though the plants are usually pretty tough, the first introductions were soon lost, to be reintroduced only in 1789. The enthusiasm for them started about 1800, and soon reached 'craze' proportions. By 1808 eight new sorts were imported directly from China by Sir Abraham Hume and a Mr Evans. Between 1816 and 1823, seventeen new sorts were added. A year or two later there were more than fifty sorts, mostly new hybrids, comprising singles, doubles, quilled and ranunculus-flowered types. A writer of 1835 pointed out that 'the Chinese chrysanthemum has been subjected to British improvement, and a number of new and beautiful varieties have lately been raised from seeds saved at Oxford, and other places in England, and in Guernsey'.

Plants were grown to prodigious sizes, and six-inch blooms were common. At shows, some gardeners exhibited plants that were up to twenty feet in circumference and six feet high. The famous collector Robert Fortune introduced the first of the pompone sorts from Chusan in the late 1840s, and by 1854 the most enthusiastic of the nurserymen were presenting lists which often had 700 varieties. Soon show plants had special houses built for them, just as tulips and auriculas had in the past. At the shows themselves the flower shapes were often adjusted by gently removing any petals that spoilt the perfect symmetry. Soon, the magazines were giving lists of varieties by height so that obsessed readers could design a whole border just of chrysanthemums.

Of course the new Victorian flora wasn't all just bedding plants and other garden 'soft furnishings'. There were immense numbers of both trees and shrubs, and while many of these underwent little further development by breeders or nurserymen (or the upmarket variant of the florist – it needed rather more space to be an enthusiast for rhododendrons than for auriculas), quite a number became important areas of new variety making.

The camellia, for instance, had been known since the late eighteenth century, and had begun to become popular in Regency gardens, when numbers of elegant camellia houses were built especially for them (early plants were thought not to be hardy). By 1847 the redoubtable Robert Fortune was in China, busily buying up all the interesting camellias (as well as moutans, paeonies and lots of other 'goodies'). Camellias survived the rigours of the journey and soon helped swell the ranks of lovely flowers, already popular garden plants, and important flowers in the markets of the major cities. There were soon long lists of varieties available, many with flowers spotted and striped in shades of pink. Imbrication of petals was much admired, as was good foliage (still important points in choosing varieties). By 1850, even supposedly cottage gardeners were expected to be growing them, in spite of the fact that ' ... at the season, when they make their annual growth, and form their flower buds for the succeeding year, they require a higher temperature, and greater amounts of atmospheric moisture and shade, than any other greenhouse plants'. There must have been some rather grand cottagers.

Camellias have rather lost their power as garden plants for

some reason (though they seem to be making a comeback in metropolitan gardens). However, the rhododendron has gone from strength to alarming strength. Among the first Oriental types to appear was, unluckily, one of the most gorgeous. *Rhododendron arboreum*, brought from Nepal in 1820, was at first thought not to be hardy. Nevertheless, its glamour captured the imagination even of gardeners unable to give it a conservatory, though they had to content themselves with some of the American sorts known to be tough. Loudon's *Suburban Gardener* of 1838, for instance, gave plans for an astonishing Tudorbethan villa, whose Tudorbethan back garden, with raised terraces all round, had beds with a suggested planting of kalmias and rhododendrons (in effect, a geometrical 'American garden').

By 1842 even provincial nurseries like J. & C. Whalley, St George's Crescent, Liverpool, could advertise lists of 'Choice American Tree and Shrub Seed' which contained many new rhododendrons. Breeding soon began. Within the decade the London Horticultural Society's garden at Turnham Green had an exhibition of American plants being sold by Hosea Waterer, which included new rhododendron and azalea hybrids in which Indian species were newly crossed with American ones. By 1862 Waterer's were showing a vast collection of new rhododendrons at the Royal Horticultural Society, with what was diplomatically called the 'high coloured' seedlings being very much admired (a taste which survives in many country house gardens). Less shatteringly colourful ones were used only for contrast. At the show, plants were displayed in elegant beds with gravel paths edged with turf between. Among the lesser beds were earth mounds planted with single ancient standard rhododendrons, including the marvellous-sounding brown-flowered 'Prince Albert'. A little later in the decade, 'rhodos' had become conventional shrubbery plants, mixed with the dull Portugal laurels, *Robinia inermis*, roses, and some species of *Cytisus*.

Azaleas, too, were a fashionable group, particularly the Ghent hybrids which were raised near that town in the early nineteenth century as crosses between some of the recently introduced North American species and the lovely and heavily perfumed *Rho-*

dodendron luteum from Turkey. London flower-sellers were importing large quantities in the 1830s, and by the 1860s the trade was so considerable that huge consignments were being auctioned regularly in the same city. 'Indian' azaleas (miscalled, for they were in fact Chinese garden plants, first appearing in Europe about 1810) became another popular group found in almost every greenhouse and conservatory in the 1880s. All were so admired that British breeders soon started work on them, and most florists' shows had classes for azaleas by 1870. The hardy American species were denizens of many 'American' gardens, and were also important in the 'fernery' as a means of alleviating the flowerless green.

So far, most of these new developments have been of almost entirely new groups of plants; developments of entirely familiar genera were often just as extreme and just as exciting. For many genera, all sorts of new relations had flocked in, adding new genetic possibilities to the breeder's palette and also creating new demands for the older varieties. In any case, what is newly possible is immensely attractive, and many nurserymen must have tried crossing the old with the new as much for the sheer fun of breeding as with the deliberate hope of finding fame and fortune.

The old garden flora, of course, contained such potential-packed groups as the roses (the new Victorian groups like the Ayrshires, Bourbons, Scottish, Teas and so on, we look at below), delphiniums, paeonies, hollyhocks, lupins, sweeet peas and tulips. A group like the tulips, almost entirely a florists' flower, and therefore rather rarely part of the flower garden proper, continued as a vastly popular fancier's plant but were also pressed into service for bedding. In spite of all the excitement about garden design, the old-fashioned system of planting tulip beds survived and the flowers remained immensely popular. Nurserymen like Mr Groom at Walworth kept trade going by producing expensive and glamorous new sorts. Groom wrote that it was only the patronage of the wealthy looking for such things that made a nursery viable, for the return on cheap varieties was very low. He must have done well, for he bred some quite marvellous tulips, especially a famous but vanished variety called 'Groom's Prince Albert', in which the soft yellow petals had a blue-black feathering.

In the 1860s grand tulips like this were never used as border flowers, though there were numbers of cheap and colourful border ones. Shirley Hibberd, and many of his readers, liked to see such varieties against evergreen shrubs, where they were planted as a brilliant margin to the shrubbery. He added that ' . . . it is not MERELY the colour which determines the value of a Tulip, but colour is all that ordinary persons require; and, that can be had in extravagant abundance from Tulips of the commonest kinds'.

As with so many grand flowers, there were auctions of particularly good collections; in 1851 'The most superb bed of Tulips in Europe! Mr R. Lawrence, of Hampton, will sell his unrivalled bed of Tulips . . . Catalogue forwarded to principal Seedsmen, or available from the Subscriber . . . ' Twenty years later, the prize lists name tulips that were still in commerce until the 1950s, like 'Talisman', 'Sir Joseph Paxton', 'Polyphemus' and so on. Many were bred by the extraordinary Mr Sam Barlow, who consistently won almost all the prizes at the London shows of the decade (he also has one of the most beautiful of all the 'bizarre' tulips named after him, and one which is still to be found).

35. 'Yowell's Zenobie', a famous picotee carnation of the 1840s.

Much the same sort of thing happened with other florists' groups, especially anemones, narcissus, hyacinths, pinks and carnations. However, one genus which had been in gardens for centuries, though it had never yet become a florists' flower, suddenly went through some extraordinary developments to become one (and indeed, it so remains). The clematis had been known only as the scented wildling of the hedgerow and as some of the lovely blue-flowered species from Europe. However, in the 1830s all sorts of interesting ones were being introduced from Japan by Dr von Siebold – including *C. coerulea*, with marvellous blue-shaded petals (rather similar to today's 'Lazurstern'). A few early hybrids were available in the 1840s, when an anonymous writer had to 'have some musk and noisette roses, and jasmine, to run up the mullions of my oriel window, and honeysuckles and clematis, the white, the purple and the blue, to cluster round the top ... '

The origin of Jackman's clematis hybrids has already been described; by 1870 even William Robinson liked them, for they could be cultivated in so many different ways; pegged down, put up stakes, against walls, down rock faces, or draped over rustic bridges. He thought the best sort was 'Jackmannii', though he also promoted species like the vigorous and perfumed *C. flammula* for clambering over tree stumps and spent plants. Miss Jekyll must have read this carefully, for she used this technique extensively at Munstead Wood. By the 1870s clematis was thought of as a cottage flower and 'To speak of a posy carries us back to quiet country villages where sweet-scented Jasmine and Woodbine, purple Clematis and monthly Roses fight longingly for a place beside the rustic porch'. Other species, such as *C. montana*, were soon being mixed with honeysuckle and wild vine to scramble through the branches of picturesque trees, and Miss Hope of Edinburgh was growing a mix of clematis and roses up a wire netting wall as background to a border (still a good idea, especially against a boring boundary fence). By the 1890s, American gardeners were busy growing the new British clematis hybrids recently introduced there and becoming popular.

Other fast-developing genera included a whole range of flowers still widely grown today, especially some of the primulas (both hardy and tender) and, even more important, the pansies and violas. The word 'viola' seems to have been in use at least since the 1830s, and originally applied to almost any hybrid between any species of that vast genus. More modern usages refer to a slightly more precise series of hybrids. The old name, also, for some of these older hybrids, as well as for *Viola bicolor*, was heartsease. To make things difficult, the name heartsease was also taken up for some of the Regency hybrids, so that even by 1840 one writer could say: 'I really liked heartsease till the florists called them pansies – a pretty name though, and Shakespearean too, – and put a thousand and one varieties in their catalogues, advertising flowers "as big as a penny piece".'

Following the sudden burst of hybrids that started in the 1820s, the flower was rapidly taken up by florists, by gardeners grand and humble, and by nurserymen. Societies for its promotion started forming in the 1840s, the first being in the rather unlikely location of Falkirk. In other parts of the country, too, breeding was marching forward with speed. Black pansies were being produced by J. Pearson at the Chilwell nurseries near Nottingham (similar plants still excite gardeners today). New varieties were quite extraordinarily expensive – 'Shepherd's Laura' cost the enormous sum of 7s. 6d. each, and even the pansy 'Maid of Athens', an Edinburgh variety, was successfully sold to local gardeners by Thomas Handasyde at 5s. each.

By the end of the 1840s viola hybrids had already become part of the cottage garden fantasy, as if they'd been there as long as the other denizens. They suited country cottage gardens rather better than urban ones, for none of the new hybrids liked heavy smoke and so needed to be grown beneath bell jars in city gardens. Naturally there were soon various classes of the flower, like 'show' and 'fancy' sorts (now often difficult to distinguish). A contemporary writer gave their history thus: 'It is exactly forty years since three florists instituted the first pansy society, and held the first Exhibition of these at Falkirk, Scotland. At that show the blooms staged were all show kinds, not one of which would be looked at today.' He goes on to say that the show sorts were older and more refined than fancy ones. The 'fancy' ones ('fancies' have a larger black central blotch and larger size) had been developed over the last ten years by Mr Salter (a Frenchman) in London (i.e. from 1840), a separate florist in Lille producing the even larger Belgian types. Mr John Downie in Scotland (now mostly remembered in an attractive sort of crab apple) went on to produce innumerable gorgeous things.

In the 1860s, with the increasing number of new varieties coming forward (some were already thought of as old, though they'd been in the garden for less than thirty years), gardeners began to see the bedding possibilities of the group. After all, though they were short of anything resembling red, there were endless numbers of stunning blues, violets, yellows, some perfect whites and even a 'bronze' sort. Bedding violas were almost the democrats of the flower garden, being cheap and hardy.

The disadvantage with the show and fancy pansies was that they were not reliably perennial, and were very apt to grow scrawny. Also, the black markings on the flowers detracted from the purity of the ground colours, making beds look too 'busy' when seen from a distance. Pansies were therefore soon being crossed with the horned violet (*V. cornuta*), a slightly variable species which shot to favour after 1860 and which is still an important garden plant. The new hybrids, often without any markings whatever, were soon to be found in some sumptuously grand colours, from rich smoky grey or amethyst, to gold and velvety purple. Soon there were hundreds of named varieties, like 'Perfection', 'Lavender Queen', 'Enchantress' and so on. Some of the loveliest were in shades of soft mauve, all looking well, it was thought, with some of the silver variegated geraniums (that's a combination that is still easy to make; try the lovely pale violet 'Lorna' with the geraniums 'Mrs Parker' or 'Caroline Schmidt', but don't let 'Mrs Parker' flower).

Even the new railway companies got their station masters to grow violas, using the company colours. Station gardens, for which competitions were held, were soon dazzling with yellow crocuses teamed with purple violas (or vice versa), or white or yellow variegated geraniums with yellow violas, or green-leaved red-flowered geraniums teamed with purple violas.

A few other species of the genus were taken up. The ancient garden forms of *Viola odorata* were further developed into a wonderful range of new colours (the litmus paper so essential for all Victorian chemists was derived from the same flowers). Parma violets began to be seen in the flower markets of London, and by the end of the Victorian period, garden connoisseurs were beginning to grow Americans like *V. cucullata* and *V. pedata.*

There remain two quintessentially Victorian groups. The first was part of the long-cultivated developed flora, the second of initially wild-collected species, dependent on tropic trade links abroad and highly developed technology at home, which suddenly burst into a vast flora of hybrids. The first group went on to become contaminated with the whole bedding idea and survived to be seen today in almost every single garden in the country. The second has dwindled into a long obscurity, though with developments in today's new sorts of garden and garden prosperity, it may perhaps make a comeback. The first group is the roses, the second the orchids.

Orchids of the tropical kind, mostly needing both jungle heat and humidity, were considerable status symbols from the moment of their introduction. To grow them needed 'stove' houses, kept constantly warm by the heat of fermenting horse dung or by one of the many types of boiler system developed from the 1800s onwards. The flowers, waxen, exotically coloured and sometimes equally perfumed, were an irresistible draw to the rich of the age. By 1839, for example, the glasshouses at Chatsworth were packed with orchids, many collected specifically for the Duke of Devonshire. In that year, Paxton published a magnificent plate of the gorgeous *Dendrobium paxtonii,* supposedly the most splendid example of the genus in existence. It had only just flowered, the immense plant having been shipped whole from the Amazon. By 1850–51, even cheap part-works began to include pictures of only slightly less glamorous orchids among the moutans, passion flowers, new species of *Ceanothus, Viburnum* and caladiums. In 1852 there was even a ticket-only sale of Guatemalan orchids to benefit the Gardeners' Benevolent Society, and a few years later

36. *Dendrobium paxtonii*, illustrated by Paxton in 1839.

the *Cottage Gardener* ran a series on plant collectors to encourage its readers to greater efforts. The longest article was on Thomas Lobb's collecting trips, particularly one to Java, where he collected vast numbers of new orchids.

By 1861 florists' classes for orchids appeared at provincial flower shows, and even the *Garden Oracle* began to list new varieties and the many new species of orchids. They were big business; in 1877 a report on British horticulture said that

A visit to any large nursery, say that of Messers Veitch and Sons, in the Kings Road, Chelsea, for example, will be amply sufficient to show that the trade industry of gardening is a most important one. In many of our leading metropolitan nurseries, the capital employed varies from £10,000 to £50,000 or even more, and it is a matter of some surprise to find that these large sums are invested in plants and seeds . . . one of the most profitable branches of the nurseryman's business of late years has been the collection and importation of the Indian and South American orchids, lily bulbs from America and Japan, and seeds of various kinds . . .

A year or two later it was common for orchids to be used to decorate the drawing-room.

Naturally interest slipped over to include the wild orchids of the countryside, and, early in the period, native orchids were often to be found growing in fashionable 'rootworks'; later, even humble cottagers included them in the bowlfuls of wildflowers exhibited at the local cottage garden flower shows. One commentator wrote that 'Some of the collections of cut flowers were very beautiful, and I recollect a bouquet of these (in an old china vase) composed of Ferns, Foxgloves, Grasses, Orchids, honeysuckles, eglantine etc. managed so artfully and elegantly that the Queen herself would have been proud of it . . . '

But queen of the garden was the rose; indeed, roses are almost *the* Victorian flower, for the great development which started in the latest part of the eighteenth century really took off from 1820 or so onwards, and by the 1840s was in fullest flight. Immense numbers of new varieties appeared, mostly in France, with some breeding taking place in Britain and America. New species were introduced to Europe from all over the world, and many of these were incorporated into existing types. The results were extraordinary, ranging from the tiny, spiky, creeping but deliciously perfumed Scots roses to vast sprawling things like the Ayrshire hybrids, the huge multiflora roses, the beginnings of the bedding roses like the 'teas', the first appearance of large numbers of pure yellow roses, and so on. Every garden that could (which was all except the most centrally urban ones) had roses, from the humblest cottages to the very grandest mansions. The powerful National Rose Society was started up in 1858, and rose books began to appear to cater for all social levels of the reading public.

The period opened in 1831, with the colossal *General System of Gardening and Botany* by David Don. Though this listed every species of rose known, and gave enormous lists of all known rose cultivars (though, alas, without the tiniest descriptive phrase), the project collapsed because, not unexpectedly, no one would read it. It perished after four immense volumes. However, it is of interest because it shows exactly the state of the rose in 1831,

37. A lush display of flowers and foliage, set on an industrially produced rustic stand.

when there were 211 Scotch roses, fifty-four damasks, sixty-eight centifolias (provins), and 706 other roses belonging to the centifolia group – almost all with French names.

However, things were soon to alter, for with the gathering interest in flower shows and exhibitions, more gardeners became rose-conscious, if not yet potential rose breeders. By 1835 a letter to the *Botanical Magazine* could suggest that 'One of the effects produced by the great number of flower shows established throughout the country is the great demand which they have created for new plants. This has been met in two ways: first, by occasioning large importations of herbaceous flowers and flowering shrubs from the Continent, such as the Dutch anemones, the German asters, the Ghent azaleas, and French roses . . . ' However, in the following decade, while the fabulous garden at Dropmore had its borders decorated with huge numbers of roses, mostly still French, and its walls embowered with thousands of Boursalt and de Lisle roses, through which, to quote a contemporary admirer, 'the sunbeams shed a ruddy and broken glow', and cottars mostly seemed to live in 'a cottage covered with woodbines, roses and jessamines', the British collector Robert Fortune was finding plants that were to alter for ever the direction that rose breeding was eventually to take. By 1847 he seems to have collected many new sorts of China rose – yellow (soon to be important), doubles, and even reds and whites on one plant. Two years later he found the now immensely popular *Rosa rugosa* in Shanghai.

Throughout the 1850s new things appeared; the architect Nesfield had at his Muswell Hill garden a baroque ramp topped with an eighteen-inch-high hedge of dwarf china roses, jasmine and sweetbriar. Kemp's *Landscape Gardening* gives a plan of a rose bed that he designed for a garden in Dulwich, basically circular, but with sausage-shaped beds of provins roses, the new hybrid perpetuals, damasks and so on.

Soon there were roses that still survive today, like many of the moss roses, and wonderful ones like 'Souvenir de la Malmaison' (which was widely grown as a potted rose – it grew well under those circumstances, and still does), 'Gloire de Dijon', 'Louise

Odier', and others (all good for pots, though 'Gloire de Dijon' is now more often seen on the walls of country rectories). All the Scots roses were widely thought to be excellent. Many of those have lost their names, though there still seem to be thirty or forty left of the vast numbers available at the beginning of the period. They are so tough that it seems likely that many remain to be rediscovered. New were the grand hybrid perpetuals, which included the marvellous 'Souvenir de la Reine d'Angleterre', many new bourbons, new mosses (some of the nicest from the firm of Shailer), new tea roses like 'Isabella Grey' (a close relative of the still wildly popular and similarly coloured 'Alister Stella Grey').

By the 1850s, as well as to drape walls, swamp borders, and be crammed into rosariums, standard roses were being used for vertical emphasis in the parterre. At the Priory, in windy Argyll, a simple eight-part square had each plot filled with different bedding plants in a single colour, the corners of each being marked with standard roses (the description doesn't say if these were all of the same variety). To us it may seem that this arrangement may have looked rather odd, a possibly motley collection of roses failing to unify a motley collection of bedding annuals. However, it is possible that it may have looked odder still in practice, for there was a popular protection device for standard roses, particularly where they were likely to get damaged by bad weather, or coated with soot, called 'SANGSTER'S FLOR- UMBRA'. This was a small umbrella on a universal joint atop a pole, intended to shade the flowers. There was even a bag which could be tied over the whole thing and used with 'Brown's Patent Fumigator', to get rid of Victorian greenfly and earwigs.

Everyone in London wanted standard roses, and these were often sold potted, having been imported in vast quantities from France. Presumably, their being potted meant that they could be used where there was no suitable garden for their planting, or be stood on balconies or terraces, or taken into the drawing-room. However, potted standards were much more difficult to manage than potted bushes. Writers of the day suggested that short standards were better than tall ones, and even those should be bought from a country nursery, where the roots might have been less badly hacked to get them into the pot.

Of course, London gardeners had worse problems than unscrupulous nurserymen, for the 'smokes', even in summer, were so bad that within a mile of St Paul's, only old cabbage roses, the York and Lancaster, 'Maiden's Blush', and the charming 'Rose de Meaux' would survive. A few miles further out and the list was a little longer, including some of the newish hybrid perpetuals. Beyond three miles, hybrid Chinas and noisettes became possible. However, there had to be no smoke at all to grow the moss roses or the new and fashionable teas. Bearing all that in mind, a design for a Victorian town garden rose bed of 1855 suggests something twelve feet in diameter, centred with a standard 'Aimée Vibert' (still available), and a ground of 'Jules Margottin' (available) and 'The General' (lost), alternated. Failing those, the gardener could once have planted 'Géant des Batailles', surrounded with 'Duchess of Sutherland'. Some districts of the city, however, especially the poorer ones, were so polluted that roses had to be grown under bell jars. These could be removed at weekends, when the air was less polluted (much of it must have been caused by industry). On a good summer Sunday morning in the city, with the bells ringing, attic dwellers in even the most central areas could just smell the hay of the countryside.

Ten years later, roses were twined through all sorts of artistic wirework, baskets, stages, rose arches, and the rest (incidentally, if you have a suitable set of garden railings, the rose 'Aimée Vibert' was thought to be the best for twining round them). Soon at least some breeding was being carried out in London and the Midlands, though this doesn't seem to have helped Mr Shailer, whose Battersea nursery was sold up in the early 1860s.

In 1862 the editor of the *Gardener's Chronicle* was sent a batch of English seedling roses; he was delighted that anyone in England was trying to develop new things, but he was not enthusiastic about the results. He wrote, dishearteningly for the sender of the flowers, that the French 'Duc de Rohan' (probably lost) was still the most gorgeous rose of all. Britain's 'Beauty of Waltham' was also superb (new in 1861, it too now seems lost).

He was even sent one called 'Robert Fortune', but something ate the buds.

Ironically, the same editor, at the Rose Show at the Royal Horticultural Society's site at Kensington the same year, writes: 'Both among old and new varieties, the exhibition of the 26th inst, offered unmistakeable evidence that the race of Hybrid Perpetuals is the dominant one, if it be not destined indeed to become almost the exclusive occupant of our Rosariums. The Teas, in fact, were the only rose besides them that made any figure in the assemblage. Another observable and notable point was that the varieties of cupped or globular form, which present the very perfect BEAU IDEAL of a perfect Rose, are gradually but certainly expelling the flat hard-looking ungainly varieties which were once so numerous ... ' He goes on to suggest that all the boring old flat ones be ditched, and almost every gardener seems to have followed his advice; that is until recent times, when rose connoisseurs have been busily hunting out every old flat one that they can find.

A few years later the influential prize lists of flower shows contained 200 hybrid perpetuals, thirty teas, and only 100 drawn from all the other groups. These new roses soon came into their own, being grown by gardeners all over the country, drawn (as rose admirers still are) from all social classes. Dean Reynolds Hole describes the growth of the enthusiasm in his *Book about Roses*, dating the wildest part of this to just the last twenty years (from 1865 or so). He describes, too, visits he made to the allotments of Nottingham, where minute glasshouses produced some of the best March roses he'd seen. He comments that though roses have now been taken up by everyone, not one in a thousand is well grown. In Nottingham they were grown, using his charming phrase, 'de l'abondance du coeur'.

One of the growers told Dean Hole: 'It's more nor a mile from my house to my garden but I've been here for weeks, in the winter months, every morning before I went to my work, and every evening when I came from it, and not seldom at noon as well, here and back, and my dinner to get, between twelve and one o'clock.' 'How do you afford,' he inquired of another, 'to buy these new and expensive varieties?' He goes on: ' ... and I would that every employer, that everyone who cares for the labouring poor, would remember the answer, reflect, and act on it. "I tell you," the workman said, "how I managed to buy 'em – *by keeping away from the beershops*".'

In the same book, Dean Hole began to express a nostalgia that we shall meet in more detail in Chapter 10. He wrote:

Sixty years later [after 1772] in my own childhood, there were in the garden before me as I write – and now little more than a subdivided flower bed – those bowers and meandering walks, many a pleasant nook, where the aged might rest, young men and maidens sigh their love, and happy children play.... But what do I see, as the mist clears? A garden which like a thousand others, has obeyed the command of imperious fashion ...

He bemoaned his vanished grottoes, walks of laburnum, lilac and the rest. In, of course, came geometrical bedding: 'Do you require examples? Copy your carpet, or the ornaments on your pork pie.' For his new rose garden, in which he hoped to recreate some of the qualities of the past, he got Marnock, Robinson and a Mr Ingram of Belvoir to help him recreate a 'real' garden.

That may perhaps have looked like a committee garden; however, all rose enthusiasts are indebted to him. Though he was a very prolix writer (indeed, some of his publications have no discernible material whatever), he did assemble an extraordinary collection of roses. In his day, the tea roses, a new and treasured group, were pampered quite as much as the valuable tulips and auriculas of seventeenth-century florists; they were grown under a framework so that they could be sheltered from inclement weather and strong sunshine. He had 3,000 sorts in cultivation, wrote vast amounts on them, and won more prizes than any other grower. In *The Florist* of April 1857, he first suggested a Grand National Rose Show. There was no initial response. By no means deterred, he then wrote to Mr Rivers, Mr Charles Turner and Mr Wm Paul, outlining his ideas. They, all good businessmen, saw what potential the idea had, for the general public as well as for

38. Handsome auriculas like this survived in florists' gardens throughout the period.

themselves. Great excitement followed. The first show proved excellent. The second was a more splendid affair than ever. The third was held in the Crystal Palace, and thereafter became a fixture at Kensington. Oddly, the pressure of the new is well illustrated in some of the prize lists for the early rose shows; by the late 1850s there are no variety names in common with the roses listed in the Loddiges catalogue of 1830, and yet just as many are of French origin.

By now the use of the rose as a large bedding plant had become part of every gardener's baggage, and the rose beds, together with the rockery, were part of what every garden had to have. Robinson, as ever, inveighed against the conventional belief that no rose looks good in association with other plants (which was why they were so often confined to a particular area). He wanted a rich underplanting of rose groups or beds, using bulbs, saxifrages and periwinkles, and wanted the roses not to be pruned, but to be left to grow into handsome and floriferous bushes.

Soon, while advanced gardeners were sighing for the past, most other gardeners were in frantic pursuit of the new. Even in

Japan, the inhabitants had just gone through a craze for the rose, which fetched vast prices for a couple of years. So many were soon being imported that the price crashed, and everyone lost interest.

By 1900, and after, country houses, town houses, and anything in between all had gardens filled with roses; at Bowood, photographs of the empty parterres of winter show the central diamonds still with standard roses. Hatfield, for all its seventeenth-century design, still had central standard roses or yuccas in the parterre beds; Broughton Castle had (and still has) a lovely rose garden, complete with rustic chairs and too much gravel. Arley, Belton ... the list of great Victorian rose collections goes on and on. The rose garden had become the most popular of all garden elements.

CHAPTER
6

NEW
ELEMENTS

ICTORIAN GARDENS WERE NOT JUST ABOUT
the extraordinary developments of the various styles
of bedding or of the garden's flowers. The appearance
of Victorian gardens was just as much determined by a whole set
of new, or at least further developed, garden elements. Some of
these were to provide places to grow some of the new plants
being introduced from the furthest corners of the earth, or for
some of the many new sorts of flower being bred by the nurserymen of Europe, America and the Orient. Some new elements
were designed for new classes of gardener, for example, simple
rustic pergolas or summerhouses (so much cheaper, and so much
more 'honest', to build from fallen timbers from the woodland
than from finely cut ashlar designed by the architect) for simple
middle-class families, or grand conservatories for the very grandest of people and plants. They varied from the 'Arborets' of Mr
Hudspith of Haltwhistle, who was exhibiting and selling 'very
tasteful' stands for pot ferns, made from 'skilfully altered' knotted
tree trunks at the Great Exhibition of 1851, or real arboreta
containing the very latest trees from North America or China, to
the many newly built rock gardens in which to grow alpines
from all over the world, or the rosariums, heatheries, and even
'American' gardens.

183

Some of these elements naturally had earlier antecedents. Arboreta, for instance, had existed in one form or another at least since the seventeenth century. They had become commoner in the following century, especially once new and spectacular species began to be introduced from North America towards the end of the eighteenth century. When the trickle became a flood, the possession of an arboretum became a necessity for those with sufficient land to hold one. The study of botany had become popular all over Europe in the late eighteenth century, and a rage, especially for idle ladies, a few decades later. Having a collection of trees available for instant study was obviously more status-full than having to find weeds from the hedge bottom, or a few flowers from the garden.

Some of the grandest arboretums were very handsome indeed; many survive in the grounds of the larger country houses, and quite magnificent examples can now be seen at Scone, Killerton, Westonbirt and elsewhere. By 1839 a writer in Paxton's *Magazine of Botany* was thinking that

An arboretum, vaguely considered, is merely a collection of indigenous or exotic trees, disposed according to the taste of the proprietor ... In modern arboretums, every genus or tribe of plants is grouped together, more or less densely in estates of considerable circuit, or in botanical or other public gardens; such departments create a variation, and sometimes a pleasing one. They also furnish the beholder, at one gaze, with a knowledge of the hardy ligneous species of every genus, tribe or order of plants, and their position in the natural system of botany ... the practice of attempting to arrange plants ... according to their natural affinity ... is radically erroneous. It creates both a dull monotony ... [and] paradoxical as this may appear, it is not the less CORRECT.

If the lady of the house couldn't have an arboretum, whether correctly planted, or just good to look at, everyone with a garden could have a rockery; they weren't just a feature of grand gardens like those in Chapter 1. Rockeries were beginning to become popular at the very end of the eighteenth century, and were closely related to the grottoes of the earlier part of that century, as places to excite the senses (the sense, that is, of Gothic horror and awe if the grotto was got up to look like a ruined castle or a rock-strewn and haunted cave, or the sense of classical serenity if the grotto had a statue of a water god or a half-naked spring nymph). The entrances to grottoes of all sorts were often planted up with saxifrages and alyssums ('ruined castles' were made to look venerable by draping them with ivy). For some gardeners the planting became more interesting (and less childish) than the associations, and the resulting piece of builder work to support the plants was called 'rockwork'. It became home for various mountain plants, mostly those of Europe.

Such rockwork became more and more popular in Regency gardens, and soon became a necessity in even the tiniest urban ones. Standards were soon heavily debased. That process had started by 1838. Paxton's *Magazine of Botany* suggested some pretty little rockworks thus: '... the turf on which the pedestals stand is to be inclined at an angle of 45°, and the pedestals [for vases] are enclosed in small circular borders, on which may be placed fragments of rock, or shells, and by the introduction of a little soil amongst them, alpine plants may be successfully grown'. The design is both elaborate and geometrical, consisting of a large rectangle of ground with a guilloche-pattern band of planting outside, with grass pyramids in the corners to hold statuary (there's rockwork at the base of these too). Inside all this is an inner parterre, with more beds around four subsidiary fountains (with rockwork margins), and then a pergola over the central feature. The whole thing is surrounded by shrubbery.

> The introduction of fountains, of chaste and unique structure, and ornamented with every variety of rock and shell, into the central compartments, with jets of water issuing from every crevice, and propelled with diverse and ever-varying degrees of force, would form most delightful and refreshing spectacles during the summer months.

Perhaps.

However, many gardeners had already gone beyond the idea of merely using 'fragments of rock or shells', and J. C. Loudon complained that most suburban rockeries were often just a pile of stones around the roots of a tree, or, worse, consisted of a pile of stone, broken bricks, glass debris or old tree roots. He correctly pointed out that to get the construction of such things to look good is exceptionally difficult. Failing inspiration on the part of the owner or gardener, resort could be had to a professional rockery builder like a certain Mr Gray, who did the Colosseum grotto at Regent's Park, as well as a rockery at Clumber, and many in London. Elsewhere in the book, however, Loudon (or more likely one of his contributors) suggests that beds in the front garden could well be decorated with 'historic or antique stones' (so easy to come by), shells, ammonites, or lumps of spar.

It is difficult to know how rockeries sank so fast, for soon they included even broken cups and saucers, like a medieval midden. Mrs Loudon, writing two years later, confides:

Rockwork, though composed of somewhat ponderous materials, is very frequently arranged according to female taste ... there are many kinds of rock-work; but they may all be desirable as collections of fragments of rocks, stones, flints, vitrified bricks, scoriae, and similar materials, so arranged as to afford a striking object in the landscape; and, at the same time, so as to form a number of little nests or crevices for the reception of alpine plants.

At Redleaf, Blenheim, Hoole and in rockeries well into mid-century, the plants were grown in clearly marked and individual 'cells', usually delimited by four flat stones.

Hoole remained fashionable at least until 1850. The estate was, at base, a rather grand *ferme ornée* of twenty to thirty acres, with lawns around the house and an extensive kitchen garden. The rockery, 'being one of the most remarkable specimens of the kind in England', was vast. Yet in spite of its scale, and the fact that 'it has been the work of many years to complete', it had problems. The worst of these was 'the difficulty being to make it stand against the weather ...' This suggests that it was only made from painted plaster; this wasn't unusual. Although many early writers, like Jane Loudon, suggested that to make naturalistic rockeries the stones should be piled 'one upon another so as to imitate the stratification of a rocky outcrop', the advice was rarely followed.

Whatever the difficulties, and however improbable most of the results, by 1841 such good picturesque advice persisted:

... rockeries have been made principal features in flower gardens; sometimes by accident, that is, when rocks happen to be about on the spot, but more frequently by design ... [which] after all ... can hardly be called good taste. Rock work, whenever it is intended to be formed, should always be constructed with ONE KIND of stone; not, as usually seen, made up of petrifactions of building bricks from kilns ... altogether a rubbish-like assemblage, and as a work of art, quite contemptible. But when stone is used, and laid in horizontal strata, as it probably lay in its native bed, it has an artistical look, and the interstices answer well for the reception of plants.

Structural honesty was not always possible or followed.

Of course any rockery large enough to inspire any truly alpine excitement was beyond the means of most middle-class gardeners. In small gardens rockeries could only proclaim artifice, never the Sublime. They became inextricably mixed up with the picturesque 'rustic' ideal, which admired trellis-work, plant stands, fences of wirework, together with vases, rustic cascades, and moss houses. There, together with the rosery, the rockery and the heathery, and just beyond the lawns by the drawing-room, were crammed all the new garden elements of Victorian Britain.

There, according to Shirley Hibberd's splendid work called *Rustic Adornments for Homes of Taste*:

A circular pond of five feet diameter, may be surrounded with a border of rockwork of twelve or fourteen inches, the dark stones being merely loosely laid on an even surface, with no pyramids or ruggedness of surface, and beyond this a ring of turf two feet wide ... The rockwork should be wholly formed of dark stones of small size ... and the edge next to the pond sloping down towards it. Around this a light fence of wire-work should be placed, and on the turf about eight or ten standard roses should be planted, so as to form a ring. The stones should be planted with one or two junipers ... and the pond furnished with a fountain and gold fish.

Although he later avers that 'Men of taste generally eschew rock-work in a garden; and well they may, considering how, in too many instances, taste is violated by the introduction of oyster pyramids, plaster busts with dilapidated noses, conch shells, mineralogical specimens, and even broken crockery, under the general denomination of rock-work ...' he thinks that, properly treated, every garden should have one – especially all urban gardens.

39. Rockwork, hanging baskets, and plenty of heat in Mrs Hibberd's fern house.

Next to the house was apparently the standard position for such a garden feature, where it was not so much a rockery but more a showy raised bed to tease the eye. His illustrations make clear that it was all decidedly artificial, for

Where a considerable elevation can be attained, a dark cave may be constructed, both for general effect, and for the growth of mosses and ferns ... Around the cave, ivy and *Stauntonia* may be thickly twined, and the face of the rockwork and each side of the cave planted with the gayest of alpines, but not too profusely, or they may hide the picturesque blocks of which it is composed. The Scotch thistle will be an appropriate addition if planted in the most elevated spots.

This seems a decidedly odd top-knot for such a thing. If anyone carried out such works, they might have been odder still if they'd carried out the next of his suggestions that 'A few birds might be domesticated in such a cave; a pair of owls, for instance, whose hooting at night would be no unpleasant music.'

For town gardens with long narrow sites, he suggests that this garden element (and its owls) should be

at the wall most remote from the house, [where] you may throw up some rockwork, and on one side a mound, to be covered with ivy and surmounted by a good sized shrub. The outside of the rockwork should be built up tastefully with large clinkers, and covered with any large dark masses of rock, and the inside filled with rich mould. It should not be less than two feet six on one side, and should run down in the centre to about ten or twelve inches, and rise again to about two feet on the other side. If this, and a low mound be constructed, and formality of outline studiously avoided, it will add very much to the apparent size and picturesqueness of your ground as viewed from the window...

A few years later, in 1864, the author of *How to Lay Out a Garden* could write, in a very superior way, that

... those who would steer clear of the vulgarities and irregularities of mere cockneyism will do well not to permit anything of the kind I have been describing around their houses. When composed of such materials as shells, pieces of old porcelain, scoriae, and other small artificial or manufactured articles, and interspersed with grotesque-looking busts, heads, etc, as is frequently the case, their use in connection with houses is all the more to be deprecated.

By that time the rockery had evolved into a number of different types, suited to particular groups of plants, and the word 'rockery' included both the usual alpinery and the fernery, a place for such

189

ferns as would actually grow on 'mountains, rock and clefts in old walls'. Such plantings were usually mixed with small azaleas and other American plants and the soil surface planted with moss.

Ferns became the 'vogue' plants of the later Victorian period. The fernery was usually made of rockwork, for they were 'more effectually displayed when their bright green tufts rise out of grey stones or dark burns from the brick kiln'. Hibberd, who played a large part in creating the fashion, deleterious as it was to almost any wild population of native fern, could continue: 'You'll eventually need a grand fernery, with, perhaps, a model of a ruin for the main feature of the scheme . . .' It was deleterious because, as he wrote in *The Fern Garden: How to make, keep and Enjoy it; or, Fern Culture Made Easy* in 1896:

Allow me to remark, further, that the passion for fern collecting has in many instances been carried to a ridiculous excess by persons who merit the title not of fern collector so much as fern destroyers. Let every genuine fern lover be on his guard to discourage reckless fern collecting ... It is not many years since I saw ... in the possession of a lady, a sheet of Tunbridge fern nearly a yard square ... brought forth as a trophy, and preserved as a memorial of the days 'when we went gipsying ...'

The fern was extinct.

London was by then well supplied with itinerant fern vendors, though their plants, pulled up from the wild, rarely survived in town, for the air was too polluted. However, this seems to have deterred no one, and indeed it was urbanization that was the driving force behind the fernery, for it had become, in a way, emblematic. Its function was to remind the urban gardener of rocky wastes, mountain glens, wooded waterfalls, indeed all of the lost and romantic world.

Some outdoor ferneries were constructed of tree roots and banks of earth, 'picturesquely disposed and planted with ferns severally adapted to the sites and positions the scheme affords . . .' Hibberd's own fernery was illustrated in the *Floral World* of January 1867, and was a long and winding double wall, made of

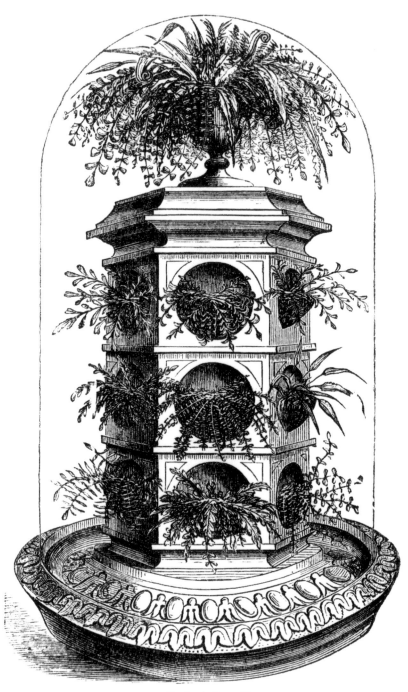

40. Rosher's fern pillar.

clinker, with both sides and top planted, using a mix of ferns and alpines. It had only the merest suggestion of a 'ruin'.

Like the infatuation with bedding, the passion for the rock garden swept everything, including sense, before it. William Robinson, sensible even in illness and old age, wrote in 1914 of the rapidly increasing range of rock plants as 'this wondrous flora'. He pointed out that the love for rock gardens was now widespread throughout the gardening world, and that though '... the English were first to take pleasure in it: their first attempts were futile'. Mocking Loudon's awful early Victorian suggestions, he sensibly points out that large numbers of rock plants were (and of course remain) perfectly hardy in the ordinary garden, where even some of the more difficult things are happy in raised beds – easier to manage and better to look at than the usual 'rockery'. As a final irony he describes a journey to Switzerland to look at a famous alpine collection, where he was astonished to find them grown on a St John's Wood style rockery rather than on the natural rocky slopes of their native land.

The rockery's early companion, the 'rootery', seems never to have caught the public imagination in the way that its stony cousin did; perhaps the flora for it was too obscure. They were often planted up with orobanches, saprophytes whose flowers should surely have suited some of the period's subtler colour schemes, wild orchids, and woodland plants. Even though there were grand examples, like the one at Biddulph that led to the Chinese garden (which perhaps eclipsed it), or the extraordinary one at Drumlanrig built 'in a low and obscure ravine near the splendid flower garden' made of old tree stumps dug from the local peat, they didn't catch on.

The 'mossery', too, played a rather minor role, and only one or two survive, though mosses themselves played an important role in the whole rustic movement. Moss houses were their particular abode, though as dead plants rather than living. They were already popular by 1840, and Jane Loudon gives her lady readers full directions for their construction: they were to have concrete foundations, with rustic pillars stuck in to support the roof – generally trunks of young larches or spruce (both with the bark left on). Then the rafters, laths of hazel rods, were nailed on. Mosses of various sorts were then pushed between the laths with a wooden wedge; different sorts of moss were used to get a pattern (the pattern was chalked on the laths to give a guide – rather like an embroidery plan). She wrote:

... a very rich and at the same time original effect, might be produced in a moss house, by arranging the moss in an arabesque pattern with different colours combined something like those of a Turkey carpet ... or the walls might be of some plain colour with only the crest of the family, or the initials of the designer's name in white or colours...

The floor was sometimes finished with

... other pine cones, or with small pebbles, some of which are white and are arranged in a kind of pattern; the windows are frequently of

41. A pretty rustic boathouse, whose interiors would have been decorated with 'moss work'.

coloured glass; and a curious effect might be produced by having those in the back of the building purple, which would make the ground and every object seen through them look as if covered with snow; and those in front of the building filled with yellow glass, which gives every object the rich glow of summer.

By 1853 moss houses were still popular: 'Structures such as arbours, moss houses etc., should always be placed in positions to command a perfect view of some object of interest ...' One such, at Dalkeith, was furnished so that

The seats are all portable, and consist of a sofa and six chairs, two of which are representations of arm-chairs, hollowed out of the trunks of two old oak trees, very much covered with excrescences; the others are light chairs, formed of hazel, and the seats cushioned with *Polytrichum commune*. The sofa is also cushioned with the same, the back being open wickerwork. The table is circular, set on a clawed stand, and is covered with a matting of *Polytrichum*.

The side walls are covered with moss. In the centre of the back wall is a representation of a ducal coronet, done in fir cones. The roof is of *Sphagnum palustre*, a white moss; and in the centre is a stag, three fourths of the natural size ... done in a very ingenious manner with small rods of young larch.

Of all the new Victorian elements, however, the rockery was really rivalled only by the rosary. This had started life in the early years of the century (it could also be called the rosery, the rosarium, or more simply, the rose garden). By the early part of the Victorian period, all roses were in fact shrubby sorts or climbers. The first needed little in the way of pruning, most eventually making large and romantically sprawling plants. By the end of the Victorian period the bedding system had even tamed the rose itself, and the Bourbons and early tea roses were adapted for rose 'beds' in which the once grand and untamed rose was treated just like any other Victorian bedding plant – as a patch of colour.

Rose gardens varied in style from the Celtic, with interwoven beds around a complex arched pergola, surrounding a pool, to the geometric, and to the entirely gardenesque. Bad taste showed itself very early, eventually provoking Dean Hole in his *A Book about Roses* (1884) to say '. . . nowhere is the formal, monotonous, artificial system of arrangement more conspicuously rampant . . .' He wanted informal rose gardens planted up to show the full variation of the rose, with varieties in all heights, growing up pillars, pergolas, baskets, hedges and screens. Many gardeners must by then have agreed, though the Dean's own design suggestions were not of great visual interest. Robinson, too, took up cudgels on behalf of the rose, and lambasted conventional belief. Naturally, Robinson disliked it, saying that roses 'should be everywhere in the garden where they will grow. We never saw a garden yet where either places or position needed to be invented for roses . . .'

Rose gardens could be places either for private meditations or for public display. If the latter, then they could simply be planted in the front garden, where socially competitive gardening reached new heights. Most garden writers of the age, realizing the importance of this new element of domestic life, give suggestions for its planning and planting. Loudon gives large numbers of ideas (useful for any modern gardener with an early Victorian house wanting to have an authentic-looking garden), usually in the gardenesque style. By the late 1820s an average-sized front garden would be bounded by a narrow shrubbery and the lawn would have four batswing beds, each bed with a central standard rose, with the rest of the area in two of them planted with pansies and a mix of fuchsias, calceolarias and annuals in the others. By the time of the *Suburban Gardener*, Loudon gives various planting schemes for suburban gardens using shrubs, herbaceous plants and bulbs. However, he also suggests some more advanced ideas for 'Planting with bulbs, to be succeeded by showy annuals'. Though all the bulbs had been known for several centuries, he adds that 'All these annuals are new, and eminently beautiful; and seeds of them may be procured in most of the principal seed shops.' He suggests planting them in the manner of the previous decade, using one sort of each bed, though often in a mix of colours. He especially liked 'Lupinus mutabilis', calliopsis, collinsias, and the brand new clarkias.

Lower in the social scale, even by the 1830s, front gardens could be planted with edible plants. One writer suggested marrows, pumpkins and squashes, to provide winter and summer vegetables. The flowers were fried in butter and the young shoots and leaves were thought to be as good as spinach. The walls of house and garden were covered with fruit or beans. It could have looked rather pretty.

Twenty years later, middle-class front-garden design had become so conventionalized that it must have been widely ridiculed; one earnest writer clucked that

It is too much the custom to ridicule those little quadrangular spots of cultivated ground in front of the endless rows of houses in the approaches to London and most other cities, where we find three or four square yards of earth covered in weeds, intersected with bright gravel, white pavement, and brown grass, with rows of box, and a few dingy roots and shrubs, endeavouring to extricate themselves from the tight embrace, forming what is pleasantly called the 'front garden', but we hail with fullness of respect this tribute to the God of nature, as being the only approach to the living vegetable world, which stern necessity allows to many sons and daughters of toil and affliction.

A few years later, Hibberd wrote that front gardens should show 'high keeping' but no frills. He was particularly against rustic work, rockeries and summerhouses, all of which were more suitable to the back garden. The front part should have only grand species of trees and shrubs, with nothing that needed close inspection. Things must have been getting out of hand to his mind too, for he insists on a straight path to the front door, with not a single wiggle, adding that one of the nuisances of the age was that 'we have winding paths to make butcher-boys giddy, and perplex the stranger, who would find the way if he could, and which compel the visitor to make half a tour of the grounds, when his chief object is to get inside the house, to take off his hat and gloves, and sit at the table punctual to a moment'.

A little later, by 1877, front gardens of tasteful and aesthetic owners could be filled with old-fashioned flowers, enclosed by a whitethorn hedge. One elegant plan showed, within this boundary, that the borders were often only four feet deep. The lawn was scattered with occasional shrubs, box, aucubas, or with ivy up posts and pyramids. The front garden paths were to be bordered with box (hard work to keep in order), tiles (expensive), *Arabis albida*, or even houseleeks, which 'will survive the trampling of tiny feet'. In the borders stood phlox, with plenty of hollyhocks at their backs. The spaces between were filled with a tangle of sweet peas, mignonette and other annuals. Stocks and asters were to be squeezed in the interstices, for late colour. Honeysuckle was draped over the Gothic woodwork porch, and more stocks, violets, clove carnations, musk roses and mimulus were planted beneath the cottage windows.

The writer, Hobday, says that it is a mistake of cottars (whether real ones, or the sentimental fake kind) to try to have a geometric flower garden. The front garden should have only four small beds at most; after all, 'why should one person go to the expense of providing fresh plants for his flower garden annually because his neighbour chooses to do so?' Worse, 'in the formation of their flower beds let one and all eschew stars, diamonds, and all fancy patterns. A plain circle or oval or an irregularly shaped bed with easy flowing lines would present a far better appearance than a flower bed in the shape of which sharp angles prevail.' That he is not really writing for the agricultural poor is clear when he suggests small shrubs that include aucubas, arbor-vitae, catalpas, deutzias, the only recently introduced forsythias, rare retinosporas and so on. The herbaceous flowers he adds to these include *Anemone japonica*, *Zauschneria californica* and *Dicentra spectabilis*, as well as older flowers like *Lilium candidum*, *Campanula persicifolia*, *Corydalis lutea*, daisies and sweet williams.

The front garden, except in the poorest examples, became the site of another piece of competitive gardening: the lawn. Of course the great eighteenth-century gardens had had lawns, often vast, though these were either cropped by the park's inhabitants such as fallow deer, rare breeds of sheep and cattle, or kept scythed by the garden staff. In suburban Regency gardens lawns were similarly scythed, giving them a slightly textured and shaggy look (one of the great annoyances of Regency middle-class life was being woken by the sound of a neighbour's gardener sharpening his scythe). Soon, every Victorian house had a square of lawn, even if this was scarcely large enough to lie upon outstretched and could be cut with a few sweeps of the scythe. However, Victorian ingenuity was at once set to work on the provision of a mowing machine that would do the work and that could also take care of the numerous flower-beds and their complicated shapes cut out of the grass.

From at least the 1820s the minds of inventive gardeners had turned to ways of solving the problem of mowing the lawn. The first machines with rotating barrels of blades were illustrated in the late 1820s, but proved difficult to maintain and were quite expensive. Even by 1842 a magazine letter by 'An Odd Fellow' suggests some of the difficulties: 'A mowing machine costs from £7–£9, according to its size; it can only be used in dry weather [still a problem with cylinder mowers], and when grass is very short. Where a lawn is to be kept extremely short, this machine is more effectual than a scythe, and it also has the merit of not requiring any dexterity in using it. We, however, prefer a scythe in the hands of a good mower.' It is important to remember that the scythe, in the hands of an adept, could indeed be very effective; a bowling green in Aberdeenshire was kept scythed until the 1970s.

However, except in remote areas, the future was clearly with the machine. Every one of the tens of thousands of new houses being built had to have a lawn, and a cheap machine for cutting it clearly had an enormous market. Developments proceeded apace. By 1856 lawns were actually becoming cheap things to own, for the mowing machines made their maintenance so much easier. The most popular model still needed two men to operate it: one to push, one to pull. Large establishments had horse-drawn mowers, and the horses wore large leather shoes to stop their iron-shod hooves ruining the lawn's surface.

Greens introduced the first effective one-person lawnmower at a cost of five shillings. A lighter model for ladies, called the 'Parvum Miraculum', was a shilling dearer. The same firm also had a range of two-man machines in various widths, from fourteen inches (costing £6.10s) to a twenty-four-inch model (costing £9). By 1862 controversy raged over rival types, rather as it does today, and gave rise to a massive correspondence in all the garden magazines. There were even competitions to see which machines were the most effective; the largest one produced by Greens often won, doing four or five acres of hilly tree-planted lawn a day if drawn 'by a steady, active pony'. Defeated, the rival firm of Shanks began to produce an exotic range of highly decorated machines, designed for the ladies' market.

Hosepipes, too, were another important market, to water front lawns and bedding schemes. As soon as houses had become commonly supplied with mains water, or had pumps to supply their own tanks, hoses were used to water gardens. At first these had been made of leather, carefully stitched, but they were prone to rot and leak. However, with the discovery of gutta-percha hosepipes began to save hours of gardeners' time and energy. Conservative as ever, many gardeners continued to prefer leather. By 1852 there were arguments between makers of gutta-percha and vulcanized rubber pipes, but the old-fashioned leather sort was still available in 1871, when one advertiser offered 700 feet of leather hose with a one-inch bore at 6d per foot.

When the house was semi-detached, or grand enough to be unencumbered on all sides, a conservatory was easily attached to the side of the house, where it could be seen by the passing world yet still overlook the private garden. They were delightful additions to thousands upon thousands of houses, both of town and country, and could vary in size from a few yards across to ones fit to house a small piece of jungle. The main impetus was given to this new garden element once the tax on glass was repealed. By 1851 many glass companies were setting up, able to produce, and find a ready market for, new and cheap glass. They produced mostly rough plate (used for glasshouses), as well as glass tiles and sheets.

Almost all the new conservatories were heated. In the Georgian

42. Conservatories and glasshouses were status symbols of the age;
advertising reflected their importance.

age, glass was heated too (producing all sorts of exotic crops and flowers), but mostly by the fermentation of horse dung. Hothouses commonly had a long central pit along their lengths, filled every couple of months during the cold season with fairly fresh manure. This produced a good heat for several weeks, was dug over to produce a second burst of warmth, and was then discarded. Fermentation produced plenty of water vapour (which made excellent conditions for growing), but also produced a powerful odour.

Some orangeries, public spaces for much of the year, were heated by open fireplaces or by external stoves, the flue of which wound up through the back wall of the building, so heating the brick or stone. However, the heat was difficult to regulate with much finesse, and was especially intense at the base of the flue. Flue-heating also made the orangery's atmosphere very dry (encouraging red spiders and thrips), and in any case meant that some poor gardener had to remain on duty overnight to check that the fires never burnt out. When techniques of iron casting radically improved in the early nineteenth century it became possible to produce all sorts of stoves, ones in which the speed of burning could be carefully regulated, and ones which could be used to heat water, or air. Good cast-iron pipes could also be made to conduct heat around the building, using the new-found principle of convection. There were long discussions of this in the garden press, some gardeners being reluctant to believe that convection would carry heat for any distance at all. Eventually they were convinced, and discussion altered to whether water or air was the best method of conveyance. Though there were glasshouses heated by water pipes as early as 1828, it took several decades for this method to be widely adopted.

One popular mechanism was the Polmaise system, whereby a stove outside the main conservatory heated air in a special chamber which vented hot air into the top of the conservatory, or piped or boxed it (long wooden tubes were made out of planking) underneath the plant stages. Once the air had cooled, it was sucked back into the chamber from vents at the bottom of the building. The method was also used to heat the main house, though there were disadvantages. A leaking boiler poured sulphurous fumes straight into the conservatory, killing the plants at once. It was also common for the boiler to set fire to something stored carelessly in the chamber, and then flames leapt up through the wooden ventilation channels. Many houses burnt to the ground when the circulation boxes caught fire. In other systems the furnace simply heated a big tank of water, or even shallow trays of it. In both there was some convection of heat, but it was very inefficient, gave poor heat distribution, and soon became used only for giving bottom heat to rooting cuttings.

Cast-iron pipes, filled with hot water or even with steam, were the dominant heating systems by the 1860s and were easily used in the main house too. There were few fire risks and the heat was evenly distributed and easily managed. It was also fairly cheap, for by 1854 horse manure was becoming difficult to find in sufficient quantities in the towns, as the ratio of humans to horses had vastly altered. However, there were problems, and even by 1850:

> If you resolve upon heating with pipes, it will be judicious to have everything settled beforehand. Hot water engineers, though often abused, are just as honest as other people; but frequently after the contract has been made, and work commenced, what seem trifling alterations are insisted upon by the proprietor or gardener, and then there is dissatisfaction when these come to be paid for in the shape of extras. The chief objection to heating by water pipes is their first expense . . .

Once the conservatory was built and heated, it needed to be equipped and furnished. Large pots of camellias, oranges or stephanotis could be watered and sprayed with 'Read's Garden Engine'. Smaller plants were set out on tiered staging, sunk in compost, so that the plants grew well to make complete pyramids of vegetation. Numerous sample layouts were published in the garden press showing the best way of laying out a small conservatory, usually with each corner, and the piers between doors and windows, piled with vegetation. Elaborate wirework stands for a dozen or two dozen pots of geraniums, orchids and so on, grouped beneath a palm or an aspidistra, can still occasionally be found. Some conservatories were fitted up in the most extravagant way, with statuary, pools, fancily tiled areas for sitting, cast-iron columns from which to drape jasmines, fuchsias and streptosolens. One glasshouse at Cragside, the extraordinary mansion of an armaments manufacturer, even had huge tiers of vast stoneware pots for lemons and oranges, every single one on a turntable, so that the plants need never grow lopsided towards the sun.

Orangeries became rare, but a few were still built, though they were rarely the main greenhouse for the mansion as they had remained on the Continent. Mintons manufactured some very glamorous tiled tubs for citrus plants, with colourful tiles set in frames of gilded iron.

As horse manure was becoming valuable, gardeners needed to look elsewhere for manures to benefit plant growth, both under glass and outdoors. By 1881 a substance called 'Poudrette' was

43. Modern heating made domestic 'stove' houses available
to many middle-class households.

popular and was often home-made. It was compounded by using
the house's nightsoil with coal ash, and was very effective. It had
been used since the beginning of the century, and was so popular
that it was even sometimes imported from abroad. It was dependent upon the use of earth closets and chamber pots. Gardens of
grand or very modern houses that had water-flushed lavatories
were at a disadvantage. For them, tanks were commonly built in
the back garden, or in the grounds (where the lie of the land was
suitable)

. . . so as to receive the drainage from them [the sinks and the lavatories]
. . . In using this liquid manure, great care must be taken never to put
it on the leaves of plants, and either to follow it by watering with clear
water, so as to prevent the surface of the soil from being disfigured;

or, what is preferable, to use it chiefly during or immediately before rain ... The liquid manure from a house where a family consists of five or six persons, and where they wash at home, if used as it is produced, so as to allow none of it to run off by the drain, will be quite sufficient for a garden 200 feet long and 60 feet in breadth. Liquid manure, however, though powerful in a recent state, is always more efficacious after being a week or two fermented; but for this purpose two tanks are necessary.

All over Europe the search for nitrogenous material for agriculture and horticulture was in full swing. By 1842 a long article by Professor Charles Sprengel (translated from his original German) was published in the *Gardener's Chronicle*. After a mass of tables of chemical analyses of flesh, bones and offal, it continues: 'In Belgium, the flesh of dead animals, or such as have been killed on account of being diseased, is cut immediately into small pieces, which are divided over the field, and soon covered with ploughing them in ...' The animals' entrails needed chopping, mixing with 'humous' earth, rolled, and were then applied lightly 'or they will make vegetation push much too luxuriantly'.

Sheep blood was thought to be better than that of oxen, though the horn of the latter was very sought after by florists (calculation proved that 300 lb of horn-shavings was worth 1,200 lb of dung). Gardeners looked for hair and wool, for the refuse of glue factories (excellent for cabbages), for 'greaves' (the skin and cellular tissue left after suet and fat have been converted to candles and soap). That was very powerful, and needed to be rotted in pits with earth.

In some parts of England a manure was made with enormous quantities of sticklebacks, which were easily caught, and '... it has been calculated that one load of fish is equal to six loads of best stable dung', though the odour must have been stronger too. Elsewhere, in more exotic locations, even things like mayflies were used (in the marshy parts of Carinthia and Hungary). In southern France, chrysalids of silkworms were dug into the vegetable patch once the silk thread had been boiled off, and if that source was not available, cockchafers could be caught in sufficient quantity to be killed in hot water and composted.

In formal gardens even the clippings from the box parterre made excellent compost, and one which was especially popular in France. There, too, the dung from the inns of the south of the country was especially strong, perhaps reflecting the quality of the diet.

Guano had just been discovered in 1842, and went on to become a major item of international commerce. In Peru it was sown with the seed itself along the drills. In this country it was merely used in the same way as pigeon dung, a popular 'guano' in Britain and France; the French one was best as the English one was hideously smelly. Human urine was also a popular garden fertilizer though its quality depended on diet and fluid intake.

Naturally there were soon all sorts of patented artificial manures, some of quality, others more dubious. One, from the 1850s, labelled itself as 'Patented Creosoted Fish for Manure ... as good as guano ... keeps your potatoes free from disease', though that may have been because the creosote content killed the potatoes.

Insects, too, were under new attack. In the past, larger insects had often been picked from plants by hand, or the plants had been sprayed with warm water to stun them, after which they were gathered up. More difficult creatures, like the scale insects or mealy bugs that so liked pineapple or citrus plants, were attacked with soft soap pounded with mercury, and even more poisonous concoctions. One of the problems was that most gardeners had the comforting idea (comforting in so far as it excused imperfect eradication) that insects either appeared spontaneously or were created by the action of electricity on salt water. Even scientists believed the last theory, though one garden editor smacked the idea firmly on the head: '... they [the scientists] may, in their vanity, assert that they have gained the prowess of the Creator, but we are not quite mad or wicked enough to believe that the Almighty has surrendered his power to their galvanic batteries'.

For some insects, notably greenfly, tobacco smoke, powder or juice became increasingly popular in the Victorian garden (and it was certainly effective). Innumerable puffers, bellows and spray guns were designed for its application. There seems to have been no awareness that what might poison the greenfly might also poison the gardener. Tobacco was often most effective under glass; outdoors, until the introduction of pyrethrum in the 1850s, it was not at all uncommon for plants to succumb entirely to insect attack. Fruit trees were especially susceptible. If fruit ripened, especially grapes and peaches, wasps at once attacked. Blocks of sugar were wedged between the branches, and the wasps were bought off.

By the 1850s there were so many patented insect destroyers that some gardeners began to make comparative tests. 'Clarke's Preparation for Killing Mealy Bug etc.' (which was widely advertised) prompted a letter: 'I have tried this mixture, and can confidently declare that far more plants were destroyed by it than bugs. The only really efficaceous ingredient in it is turpentine, which certainly destroys the insects, and the plants also.' The writer signed himself 'Anti-Humbug'.

By the early 1860s 'Keatings Persian Insect-Destroying Powder' was widely available, and its advertisements proclaimed that 'Poultry, Dogs and Plants are effectually freed from fleas, and all other Vermin . . .' They were, too. It contained pyrethrum.

CHAPTER
7

NEW
WORLDS

*A*MID ALL THESE HEADLONG DEVELOPMENTS of new garden elements, other and older ones were still on the move. For instance, the 'American gardens' so popular towards the end of the eighteenth century were still important. Many Victorian writers have plans for them, though their definition became increasingly blurred as plants from other continents were added, especially Indian and Chinese rhododendrons and camellias. Indeed, the term became used for almost any combination of conifers, 'rhodos' and other evergreens; it became almost a style in its own right, especially in the wilder parts of Scotland, where almost every industrial or aristocratic magnate had an estate. These 'magnates' gardens' did particularly well on acid soils and in areas of high rainfall. By the time most of them were being established (using rhododendron cultivars as well as the latest species from India and America), American gardeners had become as keen on their own native plants as on the hybrids developed from them. It hadn't always been so.

In the first half of the nineteenth century in America, only the most sophisticated gardeners were at all interested in the native flora. Though there were many wealthy garden enthusiasts, there were not yet many large estates held in long lines of descent, and so there was little incentive to indulge in long-term garden planning and planting. In view of the severity of the climate of much of the landlocked states, it is extraordinary that so much of the European garden flora was treasured for so long; essential things like box, rosemary, lavender, bay, even daisies and pinks had to be coddled over the winter, often being grown in pots as British gardeners were doing with oranges, lemons and oleanders.

Even by the early nineteenth century there were few American garden books. The *American Gardener's Calendar* by Bernard McMahon appeared in 1806, and the delightful *The American Gardener* by the Englishman William Cobbett came out in 1821. Another rare American garden book based on actual American climatic conditions appeared in 1822. Perhaps not surprisingly it was concerned with the garden as an economic unit. *Gardening for Profit*, a title used hundreds of times since then, was by the Edinburgh-born Peter Henderson. Twenty years later, the next important garden work was closely based on the works of Repton and Loudon. *A Treatise on the Theory and Practice of Landscape Gardening, with a view to the improvement of Country Residences, etc etc, with remarks on Rural Residences*, by Andrew Jackson Downing, was a vast success, and had appeared in its fourth edition by 1849. Though published by Longmans in London, it had been revised and expanded for the increasingly enthusiastic American market.

Downing's preface draws a contrast between the new pioneers and their rough plots in the West, and the old families and long-cultivated country in the East. It is the first book on American landscape gardening, and is an attempt to show newly prosperous gardeners how to ensure that they gardened in the most correct taste. Downing freely acknowledges Loudon's help, as well as that of various American garden owners. After a rather confused account of European garden history, he continues:

In the United States, it is highly improbable that we shall ever witness such splendid examples of landscape gardens as those abroad, to which we have alluded. Here the rights of man are held to be equal; and if there are no enormous parks, and no class of men whose wealth is hereditary, there is, at least, what is more gratifying to the feelings of the philanthropist, the almost entire absence of a very poor class...

15. Ivies, coleus and a surprisingly wind-proof lily in this Gothic windowbox
with a wirework frame to the window.

16. A lush climbing rose, 'Princess Louise Victoria'.

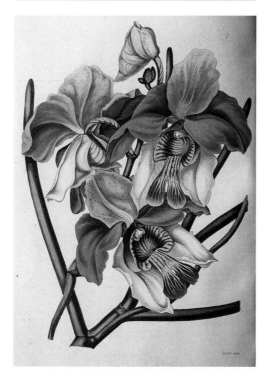

17 – 20. Indian pinks, petunias, orchids and tender primulas: plants from all
continents decorated conservatory and hot-house.

21. These shattered peaks and miniature glaciers surrounded the flower garden at Hoole House.

22. A bouquet of exotic foliage: many of the plants used for sub-tropical summer bedding.

23, 24. Exuberant fussiness on the parterre at Wilton *(above)* contrasts with
bleak magnificence at Castle Howard *(below)*.

25 – 28. Victorian favourites from 'florist's' flowers like chrysanthemums,
ranunculuses and cyclamen to hot-house stephanotis and belamcandas.

29. A bouquet of late-Victorian roses grown throughout the gardening world.

He says that the middle class, who have villas and need landscaped grounds, is increasing every day, and

... we have no hesitation in predicting that in half a century or more, there will exist a greater number of beautiful villas and country seats of moderate extent, in the Atlantic States, than in any country in Europe, England alone excepted. With us a feeling, a taste, or an improvement, is contagious, and ... is disseminated with a celerity that is indeed wonderful.

Downing clearly felt that he had a clear field, and that it should be he who became the first great American garden designer. The only 'current' designer when the book was written was the late Mr Parmentier of Brooklyn, who arrived from Holland in 1824 and established a nursery. Downing notes wanly that he did surveys and furnished plants, though he appears to have much admired some of Parmentier's work. He continues that 'the introduction of tasteful gardening in this country is, of course, of very recent date. But so long ago as from twenty-five to fifty years there were several residences highly remarkable for extent, elegance of arrangement, and the highest order and keeping.' He lists a number of these, giving thereby a conspectus of the state of design in American gardens: Woodlands, Pennsylvania, seat of the Hamilton family from 1805 (they were rich enough to employ a plant collector and botanist called Pursh to look for interesting native plants) was in the landscape style; Judge Peter's House, thirty miles away, was in the ancient style of gardening with 'long stately avenues terminated by obelisks, and gardens adorned with marble vases, busts and statues, and pleasure grounds filled with the rarest trees and shrubs ...' It was, when Downing was writing, still exceptionally fine. Lemon Hill, also once perfectly geometrical, had by now been destroyed by the extension of the same city. Also formal was Clermont, but on the Hudson River banks and in the French style. Waltham House, nine miles from Boston, had a landscape park planted with English trees (when its English equivalent would have had many American ones). Downing thought Waltham and Woodlands were the best

44. Montgomery Place in the 1890s.

demesnes in the landscape style. He also illustrated Hyde Park, and the Manor of Livingston. Hyde Park, like many others on the banks of the Hudson, was blessed with a wonderful site, one that had been decorated by Parmentier, and is, he thinks, one of the finest seats in the country.

The list goes on: Blithewood, with its manicured lawns, but also wild and picturesque ravines; Montgomery Place with a wilderness with rustic seats (very advanced), lake and perfect flower gardens; Kenwood, a mansion in either Gothic or an odd sort of Flemish Renaissance, with touches of Tudorbethan ... And so on. He praises each estate with entirely Victorian enthusiasm, though few of the houses seem especially large or grand, many being little more commodious than a first or second rate suburban house in London.

Some of his readers might have wondered quite how strong Downing's own sense of style and 'American-ness' was: he shows a conversion of a big American farmhouse with a straight drive up a field side, changed, at small expense, into an 'old English cottage', all Gothic barge boards and rustic verandahs, but with little to do with either 'old' or 'English' or even America. It is difficult to know, too, how the liberals of America would have felt about his belief that the landscaping of a farm or small estate should be designed so as to enhance the apparent size of the grounds. He suggests drives rather than the outdated avenue, because a drive can give the viewer a better (because grander) idea of the scale of the estate; to this end he suggests that an owner doesn't show the house from a great distance in case visitors get the disappointing idea that it's small. He is also rather superior about the newest money of all, saying that 'Nothing is more common, in the places of cockneys who become inhabitants of the country, than a display immediately around the dwelling of a spruce paling of carpentry, neatly made, and painted white or green; an abomination among the fresh fields, of which no person of taste could be guilty ...'

The 1849 edition of Downing's book also includes a dated British plan for 'an irregular flower garden', with a dozen amoeba-shaped beds with surrounding bushes. 'In the English flower garden, the beds are either in symmetrical forms and figures, or they are characterized by irregular CURVED outlines. The peculiarity of the gardens, at present so fashionable in England, is, that each separate bed is planted with a single variety, or at most two varieties of flowers.'

However enthusiastic Downing was for the landscape, and especially the picturesque form of such things, and however enthusiastic some of his readers, old habits of gardening died hard. By 1866, admirers of the formal could buy the newly published *The American Gardener's Assistant*, supposedly an edition of a mythical book written by Charles Bridgeman (an early eighteenth-century British garden designer), now enlarged by Todd and published in Pennsylvania. Of course, it is really only the title that Todd has taken; there's no real suggestion that gardens of the 1720s are to be resurrected.

Though the author suggests that annual flowers are best suited for ladies, he was mainly fostering a still much-used strategy for having a colourful summer garden in spite of the severities of climate of much of North America. He suggests planting greenhouse plants outdoors in the summer, a sort of sub-tropical bedding, except that the plants used are the old Mediterranean exotics such as acacias, oleanders, aloes, though with a few others, like *Agapanthus*, *Alstroemeria* and the strawberry tree, as well as *Aucuba* and azaleas, thrown in. The list of greenhouse flowers also includes much more familiar things like daisies (especially the hen-and-chickens form), wallflowers, bay, lavender and rosemary, and still lists many plants cultivated for medicinal reasons (they were going out of use in Britain at this date), though interestingly he only includes two or three native American species, taken from Indian pharmacopoeia (though this was infinitely more extensive).

Todd points out that new settlers in America copy the sort of gardens that they knew 'at home', and he asks the question (without giving an answer) what sort of gardens should subsequent generations have? He points out, too, that not only does the old European garden flora still flourish, but that so does the old formal style. The natural flora has made little impact as yet, and there is no national style.

In the South this was especially true, with many estate and farm gardens still perfectly formal in design, if not in feel. In 1861 the young Frederic Law Olmsted wrote *Journeys and Explorations in the Cotton Kingdom*, based on his travels of a few years before. Among the gardens that he described was one in which

The residence is in the midst of the farm, a quarter of a mile from the high road – the private approach being judiciously carried through large pastures which are divided only by slight ... wire fences. The kept grounds are limited, and in a simple but quiet taste; being surrounded only by wires, they merge, in effect, into the pastures. There is a fountain, an ornamental dove-cote, an ice-house, and the approach road, nicely gravelled and rolled, comes up to the door with a fine sweep.

Others were less nice...

On either side, at fifty feet distant, were rows of old live oak trees, their branches and twigs slightly hung with a delicate fringe of gray moss, and their dark, shining green foliage meeting and intermingling naturally but densely overhead. The sunlight streamed through, and played aslant the lustrous leaves, and the fluttering pendulous moss; the arch was low and broad; the trunks were huge and gnarled, and there was a heavy groining of strong, tough, knotty branches. I stopped my horse, and held my breath...

All was fine until Olmsted reached the house, where pine woods (planted because the soil had been worn out by over-cultivation) surrounded it in every direction.

A number of old oak trees still stood in the rear of the house, and, until Mr W. commenced 'his improvements' there had been some in its front. But as he deemed these to have an aspect of negligence and rudeness, he had cut them away, and substituted formal rows of miserable little ailanthus trees. I could not believe my ears till this explanation had been twice repeated to me...

When, from the 1860s onwards, at least some American gardeners began seriously to look at their own flora, not only did they, naturally, discover that the plants were perfectly suited to their climatic conditions, but also that many were exceptionally beautiful.

In terms of design, up to the middle of the nineteenth century, most smaller American gardens had been of the cottage type, where useful plants and those purely decorative were grown in a convenient and unstylish (but often very pretty) mix. Though, as we've seen, some East Coast and some southern gardens were in the latest European taste as early as 1840 or so, such stylishness remained fairly rare. As Americans of European descent moved west, few of the new settlers had either time or means to worry much about gardening. The Civil War left all parts of the country impoverished, and new designers, like Frederick Law

Olmsted, had to occupy themselves more with public than with private commissions.

Olmsted, who took over the American design mantle once Downing had perished in 1852 aboard the paddle steamer *Henry Clay* (an accident even reported in London's *Gardener's Chronicle*), followed a rather conservative 'picturesque' line, believing, as his book showed, in the preservation and enhancement of natural scenery. He tried, as far as possible, to avoid all formal elements except, as was fashionable in London and Paris, a few near the house, as an overture to a large central lawn, beds of native plants that would have been the envy of any European gardener, and a serpentine walk around and just inside the ground's boundary (an idea developed by 'Capability' Brown in the middle of the eighteenth century and still popular). Good examples of Olmsted's work were at Mount Royal Park, Montreal, Franklin Park, Boston, and (most important of all, and where he was working from 1857) Central Park, New York. He also did other important parks at Brooklyn, New Britain, San Francisco, Chicago-and elsewhere. In many of these he worked closely in association with Clavert Vaux, a designer who first trained in England and who had previously been a partner of Andrew Jackson Downing's. Olmsted's firm was very active and trained many other designers. In a way, therefore, the Olmsted office inherited the new American design tradition in a remarkably direct way.

In America, where the idea that informality of design was associated with the ideals of republicanism was more easily propagated than it was in Europe, the new formalism only began to be re-introduced to gardens around the late 1890s, though, as in so many other things, California was a special case. There, because of the Hispanic influence, most gardens before 1800 had a strong Mexican and Spanish feel and therefore an equally strong formal basis. However, most of the developed gardens belonged to the 'missions', with a Mediterranean flora of vines, olives, oleanders and myrtles but not much else. There were few other gardens; the romantic and perfumed hacienda or ranch garden seems to be a complete myth. Most were usually bare, and infinitely less exotic than their modern recreations.

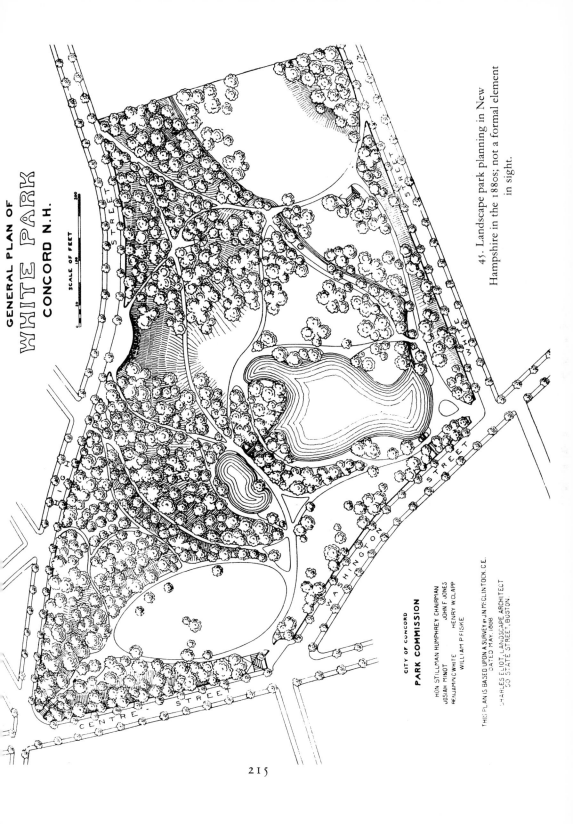

GENERAL PLAN OF
WHITE PARK
CONCORD N.H.

SCALE OF FEET

CENTRE STREET
WASHINGTON STREET
WHITE STREET

CITY OF CONCORD
PARK COMMISSION

HON. STILLMAN HUMPHREY CHAIRMAN
JOSIAH MINOT   JOHN F. JONES
BENJAMIN C. WHITE   HENRY W. CLAPP
WILLIAM P. FISKE

THIS PLAN IS BASED UPON A SURVEY BY J.N.McCLINTOCK C.E.
DATED MAY 1888

CHARLES ELIOT, LANDSCAPE ARCHITECT
50 STATE STREET, BOSTON

45. Landscape park planning in New
Hampshire in the 1880s; not a formal element
in sight.

215

From about 1850, what Californian gardens there were in formation followed the eastern states' tradition absolutely; they also had an identical flora, even if it wasn't in the least suited to California's climate. Again, there was the curious irony of the period, that Europe was busily growing many of the annuals from the Californian dry-lands, while the seedsmen of eastern America were importing seed from Thompson and Morgan, Vilmorin-Andrieux et Cie, Ernst Benary of Erfurt and so on, then selling them on to gardeners in California.

Eastern nurserymen were also buying trees and shrubs from British nurseries like Hilliers, and even from Australian ones. Gardeners found employment most readily if they had first been trained in Europe; two notable early examples were trained at Chatsworth (where Paxton had been head gardener), and at Gosford (in East Lothian, Scotland).

The first western American nursery catalogues date from around 1848 and list an eclectic flora ranging from Australian acacias to lemons from Lisbon. As life became more settled, many new nurseries soon set up, especially at San José, which rapidly became known as the 'garden city'. The Australian flora increased in strength until 1878, when interest switched to Japan (the interest was international, and of course embraced all aspects of Japanese culture, not just its gardens and plants). By the 1890s not only were American gardeners fascinated by their own native flora (and how sensible), but they were also becoming nostalgic for the old European garden flora. The reasons for this are obscure, but perhaps the fashion for gardening had taken hold so quickly that the old American garden flora had become supplanted by new garden plants, and so lost to view. *The Garden's Story* (1896) by George H. Ellwanger is an example of this new attitude. With a foreword by the Englishman C. Wolley Dod, the book, all very discursive, does much to describe Ellwanger's gardens at Rochester, N.Y. There the winter is so hard that he covers all his herbaceous flower-beds with a thick carpet of leaves. This is now necessary because, he says, over the last fifteen years American nursery catalogues have become very much better, especially in the number of roses, vegetables and herbaceous flowers; the range of the plants he wants to grow has therefore suddenly enlarged.

Like many writers of the period in both continents, Ellwanger wanted to extend gardening into the city and the countryside, suggesting that highways and drives should be lined with flowering shrubs like deutzias, hydrangeas, philadelphus, prunus, spiraeas, magnolias, exochordas, daphnes, dogwoods and so on. All this was to be mixed with herbaceous flowers such as paeonies, Japanese anemones, the taller lilies, grasses and eulalias. Lovely though that sounds, he confesses that that would not only be impossible to maintain, but also that it would suffer (as many American gardens do) an extraordinary degree of insect damage.

Like many garden writers before and since, Ellwanger likes making rules. His, though, throw interesting light on American gardens and the social mores of the time. They include:

1. Whatever is worth growing is worth growing well.
2. Study soil and exposure, and cultivate no more than can be maintained.
3. Plant thickly; it is easier and more profitable to raise flowers than weeds.
4. Avoid stiffness and exact balancing; garden vases and flowers need not be used in pairs.
5. A flower is essentially feminine, and demands attention as the price of its smiles.
6. Let there be harmony and beauty of colouring; magenta in any form is a discord that should never jar.
7. In studying colour effects, do not overlook white as a foil; white is the lens of the gardener's eye.
8. Think twice and then still think before placing a tree, shrub or plant in position. Think twice before removing a specimen tree.
9. Grow an abundance of flowers for cutting; the bees and butterflies are not entitled to all the spoils.
10. Keep on good terms with your neighbour; you may wish a large garden-favour of him some time.
11. Love a flower in advance; and plant something new every year.

12. Show me a well-ordered garden, and I will show you a genial home.

Nevertheless, despite the insects and rules, he makes gardening in America sound quite as wonderful and just as romantic as doing the same thing in the most pastoral counties of Britain.

You would know by the scent of the lilies that summer was here. How fragrant the censer of June! How profuse the scent of blossoming vegetation! – odors not alone from myriads of plants, but breathing from orchards, hedges, and thickets, rising from woods and hillsides, blown from meadows and pastures. . .

and from the gardens of 'tumble down farmsteads', where the loveliest American flowers and also the loveliest of Europe, filled the air with perfume. . .

CHAPTER
8

THE GARDENERS

I F THE VICTORIAN PERIOD SAW AN ASTON-
ishing increase in the numbers of people for whom gardening became a preoccupation or even just a mild hobby,
it also saw an equally astonishing change among the ranks of
people who serviced gardens, from the grand and almost middle-
class head gardener to the half-starved wretches, often elderly and
female, who travelled from garden to garden hand-picking the
caterpillars from the cabbages. For the best of them, life was
terribly hard, and even for the ones who prospered, the trap of
illness and desperate penury was easily sprung.

For all the gaudy brilliance of the new parterres, for all the
extravagant conservatories filled with rare orchids and the latest
camellias, for all the new parks and allotments, and for all the
charity, private as well as public, the gardens of both great
and small were rooted in the dark soil of poverty and exploita-
tion.

In 1851, amid all the excitement of the Great Exhibition, Prince
Albert was awarded a gold medal by the Metropolitan Association
for Improving the Dwellings of the Industrial Poor. Though only
'Class VII', the medal was for designs that he had done for blocks
of flats which were to be let out to artisans in the larger cities.
Each block was trimmed in a rather anaemic Tudorbethan way,
and comprised flats that were to be rented out at 4s. a week. This

represented a return to the landlord of a few per cent (each flat cost £450 to build). The lucky tenants had a lobby, a living-room ten feet by fifteen, a scullery, a meatsafe, a flushing loo, and, astonishingly both for the times and the cost, three bedrooms. Many such flats were soon built in all the major industrial cities, and wherever these model dwellings rose, fever, the bane of rich and poor who lived without running water, disappeared as if by magic.

However, such flats must have seemed impossible dreams for a vast percentage of the urban poor, and certainly for the thousands of half-starved jobbing gardeners who tidied the gardens of the fast expanding ranks of the urban middle class. Such unskilled men were badly paid, even by the standards of the times, and their pay was constantly at the mercy of the agricultural depressions that swept over the land throughout the century. During these periods destitute agricultural workers flocked to the cities in search of work, and half-starving yet often as skilled, they undercut the meagre wages of itinerant gardeners. Even a jobbing gardener with all his time filled found it difficult to earn much more than 5–6s. a day, and his weeding-woman helpers got, for much of the century, only 8–10d. a day.

Skilled and trained gardeners fortunate enough to find themselves permanent places in a household, however small, were slightly better placed. They were at least provided with a roof over their heads, though not all such were equally desirable. They also had an annual salary, clearly defined duties and a rather lowly place in the 'service' hierarchy. A manual written for servants in the 1820s described a situation that held for much of the rest of the century. It set out for the head gardener various rules along the lines of:

1. Complete every part of an operation as you proceed.
2. Finish off one job before beginning another.
3. In leaving off working at any job, leave the work and the tools in an orderly manner.
4. In leaving off work for the day, make a temporary finish, and carry the tools to the tool house...

and so on. Rule 9 was 'Let no crop of fruit, or herbaceous vegetables, go to waste on the spot' – important, for such things might have reminded the employers of how much was wasted in any garden. The manual provides a list of items that an uncertain gardener needed to impress his employers, and provides a description of what most gardeners would have looked like:

> The gardener usually wears a blue woollen apron, which, when he is pruning, he ties up before him, and then serves to hold his nails, shreds, scissors, hammer and pruning knife. He should also be provided with a light measuring rod, flat and narrow, painted and divided on one side into feet and half feet, and on the other into yards and half-yards...

To help in the negotiations which all employees had to undergo, they suggested that his salary should be from £50 to £100 a year, though this was with a cottage and generally with vegetables and fuel.

If the family was wealthy enough to need several garden staff, then the gardener was in charge of one or more under-gardeners. Such men were to do the 'digging, trenching, weeding, dunging, gravelling, hoeing, manuring, mowing etc.' and they were commonly engaged as weekly servants earning between 16s. and a guinea a week, with only vegetables coming for free. In more generous households, some also had a cottage and fuel.

The difference between being paid by the year and receiving a weekly wage was an important distinction: yearly-paid servants had four months' notice on either side, and thus at least a little stability in their lives. Weekly-paid servants could be dismissed instantly. However, being paid by the year had its disadvantages, at least early in the century. However badly their masters mal-treated them, servants needed the permission of a Justice of the Peace before they could quit their posts.

However, if women servants were hired pregnant and the pregnancy was unknown, their employer needed a Justice of the Peace's permission before they could be dismissed. If they were employed and the employer knew the woman was pregnant, the servant was paid up to the birth, but only a month beyond. Even

46. The kitchen garden.

in other areas employers had remarkable degrees of control; for instance, servants could be forced to church. Gardeners who were caught selling their master's produce, or pawning his belongings, were fined £2 in addition to the value of the goods and could be further jailed or whipped in public.

Among the rest of the servants, most had far better conditions of employment than the gardeners, though well-trained examples of the latter were highly knowledgeable. In 1841 even head gardeners were paid, for all their skills, only about a tenth of the cook's salary and half that of the footman. It gave rise to considerable discontent, and gardeners, as a class, were notoriously politicized. One such wrote to the *Gardener's Chronicle* that 'even breaking stones on the highways pays better'.

The wage levels of late Georgian Britain remained constant for much of the nineteenth century. This was in spite of the fact that the purchasing power of the pound fell more or less constantly throughout the period, leaving people in progressively worse and worse circumstances. For instance a thirty-four-year-old bachelor gardener, trained in the kitchen garden, advertised for a job in 1860 and hoped for 18s. a week. Another hoped for 14–16s. a week 'besides a House and garden, a pig kept during summer, dinner during harvest, and an allowance of 6d. or 1s. when from home delivering produce'. Both men were probably disappointed in their hopes. Such rates were sometimes to be found in the north of the country, but were down to 11s. a week in the south where competition for work was more intense. In 1842, for example, a household in Kensington advertised as follows: 'Wanted as Servant in a Small Family at Kensington, a Young Man from the Country about 21; one that has not been in service will not be objected to ... grounds half in garden, half in cattle etc. Wages 12s. p.w.' However, money wages were kept low even in parts of the North, though allowances of food, especially 'porige', were much higher. In Scotland, things were far worse than in the worst parts of England, and it was not uncommon for there to be no money wages at all, but merely 'cottage and keep'.

Public employers were no better than private ones. In 1871 the Public Parks Committee of Manchester advertised for a head gardener for the popular Alexandra Park, offering a salary of £84.4s. a year together with house, coals, gas and water. This was exactly the same salary given to the previous gardener, the 'late Mr Macmillan', whose widow and children proclaimed in exactly the same issue of the same paper that they were destitute and appealed for help to keep them from the workhouse.

Even with a husband fit and well, and earning around £70 a year (an average sort of salary for a head gardener in some minor garden), a wife could only allow her family a cup of tea once a day. Domestic economists of the mid-century suggested, for instance, that for families on this sort of income all domestic items should be kept in very specific places 'so that they can be found without needing to light candles'.

However low the salary or wages, the other important consideration was an inter-personal one, for some employing households were plainly lively places in which to work, while many others were equally plainly terrible. Many of the gardeners who took to the new media and wrote of their early careers had had delightful times, working for employers who were generous, who treated their servants almost as part of the family, and who helped selflessly with their staff's education and development. Many less vocal gardeners were less lucky; and some who worked in penurious households must sometimes have suffered terribly. For them, we can only hope that their own private family life offered compensation.

In Scotland and parts of northern England, where the infamous 'bothy system' held sway, families in the lower ranks of service were actually split up and consigned to separate bothies. For the garden staff, these were sheds built on the outside of the north wall of the kitchen garden, and offered dark and often dank accommodation. The bothy system began to alarm the philanthropists of the mid-century, and many articles about bothy life began to appear in the press. In one article of the 1860s a bothy was described as

a house set apart for the men to sit in and cook their victualls, with a sleeping apartment or apartments adjoining. In many cases the bothy is badly kept, and the sleeping apartment dirty and untidy, but there is no necessity for this and it is not inherent in the system ... Where there is a bothy, the men get their food and keep by themselves; and when a woman arrived at the years of discretion is appointed to keep their bedroom in proper order, and the bothy clean, they are far from uncomfortable, and prefer it to going into the house for their food. As regards married men, the system is radically wrong...

Once the issue was raised in public, it caused an outcry. Worried apologists wrote to claim that

In a well-conducted bothy, the master allows a female to keep the place clean, light the fires, make the beds, and at the same time cleaning out the apartments, bake the bread...

... A common arrangement of some bothies is as follows: The male and female servants sit and eat, and pass their evenings in the places where the hands sleep, and the females' sleeping place is in some off-closet, entering from it or in a separate but adjacent apartment. Sometimes the sexes have separate apartments to dwell in, having different doors ... Not always, however, is there such accommodation...

... Some landlords supply no peat or candles ... There is consequently no reading in our long winter evenings, and the darkness of the bothies encourages and facilitates deeds of darkness.

Some examples must have been quite exceptionally unpleasant, as the following:

A lad, and a big boy, and a single woman live in one room, which is badly furnished. There are two benches or forms, which supply the place of stools or chairs, but there is no table. The inmates make use of a chest lid as a substitute. There are two beds of coarse unplaned deals ... All the sheets and blankets must be provided by the lads themselves, and all the bowls, plates and spoons. Their food consists of milk, when it can be got, and oatmeal. Beef, mutton, pork or fish or flesh of any kind they rarely taste. The bothy may not be cleaned out or whitewashed for years, and their bedding is washed but seldom...

Surprisingly, the bothy system survived in parts of the country well into the twentieth century.

Of course, some servants were employed in households where even the employers were scarcely more comfortable. It was possible for households with an income of £150 (only £65 more than was paid to the head gardener to Alexandra Park) to employ one servant. Naturally this was rarely a gardener, though only slightly more prosperous households commonly employed one full-time. They probably managed this by using the often advertised arrangement whereby a gardener and his wife were employed if they had no children, with the wife to supervise the house.

In the 1850s, if such a couple were given rooms in the house, the man was paid £1 a week, his wife £10 a year. This arrangement naturally allowed employers to keep constant watch on their employees' lives, which must often have been onerous. A writer in the *Cottage Gardener* of 1849 suggested that

> Honest, sensible servants will never object to be closely watched. They will place themselves in their mistresses' situation, and be satisfied that they would do exactly the same if their circumstances were reversed. Where servants dislike being strictly looked after, they are either disposed to do that which is evil, or they are ignorant and self-conceited, and fancy that their mistress suspects their honesty, when she is only guarding against thoughtless waste.

An employer like the writer must have made the servants' lives very difficult, for the article continues:

> With a good, superior servant in the house to overlook all things, a boy or a woman might be employed for a couple of hours in the morning to clean shoes, knives etc. and to perform the little morning offices required, which would be a far cheaper plan . . . In our intercourse with the poor we must not affect to find them faultless or destitute of evil tempers, unthankful hearts, gross deception often . . . We must not expect to find the smooth tongue governed by a smooth heart, or the kindness shown always understood and valued. . .

However low the wages, and however dependent the servants' happiness was on the whims of the employer, even such bare comfort as could be expected was extremely precarious. Employers could die, lose their money, simply take a dislike to the servant concerned; gardeners themselves could fall ill, die, have too many children, or simply age (forty was considered 'old' for a gardener). The threat of total destitution was present almost every hour of every day. Only the most prosperous and provident gardeners ever managed to save sufficient money to provide for themselves or their families if and when disaster struck. Elderly gardeners often found themselves destitute on retirement, as an article of the 1840s claims, '... but the honest gardener without other means or extraneous aid to money-making, must perforce leave his wife and family a burden to posterity, pensioners on the Benevolent Institution, or a legacy to the union. And yet surely the workman is worthy of his hire ...'

It was, for a few decades, not uncommon for the better-known head gardeners or their dependants to publish heartbreaking appeals in the gardening press. An example from the same decade as the last quote runs:

We, the undersigned, appeal to the Benevolence of the Public, and particularly to Gardeners, on behalf of the widow of the late Robert Runciman, who is left with five children under ten years of age, wholly unprovided for. The late Robert Runciman was many years gardener at Coptfold Hall, Essex, which situation he was obliged to quit three years since in consequence of the gentleman leaving the place; he was not afterwards able to obtain a situation in consequence of his numerous family, and he commenced Jobbing gardener, when he was unfortunately attacked with severe Rheumatism, which confined him for many months to his bedroom; and thus the little savings he had previously made became exhausted before his death. We know him to have been a steady, sober, and industrious man, and therefore confidently make this appeal on behalf of 'the widow and the fatherless' in the hope that it will meet with that attention which the circumstances of the case deserve.

Mrs Runciman and her family do not appear in the literature again, though another example occupied the personal columns for rather longer. After the initial appeal came the following:

Henry Spare acknowledges with heartfelt gratitude the following CONTRIBUTIONS, but for which himself and family must have suffered the greatest distress and privation. He is also deeply impressed with the kindness of his late Noble employer towards his two eldest children, and he begs to add and return his special thanks to MR LOUDON for his gratuitous and prompt appeal on his behalf...

Rather cannily he published a list of the contributions, though the cost of the public acknowledgement must itself have been high. Sums sent to him range from one shilling from 'Harvey, Camden Town' to £4.12s.6d. from 'Dakin and friends, Eastnor Castle'. A later issue of the *Gardener's Chronicle* contains yet another advertisement: 'P.S. Henry Spare will feel thankful to be informed of contributions omitted or delayed (if any) which shall be acknowledged in a future number – Isleworth Feb. 17th 1842.' Sure enough, next week, he had another nine contributions, to about three pounds or so. Perhaps he escaped the full rigours of Victorian poverty.

There were, of course, various means of escape. Alcohol offered one, and a favourite. Political agitation offered a second, more exciting though no more successful. Emigration offered a third; dishonesty a fourth. And if not full dishonesty, at least some gardeners used oblique means of increasing a meagre income. Young gardeners and nurserymen felt the main impact of this.

Many under-gardeners found it impossible to get posts without offering a premium to the head gardeners to whom they applied for work. This was sometimes 18s. or 20s. a month, almost half of the under-gardener's wages. Head gardeners were also in a position to blackmail nurseries and seed firms. One nurseryman wrote:

... it is simply that the gardener has the nurseryman completely in his power. Should a gentleman visit a nursery he has not hitherto patron-ized, and selects plants to be sent to his gardener, if that functionary finds that there is no chance of his gaining any pecuniary benefit by the transaction, it lays in his power to very soon sicken the squire of that game; if large trees have been bought he will not properly secure or mulch them; choice plants he will 'shove' in a position or soil admirably adapted to 'cook their goose'; if seeds, he will in some way destroy their vitality ... Finally, the employer gets discouraged, and confining his patronage to the gardener's favourite tradesmen, the object is obtained.

47. Frames and glasshouses were key elements in the production of bedding plants

Even if the gardeners were not quite so malevolent (or simply desperately poor), some brassy gardeners asked the nurseryman for a commission of 3d. in the £, or, at the very least, a Christmas box. No wonder so many nurserymen tried to sell 'Plants for the Million', where they did not have to deal with a head gardener.

Alcohol played, at least in the media, a vastly important role in the lives of the gardening classes throughout much of the nineteenth century. Blasts against the beer-shops, and their effects on the rural or gardening male, began to appear in the 1830s. A writer using the nom-de-plume of 'Falcon' wrote: 'It is deplorable to witness the utter want of principle which induces a man to sacrifice the comfort of his wife and children, and his own respectability, to gratify his brutal appetite for intoxicating liquors ...' Of course beer and cider played a major role in the rural economy, and agricultural workers often had rations of both as part of their payment, indeed, 'such articles are necessary for carrying on the operations of agriculture, for which purpose they are still considered essential by many of those who are engaged in farming . . .'

The same was equally true of gardeners and gardening. With the increasingly religious attitudes beginning to grip the middle classes, it soon became necessary for every gardener advertising for work to claim that he was teetotal. James Carter and Co., seedsmen, ran an agency for gardeners and claimed that all the men on their books were suitably 'dry'. However, the gardening press was crammed with beer advertisements – a creative one placed by Allsopp's brewery in many publications in the 1850s featured a letter from the famous chemist Baron Leibig, who had supposedly found that many other makes of beer were flavoured not with hops or wormwood, but with strychnine.

Perhaps it was this that affected the appearance of any man who entered the awful portals of the pub. Such sins were thought to be instantly visible – 'It is astonishing to observe the difference in the LOOK between the sober man and the drinker.' This was from the *Cottage Gardener* of 1851. The writer was 'Rosa', whom we have already met. She went on:

There is always a cheerful, clean, open air look about the former, and a leary, sodden, ashamed face in the latter character. Vice always marks the man, however he may try to conceal it, and it marks his family too; for it is IMPOSSIBLE for his wife and children to look well clothed and happy when he drinks half his wages, and comes home cross, and violent, if not in a state of positive intoxication.

For those who were more fastidious or better off, or for their wives, alcohol came in many respectable disguises – for example in medicines, or more imaginatively, as perfumes like the one in an advertisement that read:

Travellers and Visitors to the Sea-Coast would do well to provide themselves with a bottle of ROWLAND'S AQUA D'ORO. This fragrant and spirituous perfume refreshes and invigorates the system during the heat of summer . . . In all cases of excitement, lassitude, or over-exertion, it will prove of great advantage taken as a beverage, diluted with water. . .

The same firm also marketed the famous macassar oil that saved so many gardeners from unbecoming baldness.

Some of the magazines aimed at gardeners rather than garden owners preached, in tones ranging from the headmasterly to the morally precious, against the evils of beer. 'Rosa', of course, adopted an enthusiastically superior voice, and wrote, in 1850,

No space NEED be lost, and every spot of ground that is turned to account adds to the beauty and the profit of the little homestead. How many beer-houses would be closed, how many empty seats in churches would be filled, how many suffering village shopkeepers would thrive ... A parish would be indeed one blooming garden.

Indeed.

'Rosa' found that almost every social activity gave rise to temptation, even the ringing of the church bells at New Year.

I wish their hearts and voices were mixed with the joyful peal. I wish, too, that my cottage readers would take a friendly warning at this special time, and strive to separate the work of ringing from that of drinking, for they are apt to travel hand-in-hand, and that which is intended as a mark of joy and gratitude, becomes a means of intemperance and sin. This should not be. Even our harmless amusements and useful employments may thus bring down a curse, and not a blessing, on our heads.

She saw alcohol everywhere, and especially in the garden. It became a matter for public self-confession, and the cheaper magazines often ran 'true confessions' of reformed drunkards. One we've already met.

Not surprisingly, with a body of men who had at least some education but were kept in a lowly position in society, discontent was rife. Both they, and the employing classes who felt the foundations of their lives shaking, wrote to the garden press. John Claudius Loudon, once an under-gardener himself, and now ever a liberal, wrote of the unemployed and discontented:

But when he is told that he is not wanted – that the thing he possesses, his bodily strength, is useless ... what CAN he do but sink in misery, abandon himself to despair ... How can we wonder, then, at his lending a ready ear to what designing demagogues may say – for what is the fabric of society to him?

It is employment that must be found, if we mean to sleep securely in our beds ... Give them something of their own that is worth keeping, and they are not the men to risk losing it...

However, solidarity was not especially strong among the gardening classes, or perhaps too many of them had been caught up in the self-righteous conservatism of the lower middle class. One quisling gardener wrote to an editor that

the sort of agitation attempted in the printed correspondence upon the subject [of gardeners' wages] I think ill-advised indeed, for I feel assured that the attempts of a few malcontents to represent the whole body of under-gardeners as a body of discontented growling paupers, meets the disapprobation of every spirited practitioner in the profession.

The fear that otherwise sober gardeners might become raging alcoholics was even used as an excuse to keep them continuously busy. In 1841, one exhausted gardener wrote to the *Gardener's Chronicle* to plead for 'liberty days' when they could visit other gardens to learn more about their craft, or to read books. The writer claimed, falsely, that drinking habits were changing fast, and so the time thus freed would not be abused.

For those impoverished gardeners who were not attracted to the multitude of raucous and convivial beer-shops, the lure of foreign lands proved strong, or the lure of new sorts of employment. One editor of 1849 was 'sorry to hear that Mr Forsyth, the talented gardener lately employed by the E. of Shrewsbury, has left his situation, and is now a guard on the North Staffordshire Railway'. 'It is truly a pity,' adds our informant, 'that such abilities should be idle.' William Ball, the owner of a market garden, and a gardener's agent, advertised a situation in India. He was deluged with replies, and had to insert an advertisement apologizing for his inability to reply individually to each applicant, as well as another one for a foreman at his own business (he was offering an excellent salary too; £100 a year, and with an annual increment of £10). It was his foreman who had gone to India.

Opportunities existed all over the globe. In the 1840s, estate owners in the West Indies were looking for experienced gardeners to tend the new crops of nutmegs and cloves. An estate near Marseilles frequently advertised for English bachelors to take up two-year contracts at 24s. 4d. a week (it advertised itself as employing many other Englishmen). Australia and New Zealand were opening up. In 1852 'A Few Friends of the Family of Mr James Corton, once Gardener at Syon House, and now wholly destitute, having formed a small purse, in order that he may emigrate with his family to Australia, solicit some further aid, in order to enable them to complete their arrangements.'

The New Zealand Society offered allotments near Canterbury in many garden magazines, and clever marketing often ensured that the offers were on the same page as various life assurance advertisements, and even as the appropriate though odd 'Lauries Patent Floatable Mattresses' to reassure anyone nervous of the high seas. Even apparently successful gardeners emigrated. Mr Tweedie left for Buenos Aires when he was fifty, and thereafter played a quite pivotal role in the development of nineteenth-century gardening. Travel to distant lands was cheap. It cost, in the 1850s, only £3 to get from London to Quebec, though the migrants had to provide their own food. Conditions on the boats were terrible, at least until the public outcry of the 1860s; after a journey to Canada of between six and eleven weeks the ships could be smelt on land long before they docked.

The gardener emigrants naturally wanted to take some garden plants with them, especially as many of them hoped to set up as nurserymen. Garden magazines published many queries from intending migrants about the best ways of transporting seeds and plants to the colonies. The techniques for doing both of these things had improved dramatically since the beginning of the century, though the fact that seeds would still germinate after packing in nothing more substantial than dry paper envelopes still caused great surprise. One editor insisted, in 1850, that 'sending seeds abroad in bottles, or sealed Indian or Chinese jars is now totally obsolete ...'

But how did the gardeners and garden staff, the ones who remained behind and were determined to avoid any temptation, live from day to day? Under-gardeners, weeding-women, watering-boys and the rest generally lived in considerable discomfort. On the whole they have left little record of how they managed, and it is only possible to view their lives from the other side of the social gulf. However, the picture of their poverty, even though there were considerable attempts to turn it into the sentimental fantasy of 'cottage life', is not pleasant.

In the 1840s, when one of the frequent agricultural depressions was filling up the poor-houses all over the country, endless schemes were discussed for creating useful work for the unemployed, especially for farm and garden labourers. Writers in all the gardening magazines tried to suggest things that the unemployed could usefully do. Some parishes tried distributing labourers to the local rate-payers, with highly rated people getting several. The scheme was intended to act as a sort of tax, for the rich then had to provide work, and therefore wages, for the poor; in fact, this system merely undercut those labourers and gardeners still with regular work, however dreadful their wages already were.

The middle classes developed guilty consciences, and some tried to improve at least their dwellings. Even if that were not possible, at least the ladies of the village could help out, for in a series of articles called cosily *Our Village*, Rosa stated that

A large jar of blackberry jam would be a very useful gift to a poor family, and a small quantity thinly spread on the children's bread would make it much more satisfying ... In my neighbourhood the poor are so extremely poor, that it is impossible to think that they could make even blackberry jam for their children's food...

In a similar vein, another writer proclaimed that

The rich are often little aware of the sufferings and privations of the poor, and how much relief they might afford by what in their abundance

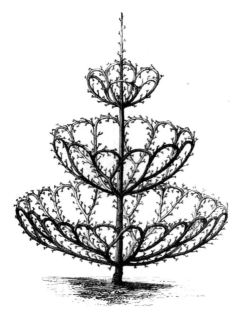

48. Feats of gardening like this elaborate piece of grafting were
only made possible by cheap labour.

they think nothing of. A few baked apples, a jug of apple water, or a
pot of apple-jam, are useful and grateful to those who are sick and
possess NOTHING.

She goes on to give various elementary recipes for basic jams and
preserves. 'Apple water' turns out to be a thin tea made by
pouring boiling water over sliced fruit, and slightly sweetening
the result; it doesn't sound very appetizing.

Inside hovel, bothy or tumbledown cottage, vermin and disease
were common. For fleas, in 1842: 'Wittering says the leaves of
the common Alder (*Alnus glutinosus*) are sometimes strewed upon
floors to destroy them, and that branches of the sweet gale (*Myrica
gale*) will produce the same effect.'

Endless attempts were made to encourage the rural poor to
make use of their gardens. As well as food, the garden could

produce other useful crops; illness had only the herbs of the field and the garden as a cure, and these were widely used by the very poor almost to the end of the century. Meadow-rue (*Thalictrum flavum*), for example, provided laxative leaves and roots, and was used in jaundice. Even the deadly *Aconitum napellus*, a nerve poison, was widely used in some areas, and *Delphinium consolida*, or larkspur, almost equally dangerous, was pounded into an ointment to remove vermin from the skin. Black hellebore (*Helleborus niger*) found a use in mania, melancholy, epilepsy (all three seem to have been very common), though the plant had to be used very carefully.

In the 1850s a retired doctor started a series of articles for the poor, using the contents of his own garden as a starting point; of his garden he was probably rather proud, saying modestly that but a page would

describe its contents, and their application in disease and sickness, but yet it is abundantly useful to my neighbours. Nay, the village doctor himself sometimes borrows from my beds, and, though somewhat jealous of what he calls my unprofessional conduct, we are, upon the whole, mighty good friends; for to tell the truth, he somewhat leans upon me. It is wonderful how much may be produced from a small plot of ground well managed; but here I must premise that to cull simples and to prepare and administer their products with success, require both skill and experience. It is a task well suited to a physician like myself, who can afford to sit down under the tree of his old age, and devote himself to such a speciality. . . .

However, even for the poor, herbal remedies were on the wane. In 1871 when Alexander Forsyth was working at the Manchester Infirmary, he had a look at the large herb markets of the city. He came to the conclusion that there were three levels of quacks: (i) those using undisclosed *materia medica*, and often especially obscurantist, who preyed on the rich or desperate; (ii) those, perhaps the most authentic, using old herbals and consulting real doctors and working largely for or on the middle class; and (iii) old crones and their believers, often working for little or no reward, and handing out folk remedies to the very poor.

In Manchester vast amounts of medicinal herbs were being sold, often with the sellers not knowing the Latin name, or even the demotic and probably ancient Lancashire ones. Plants were commonly sold by the handful or armful – even when they were deadly poison. Worse, they were sold with very little instruction about dosage. The poor simply had to take their chance in this botanical roulette, for they couldn't afford to go to a qualified apothecary. The head gardener and his family could, though they seem to have been more inclined to try the proprietary medicines produced by the burgeoning enterprise of the commercial world. It is probable that they were not much better served. Gardeners' magazines for the entire period are crammed with advertisements for all sorts of remedies for all manner of dreadful ailments.

Gardeners were assured that 'Freedom from Cough in Ten Minutes after use, is insured [sic] by Dr LOCOCK'S PULMONIC WAFERS ...' Or if the stresses of life began to tell, all they had to do was buy 'Norton's CAMOMILE PILLS for indigestion, bilious and liver complaints, headaches, heartburns, acidity etc ...' Indigestion must have been a constant problem, for every publication was packed with remedies. Only a few survived throughout the century in the way that 'Milk of Magnesia' did.

More serious ailments were still easily curable; like the 'DEAFNESS and singing noises in the head cured in a few days, whatever the causes may be. For 7/6d. from Dr Alfred Barker, 48 Liverpool St, Kings Cross.' Gardeners who read the advertisements carefully would discover that they could apply to the same address for 'Miss Dean's CRINILENE', guaranteed to give them perfect hair. They needed Keating's cough lozenges for asthma and incipient consumption, as well as 'Parr's Life Pills, Ozonised Cod Liver Oil (as used at the Consumption Hospital)', or even 'Dr Robert's Celebrated Ointment, called the Poor Man's Friend', as well as his 'Pilulae Antiscrophulae' and 'Smith's Tasteless Dandelion Antibilious Pills'. Mr Smith hadn't read much in the way of modern medical books, for he still uses the herbal terms of the seventeenth century, and talks about 'humours' of the skin. Every gardener's household must have bought the widely advertised and almost universally applicable 'Holloway's Ointment and Pills', which were supposed to cure everything from bad legs to old wounds, sores and ulcers, sore breasts, glandular swellings, tumours, scurvy, and diseases of the skin.

Not even the gardener's children were safe from all this; they were fed on 'Dr Laycock's Powders for all Disorders of Children, including Chicken-pox, nettle rash, measles, scarlatina, sore eyes, wasting, rickets, etc., etc.' In case some mothers were worried about stories of opium and laudanum turning their offspring into drugged vegetables, some firms denied all such contents.

The best-paid gardeners and their wives could even afford some of the vanities of life. To encourage them to buy, advertisements had thrilling testimonials, such as:

Sir, – I have much pleasure in informing you of the extraordinary effects of Rowland's MACASSAR OIL. For above nine years, I had not a particle of hair on my head, when I was casually recommended to give this celebrated Oil a trial ... After five months perseverance, I can now boast of as good a head of hair as any man in this city – Prices from 3/od. to 21/od. a bottle.

Houseproud wives were induced to use the services of cut-price interior decorators, offering cheap Brussels carpets, and silk or damask hangings. The largest advertisement for all this didn't appear for very long, so perhaps it was found that few gardeners' wives could afford them. More useful was an advert of 1852. 'The Comfort of a Fixed Water Closet' for £1. 'Places in garden converted into a Comfortable Watercloset by the PATENT HER-METICALLY SEALED PAN, with its self-acting valve, entirely pre-venting the return of cold air or effluvia ...'

In whatever comfort they did manage to afford, and in the time they had to spare, they read. Magazines, part-works, penny dreadfuls, almanacks, books of prophecies, *Rienzi* for the pol-itically aware, joke books for those who weren't, books that had been in print since the late seventeenth century, all were advertised on the pages of the cheap garden journals. In the middle of 1852, for instance: 'This day is published, price 3s 6d in cloth, the Second Edition of THE LIFE AND DEATH OF LITTLE RED RIDING HOOD, a Tradgedy [sic] adapted from the German of Ludwig Treck. By Jane Browning Smith . . .' But there were also complete editions of Shakespeare's works, edited by Bowdler, or, for the less cautious, the works of Byron and Scott. If none of that gave the reader sufficient insight into him or herself, then the advert 'KNOW THYSELF – The secret art of discovering character from handwriting . . . 14 stamps to be sent with a specimen' offered no doubt much-needed help. If the gardener was more interested in the vagaries of weather than in those of self, he could protect himself by subscribing to 'The Farmers and Gardeners Hail-Storm Insurance Company (Capital £200,000) One Duke, 4 Earls as Hon Directors'.

And after a life of church-going, domestic economy, and patent medicines, there might perhaps be a small pension from the savings so carefully secured, or from a kind employer. For some there was the comfort of a tiny pension from the 'Gardener's Benevolent Society'. This was founded in 1838, largely by members of the Floricultural Society of London. It grew rather slowly. By 1842, members of the Benevolent Institute met to discuss the current year's subscriptions of £200. The new pensions paid out totalled £33.8s.0d., so two new pensioners could be added to the then pitiful list. However, already the funds were invested and doing well. By 1852 the Institute supported thirty-five elderly gardeners or their widows, of whom the average age was seventy-seven. The sum of their pensions amounted only to £500 a year, and to be eligible they had to have been 'either head gardeners, or their foremen, market gardeners, nurserymen, and seedsmen, for twenty years at least, subject to the following conditions . . .' The conditions were of some complexity: for instance, market gardeners must have had at least five acres for twenty years, and nurserymen and seedsmen had to have been in business for the same length of time. All had to be over sixty, unless incapacitated. Their widows couldn't apply if they later remarried non-gardeners. Naturally, preference in the pension lottery was given to subscribers of more than fifteen years' standing, though the pension was only £16 a year for males and £12 a year for females; it was paid quarterly and was also means tested. No one was eligible if other income exceeded £20 a year. The Institute's pension helpfully included a grant of £4 as funeral costs.

Naturally, for Victorian Britain, the chances of getting a pension were higher if the original subscriptions had also been higher. The annual subscription of one guinea bought one vote, and the number of votes increased *pro rata*. Election to pensions was by ballot. In the late 1850s the pensions paid out annually amounted to over £500, though the Secretary's salary was £60. In 1858 five pensioners died and one was struck off because it was discovered that she was getting parochial relief. Only one lived in Scotland, and one in Wales. There were a few in the north of England, but most of them lived in the home counties. In that year's list of subscribers to the funds, a D. Guthrie, 377 High Street, Edinburgh, was the only Scottish subscriber (he had a vested interest too, as he owned a magazine called *The Scottish Gardener*.) Most subscribers were, naturally, gardeners, though some were businessmen and a few were wealthy aristocrats. However, the Institute was beginning to attract notables to its ranks, and funds to its coffers. In 1852 it held a sale of Guatemalan orchids to benefit the Society, and in the same year had an anniversary dinner with Charles Dickens in the chair. Paxton, Knight and Mecchi (who was rapidly building up a fortune from the sale of the new papier-mâché furniture and domestic knick-knacks) were also present. Dickens, in his address, laid 'great stress upon that honourable characteristic of the charity [no less than that of judging the moral character of the applicants before offering them a pension], because the main principle of any such institution should be to help those who helped themselves (*Cheers*)!'.

A decade later, of the estimated 10,000 parishes in England alone, each of which must have had at least one head gardener, and probably more, there were still only 294 subscribers to the

Gardeners' Benevolent Society, and of those, sixty-seven were in London. The main fund (£5,200 in 3 per cent Consols.), was still not enough to allow decent pensions to even the most deserving applicants.

It must have seemed to many that being a gardener in trade, either as a nurseryman or as a seedsman, might be more rewarding. For some it was, and nurseries that found success could quickly make substantial amounts of money. Then, as now, the top end of the market was by far the most lucrative, though to tap it needed substantial supplies of capital. Many nurserymen were kept afloat by the richest of their clients, those willing to pay for the newest and most fashionable of plants. Then, as now, too, the majority of nurserymen were attracted to the vast popular market, where competition was much keener but the cost of entry much smaller. Countless nurseries were selling, by mid-century, cheap Chater's hollyhocks, dahlias, daisies, geraniums of all types, penstemons, tree carnations (and Malmaisons) and calceolarias, or were advertising 'New Cheap Plants'. Some, like Henry Walton of Edge End, near Burnley, specialized in last season's geraniums, fuchsias, cinerarias and pansies, presumably buying job lots at auction and selling them on. Others, like John Hayes of Farnham, Surrey, sold 'CHEAP BEDDING PLANTS FOR THE MILLION' at between 1s. and 3s.6d. per dozen, with catalogues for a penny. Lancashire nurseries sold cheap carnations, pinks and picotees, with a free hamper for every twenty-five pairs of show carnations (at £4), or show pinks (at 4 guineas). Seedsmen could buy a quite remarkably wide range of killed seed (baked until there was no possibility of germination), sold as 'ooo' grade. This was for mixing with good seed of expensive varieties.

It was easy to find land to rent or lease, or, if capital was available, to buy. Many small nursery owners became rich when the land they used for growing crops became needed for urban development, and there were endless auctions of nursery stock throughout the period as businesses were swallowed by new suburbs.

Not all auctions were due to urban expansion; many were, like the following, the result of financial misfortune: 'To be sold by

Private Contract, by order of the assignees of James Bishopp, of Westburton, a Bankrupt, ONE THOUSAND SUCCESSION PINE PLANTS of all sizes, and One Thousand very fine Fruiting Pine Plants.' The plants referred to are pineapples, a popular fruit of the period, though they were being shipped direct from the tropics by the 1820s and it may have been becoming uneconomic to grow them in Britain, hence the bankruptcy. Companies like Protheroe & Morris began to specialize in such things. They advertised at least half a dozen auctions a month near London alone, whether 'AUCTION of 20,000 bedding plants', or 'Nursery equipment and 40,000 well grown bedding plants', or even the notable collection of breeding material assembled by Mr Hogg, whose carnations, picotees, pinks and auriculas were all being auctioned as his lease had fallen in (Protheroe & Morris at Paddington Green, 12 December 1842).

There were other and fashionable auction sales of plants and bulbs at 38 King St, Covent Garden. There, both imported plants like Ghent azaleas and French potted roses, fruit trees and camellias, as well as those from private growers, went under the hammer. Poultry, pigeons and plants were sold on the first and third Thursday of every month during the season October to May.

Some nurserymen, too, started trading in related garden products, from lawnmowers to decorations. One even published quite marvellous advertisements in full colour for 'canary guano', showing a vast flight of canaries around a sunset mountain, with the text 'Perfectly clean, may be used by a lady'. It's not clear exactly what it was.

So it seems that even going into business saved no more than a few gardeners from poverty, and for all the thousands of peaches, pineapples, bunches of camellias, pots of new and even Guatemalan orchids grown for their employers, for all the auctions and advertisements, for all the moral rectitude and abstinence, innumerable respectable lives must, on ill health or the death of the husband, have ended in destitution, despair or the poor-house. Only a tiny fraction of this vast section of the popu-

49. The success of South American guano started a search
for manures nearer to hand.

lace made enough money to retire in comfort. A few may have done it by turning to trade; a few others became almost rich, with gardeners of their own, but they did that by becoming media 'stars'.

CHAPTER
9

STARS

T HE VICTORIAN PERIOD, BECAUSE OF THE COL-
ossal increase in personal wealth of sections of the population previously denied it, and because of its extraordinary economic activity, was also an age of tremendous
personal possibility. The old-established and traditional society
lost its strangle-hold on what a man could be, and anyone
sufficiently blessed with energy, talent, good health and some
good luck could easily better himself (or herself) in ways that
their immediate forbears could not.

Even in the gardening world there were some remarkable
success stories, many almost quintessentially Victorian. Of course
previous garden ages had had 'stars', men like Charles Bridgeman
or 'Capability' Brown, who started off in the humblest of circumstances but who ended as a modestly landed gentleman.
Slightly earlier, William Kent, again of modest birth, had become
a society figure whose company was sought by great aristocrats,
and much of whose life was spent amid the very grandest surroundings. However, such stories had really been very few, certainly since the end of the seventeenth century, and in any case
the real 'stars' of earlier periods had been the rich patrons for
whom the work of these men was done. While a few of them
had, even in their own day, been household names among
the gardening classes, there were rather few vehicles for the

50. Alfred Smee in his chilly looking summer-house.

promulgation of their ideas or the bolstering of their fame.

Such refined exclusivity was doomed, and once the Victorian media became economically important, then 'fame' and its attendant financial rewards became an enticing prospect for gardeners who could write, or who were potential entrepreneurs, as well as for the owners of the media, who needed famous contributors to help market their books and magazines.

In any case, the Victorian passion for experts (or 'practical' men, as famous gardeners were often called) seemed to ensure that most gardeners who reached the top of the gardening tree, for example those who became head gardener or curator of one of the botanic gardens, or of a major public park, or even for one of the great landowners, had quite considerable status, almost that of minor stars. They seemed to have easy access to the media, to wealthy clients needing new gardens designed, and even to venture capital sufficient to set up magazines and other businesses. Most of their erstwhile employers seem also to have been quite happy to give their head gardeners sufficient time and opportunity to develop themselves. Perhaps their protégés' hoped-for fame reflected on a patron's garden.

One of the male garden stars, Paxton, achieved a knighthood and a comfortable 'first rate' Italianate stucco villa. Another, Robinson, ended up with a Stuart manor house set in a very pleasant estate. Several of the others retired into prosperous middle-class life in remote Aberdeenshire, or in the less accessible suburbs of London. All of them started virtually penniless.

51. Paxton, before knighthood, already surrounded by emblems of his success.

Paxton was born in 1803, the seventh son of a poor farmer, and started work as a garden boy in the nearby 'big house' at Milton Bryan at the age of seventeen. His employers were astute enough to encourage him, and three years later he was sent to work among the circular flower-beds of Wimbledon House (then owned by the Duke of Somerset). He soon began working at Chiswick House, where the London Horticultural Society had leased a garden and where he had his first momentous meeting with his future mentor and employer, the Duke of Devonshire. Moving swiftly to Chatsworth, he soon began experiments both with glasshouse design and with publishing, and was almost immediately taking a hand in the history of garden design, engineering and architecture. An indulgent and delighted employer furthered his career, and exciting projects flowed in almost ceaselessly, culminating with the fantastic Crystal Palace. He was soon an M.P., and became more interested in town planning (macrogardening almost) than in gardening.

A comparable though less spectacular story is that of Donald Beaton, born in 1802 near Strathconon in Ross-shire (continuing the tradition of the previous century, when many of the well-known gardeners and almost every head gardener were of Scottish extraction). The family (his father managed a firm of cattle dealers who exported black cows from the Highlands) spoke Gaelic and his grandmother fed him on fantasies of lost nobility; he was, apparently, the twenty-third generation of first-born men after the loss of the Isle of Skye, when two brothers and their followers had raced for it in boats. He started his studies expecting a middle-class career, but bad harvests and the Napoleonic wars ruined his father's business so that the young man had to go into service. He was educated by his first employers, who sent him to Inverness Academy as a companion for their son. Beaton wasn't an academic success, and had to take up employment as a gardener with Sir William Cumming Gordon at Forres. In spite of the 'bothy system', it actually seems to have been an enjoyable experience, for the servants were treated as part of the family and there were dancing, frequent 'routs', and hunting.

Beaton next worked for a nursery in Perth and for the Botanic Gardens in Edinburgh, then took fortune into his own hands and sailed for London in 1830. The move worked, and he soon had a job; only a few years later he was working as head gardener at Shrublands, an important Victorian garden with one of the few terraced sites of which Robinson would eventually approve (not surprising, as Robinson was called in as a design consultant). Thereafter, he began to write for the *Gardener's Chronicle* and the *Cottage Gardener*, and became a notable hybridizer of new flowers, making enough money to retire at the age of fifty. An engraving of the man shows a large raw-boned Highlander, tight-lipped, close and opinionated; rather a daunting man to have as a gardener.

In contrast is a man whose obituary of 1889 described him as the most prominent gardener of the age, who designed gardens great and small (mostly great) all over the country and in Europe, but who seems to have been modest enough to keep insisting that he be called 'gardener', and who wrote rather badly (though he did edit two unexciting magazines: the *United Gardeners' and Land Stewards' Journal* and the *Gardeners' and Farmers' Journal*, Robert Marnock was born at Kintore in Aberdeenshire in 1800. He became a garden boy and soon a skilled gardener, and moved south. He won a competition for the design of the new Sheffield Botanical Garden, and at once became its curator. Soon after that he made what was widely thought to be an outstanding design for the Regent's Park site of the Royal Botanical Society of London, so naturally, in 1841, he was appointed curator of that garden. He seems to have also had time to set up a business, for he advertised in various magazines that as his new duties were to be onerous, he was taking a partner in his seedsman and nursery venture based in Hackney. The new partnership called itself Marnock & Mawle, and was selling various rare plants certainly for the next few years.

Marnock's work as a designer seems to have followed on from that of Humphry Repton; he produced ingeniously contrived landscapes, with informal flower gardens near the domestic quarters. He eschewed terraces, vases and stonework almost entirely, so when he retired from Regent's Park (he was presented with a service of silver plate at a dinner at the London Tavern, Bishopsgate, on 7 August 1862 – tickets were a guinea each) he eventually began to write for William Robinson's *The Garden*, and formed part of the anti-bedding claque (this included Wolley

Dod, Canon Ellacombe, G. W. E. Loder, William McNab and Miss Jekyll). It was Marnock who helped Robinson's early career, and this was no doubt why he remained a contributor to Robinson's magazines; however good he was at the design of gardens, he wasn't much good with a sentence (Robinson perhaps accepted his material out of friendship). He finally accumulated enough money to retire once more to Aberdeenshire, where he lived quietly with his daughters until his death.

Robinson himself, of course, was a perfect contrast, handling the language with brio and money with great astuteness, but gardens with a much more leaden touch. He was born on 5 July 1838 in County Down, into a poor family suffering the indignity of having prosperous and sanctimonious relatives. His father left home when William was ten, and the family thereafter subsisted on the relatives' generosity. William became a watering-boy at Curraghmore, but was head gardener there by the age of twenty-one. After a disastrous row with his employer he went to the Botanic Garden at Dublin, and thence to work for Marnock at Regent's Park (he was paid 9s. a week). Although he rose rapidly, he soon discovered his gift for words (and indeed, invective) and became the garden correspondent for *The Times*, which he represented at the Paris Exhibition of 1867 (this visit was quite profitable, for it engendered two books, both of which have been extensively quoted in previous chapters). Book followed book, and the magazine *The Garden* started to appear from 1871, almost at once making a profit. *Gardening Illustrated*, using the most modern technology, started up eight years later. On the proceeds of all this Robinson began to buy property in London, which quickly appreciated in value; then, in 1884, as land prices were severely depressed by the latest agricultural difficulties, he bought the Gravetye Manor estate.

He at once set about gardening in the grand manner, though he found it impossible to make the estate economically viable. Even the almost constant addition of more farms didn't help. However, the excitement of becoming a landowner proved rather strong and, forgetting his own extremely humble origins, he began rather to oppress his tenants and to adopt somewhat unrealistic and seigneurial attitudes. He proclaimed that all modern houses were awful and ruined the landscape, that all houses should have a fireplace in the hall large enough to burn cordwood (substantial baulks of timber), and that no one should use a coal range for cooking, wood giving greater savour to the food (true, of course), and no black 'smokes' to spatter the garden.

The men mentioned so far were all, at least partly, real gardeners. However, some of the other garden 'stars' were drawn from different aspects of gardening. Robert Fortune, whose name has already appeared several times in previous chapters, was a plant collector. Yet another Scot, he was born in Berwickshire in 1812 and eventually became a gardener at the Edinburgh Botanic Garden. From there he moved to Chiswick, where he looked after the tropical collection. At about the same time, China was opened to foreigners; so, following the treaty of Nanking in 1842, Fortune was sent out to find as many good garden plants as he could. For a man who had never travelled out of Britain, and hated the passage from Leith to London, this must have been a daunting prospect. It was a dazzling success. In spite of thieves, con-men, obstructive mandarins, brushes with various oriental diseases and, finally, a number of pirates, he returned to London loaded with gorgeous plants (he was the first botanist to travel with a Wardian case, and so many plants that would otherwise not have survived the long and arduous journey were soon in full bloom at Chiswick). He too now turned author, and though he was by no means a born writer he communicated the full excitement of his first journey. His *Visits to the Capitals of Japan and China* was deservedly a best-seller.

After several further journeys, and another book, Fortune spent the last years of his life comfortably ensconced in Kensington, secure in the knowledge that British gardens would always be growing the results of his endeavours. British gardeners were soon drinking it, for it was he who first brought living tea plants out of China. Soon the plantations of India and Ceylon were providing cheap tea for the poor.

Among the slightly lesser figures of the age were men from all sorts of backgrounds, whether sons of very rich parents indeed

52. John Claudius Loudon.

(like Henry Elwes), of prosperous manufacturers (like Samuel
Reynolds Hole), or of minor gentry (like Canon Ellacombe).
Among the female 'stars', all were drawn from the middle or
upper middle classes. Even Jane Loudon, who married John
Claudius Loudon, a man of more than twice her age, when she
was twenty, was the daughter of a prosperous Birmingham family.
Loudon himself followed the general male life-history rather
closely; he was the son of a poor farmer, joined an Edinburgh
nursery at a tender age and moved to London when he was
twenty. Starting out as a garden journalist, and battling against
dreadful health, financial hazards, and an incredibly hard schedule
of work, he achieved eminence but not wealth. After her husband's death in 1843, Jane Loudon, with no money from her
family, had to carry on to produce several rather successful works
for the women's market, including *Mrs Loudon's Gardening for
Ladies* which is quoted throughout this book. She managed to
maintain herself and her daughter in the pleasant semi-detached
Bayswater house designed by her husband, dying there in 1858.

Mrs Lawrence, whose garden she had so disliked but who was undoubtedly a star of the mid-Victorian garden, was born in very comfortable surroundings too. She was fortunate, though, to have a husband whose own successful career soon enabled her to leave the cramped garden of the Lawrencian villa when he bought the estate of Ealing Park. There she grew endless rare plants, getting some of them into flower even before Paxton managed it at Chatsworth. The Queen visited her on several grand social occasions.

Visitors, royal or otherwise, were not much encouraged to visit Munstead Wood, the garden Miss Jekyll made for herself once she'd left her mother's Munstead House. While she loved her cats, and often enjoyed the company of architects, musicians and artists, she seems to have been the first 'media' gardener to have been seriously bothered by members of the public anxious to visit her garden and have intense conversations about gardening. She pleaded pressure of work, and in one article even pleaded with the public to leave her in peace; she was certainly very busy. Her frequent books were remarkably successful; she produced many articles for the grander magazines, and though she had several gardeners (for a while she conducted a small nursery for the propagation of the plants necessary for the style of garden she was promoting – and which now makes modern gardeners weep for the plants no longer to be found), she did much real gardening herself.

So did the redoubtable Miss Hope of Edinburgh, whose articles on flower arranging in the *Gardener's Chronicle* and *The Garden* were widely read. She was the daughter of a prominent Edinburgh lawyer and a descendant of an eighteenth-century 'King's Botanist for Scotland'. She scoured nurseries and gardens looking for interesting old plants, soon having an extraordinarily rich collection. Much of the produce from this ended up in the tiny posies of flowers and herbs which she and her circle of charitable friends and relatives made up to be distributed to the poor and sick. She helped promote this practice, and soon grand ladies all over the country were making posies. Miss Hope herself once made up 400 in a day, of polyanthus, rosemary and snowdrops, proclaiming that simple flowers, or plants with a nice smell, were most appreciated by poor folk; some of her readers were making up bunches of orchids and hothouse flowers. Curiously, she got her poorer kinswomen to take the flowers to the Royal Infirmary; she herself never visited a hospital. However deep her charity may have run, she had a wonderful grasp of how flowers can work together in a vase, and a number of her schemes have been quoted here. All her work is worth looking at by modern arrangers with a Victorian room to decorate.

Perhaps better known was Mrs Earle, whose *Pot-Pourri from a Sussex Garden* (a title containing not only a central product of the fad for 'huswifry' among old-fashioned flowers, but also the county that almost seems to have been the only location where late Victorian gardening took place), was an instant success, and occasioned a series of further *Pot-Pourri* books. Mrs Earle's description of her parents' attractive garden appears elsewhere in these pages.

For all these women, though, and women were hardly represented until now in the history of gardens and gardening, the journey from the comfort of their childhood homes to attaining independent voices in the greater world must have been almost as arduous as was that of the men from underprivileged obscurity to eminence and modest comfort. Brave people, and fortunate; but as they sipped Chinese tea, or sowed seeds of some perfect rarity, the workhouses, urban slums or half-wrecked village cottages were inhabited by thousands to whom fortune had been less kind.

CHAPTER
10

SEA
CHANGE

NOSTALGIA FOR A GOLDEN PAST WAS ONE OF the strands (and an important one) in the destruction of the Georgian mode of gardening in favour of the blazing obsession for bedding. The old landscape gardens and their rolling lawns vanished beneath terraces and flights of steps, beneath gaudy tadpole- and butterfly-shaped flower-beds, 'Old English' parterres or ribbon beds so brilliant that all eyes were quite dazzled.

Still older gardens, of the sort that had bred the early Victorian nostalgia, had not escaped the madness. No gardens of the seventeenth or the early eighteenth century remained at all intact; most of them had had their ancient and overgrown yews re-cut into fancy topiary, or their box-edged parterres replanted with calceolarias and geraniums, even if they were not utterly revamped and so destroyed. Ancient avenues were replanted with monkey-puzzles, New Zealand flame tree, *Rhododendron grande* and *Wellingtonia*.

Nevertheless, though the nostalgia of the 1820s and 1830s went on, ironically, to produce gardens that were totally Victorian in both look and planting, and bore only the most superficial resemblance to the longed-for gardens of the past, there was a further level of irony to come. Part of the original vein of nostalgia of the early nineteenth century retained its purity over the succeeding decades, unaffected by whatever extraordinary glories were created in gardens of the Victorian period, and eventually became so powerful that it finally almost overthrew the style of gardening that it had itself once created, but forty years before. Even by 1841 a writer on the subject of 'Garden of a Country Residence' described how

We now sallied into the Garden, and I own I was disappointed. I expected a French or Italian taste, or perhaps both, engrafted upon the modern English; trellises, balustrades, busts, hothouses, conservatories. Except the last (of no great dimensions), there were none of these. There was an abundance of natural flowers, and some beautiful exotics; but these were, I thought, too much mingled with beds of herbs for culinary purposes, of which flowers formed the borders. This produced a style nearer the preceding, than the present century ...

The visitor queried the old-fashionedness of the garden, with its outmoded herbs and mixed borders, but the owner replied, 'I would rather have the smell of tedded grass, or kine, and that little Alderney close even to my drawing-room windows ... than all the finery of lawns and Orange trees.'

The following year, the same pure if subterranean current of nostalgia was finding further expression (in spite of Paxton's continuing advocacy of half-hardy bedding), when an anonymous woman writer complained:

If I am to have a system at all, give me the good old system of terraces and angled walks, and clipt yew hedges, against whose dark and rich verdure the bright old-fashioned flowers glittered in the sun. I love the topiary art, with its trimness and primness, and its open avowal of its artificial character ...

She disliked the contemporary 'natural or English style ... [with its] scores of unmeaning flower beds, disfiguring the lawns in the shape of kidneys, and tadpoles, and sausages, and leeches, and commas ... '

Her own garden, which she described at some length, while making use of much of the new flora, had the steps to the kitchen garden flanked by old-fashioned flowers like hollyhocks (though she had some of the new dahlias as well), China asters, nasturians (her spelling), and African marigolds. Elsewhere, she had a bowling green with clipped hedges, a maze with a central mount and summerhouse, a sundial of flowers (soon to become a popular Victorian feature), surrounded by topiary peacocks and lions, covered walks, embrasures with potted carnations and pinks, a miniature canal, and much more. Though the final result may have looked rather early Victorian, her passion was for the entire range of seventeenth-century garden elements.

Naturally, like any good and greedy gardener, she couldn't resist plenty of modern elements too, like the part where 'Rock plants of every description freely grow in the crevices of the rustic battlement which flanks the path on either side; the irregularity of the structure increases as you descend, till, on arriving on the lawn below, large rude masses [of stone] lie scattered on the turf, and along the foundations of the western terrace ... ' (Shirley Hibberd copied this idea, popularizing it, as his own, a few years later.) On the other hand, the writer called the terrace 'the nosegay of the garden', and while it was planted up with plenty of fashionable and modern flowers, it gave much of its space to the old-fashioned flora, so 'the sweetbriar and the wallflower and the clove and the stock gilliflower are not too common to be neglected ...'

By 1847 Edward Jesse had published a self-consciously 'artistic' and wildly successful book called *Favourite Haunts and Rural Studies*, in which he describes numbers of gardens, some modern, like Dropmore, but many more suitably 'Gothic' and romantic, or at least formal and rational, but by no means like the sort of thing fashionable when the book appeared. Especially admired was an ancient house called Parlem Park near Colnbrook, now long vanished. With ancient arcades,

The house appears to have been preserved with the greatest care, and nothing could be neater than its appearance. Then there was that sort of old-fashioned garden in front which I delight in ... [with] large tufts of lavender and box – the honest old English roses, now nearly

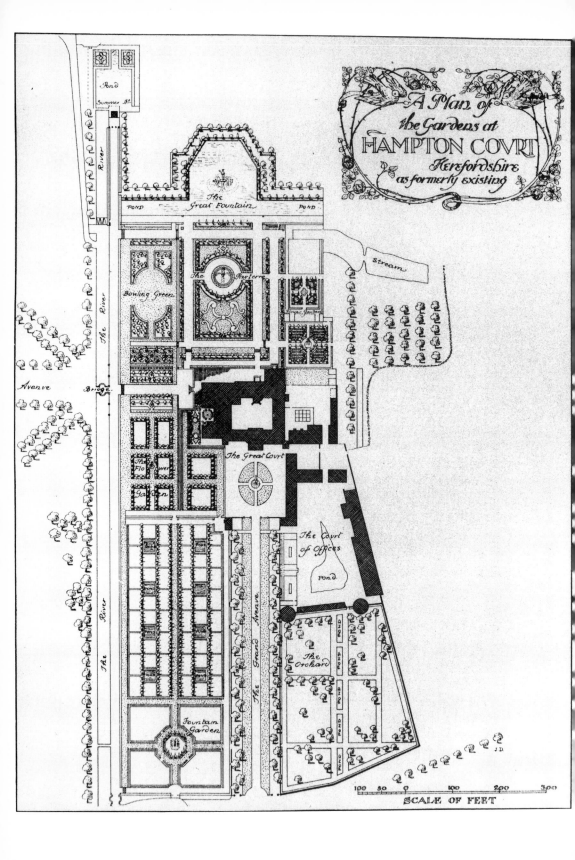

A Plan of the Gardens at HAMPTON COVRT Herefordshire as formerly existing

Pond
Summer Ho

River

The Great Fountain

POND

POND

The River

Bowling Green

The Parterre

Stream

Rose Garden

Avenue   Bridge

The Flower Garden

The Great Court

The Court of Offices Pond.

The River

The Grand Avenue

The Orchard

Fountain Garden

J.D.

100   50   0   100   200   300
SCALE OF FEET

exploded – the sundial, and other characteristics of a garden of bygone times.

It was to be only another thirty or forty years before the 'bygone' gardens were being recreated with enthusiasm all over the country.

Of Hall Barn, then with still a wonderful formal garden of the early eighteenth century (now in grand fragments), Jesse wrote:

... the gardens retain much of their original character, consisting of broad terraces of gravel and grass, sheltered by lofty screens of laurel and yew. A small lake, in the formal shape of the time, is seen at the bottom, with a banqueting house at the upper end of it, surrounded by an extensive lawn, and adorned with temples and summer houses ... The design is pleasing and elegant, formed after the taste of those times which admitted a more regular and systematic plan than would be approved of in the present day.

That set one channel for nostalgia – that of the old-fashioned 'gentry' gardens. Jesse also subscribed to the second channel (one which is still remarkably powerful). He admired English cottage gardens, where the rosy-cheeked cottager gardened with perfect taste and astonishing industry, and so 'enjoys one of the most innocent delights of human life. There the sweet briar and honey-suckle mingle together in pleasing confusion ...' – far away, as they seem, from the destitution and the beer-shops of the cottage life described by Rosa a year or two later. However patently ridiculous and untrue this 'cottage fantasy' must have been for a large percentage of the rural poor, the sentiment expressed by Jesse was widespread: it saw, through a rose-coloured glass, a cottage garden filled with the perfume of lavender, myrtle and roses, doves cluttering the house roof, and wasps buzzing among the gnarled but laden fruit trees. One of the reasons that it became more and more powerful throughout the century was that more and more of the population, and therefore the book and magazine readers, became exclusively urban.

Associated with the delights of humble country life were humble garden flowers, all so different from the over-bred and over-fashionable plants being planted out each summer for the few warm months. In the late 1840s, cottagers' gardens were supposed to be full of the old garden flora: things like *Adonis*, aubrietas, double ladies' smock (*Cardamine pratensis* 'Flore Pleno'), hepaticas, double primulas, columbines, campanulas and double sweet williams. It's not clear if they actually were, though there may perhaps have been, to some extent, 'class floras' as there are today. From the lists of cottagers' garden plants published from the 1850s onwards, it seems very much more likely that the vision of 'cottage garden flowers' was merely a projection of middle- and upper-class hopes (perhaps making them feel less alarmed for the future). The lists of actual flowers suggest that many of those cottagers with enough time and money to grow flowers were quite as keen as the magnates to get hold of the very latest thing. Cottagers really did grow things like *Gentiana septemfida* and *Anemone japonica*, within a couple of seasons of their first intro- duction. Both were plants that remained just as popular in gardens of the wealthy.

There were some sharper looks at cottage life than those of Jesse. *The Kitchen Garden* (written in 1855 by E. S. Delaware) was one of a series of small volumes called *Books for the Country*. They were published in waxed linen covers, no doubt to suit real-life grubby cottage conditions, and though this one opens with a charming vignette of rakes and spades leaning against a fashionable sundial, it does have a more realistic frontispiece showing two very depressed-looking gardeners among the cabbages. Of herbs and herb gardens (just about to become fashionable in middle-class gardens, as part of the nostalgic in- terest in 'huswifry', pot-pourri and such like), he writes, for example, of tansy: '... Tansy-pudding retains its place in old cookery-books. Few persons will regret its remaining there- in instead of appearing in proper person on the table, if the dish partakes strongly of the peculiar and powerful odour of the plant. It may be of more value as a vermifuge than as a dainty.'

Even such modest insight didn't last; too much was at stake. Shirley Hibberd, shrewd enough when he wanted, sensed that sentiment suited the spirit of the age, and of present times he wrote:

Gorgeous as is the promenade style, with its 'chain patterns' and 'panels' in colour, its terrace walks, sculptural embellishments and artistic devices, the brightest and most dazzling of flower mosaics must 'pale its ineffectual fires' when put in contrast with the arbours and avenues, the grand old trees, and the full richness of a well-kept ancient garden, where the old medicinal herbs load the air with odours, and in the fiercest heats of summer a cool shade is within easy reach ...

Writing for a female audience, he wrote of the housewives in his version of Merrie England: '... see how they gloried in their sweet-smelling dainties ... you will almost smell the cowslip wine ... and the bitter draughts that over-dressed dandies drank at the early luncheon, and the many sweet confections and pomades that good wives invented without number to enhance their own and their daughter's charms; for then the wife was head gardener', and grew laced pinks (Hibberd is being anachronistic here, for laced pinks had been grown only since the last few years of the eighteenth century, by which time few ladies had much to do with the herb garden), picotees and carnations.

By 1862 this nostalgia was no longer half underground, but in full light and flowing fast. One writer declaimed

... Where be my Primroses, my Narcissuses, my Daffodils, my Paeonies, my Saxifrages, my Hyacinths, my Roses, my Irises, my Pinks, my Picotees? Where be my storied plants (I mean my plants with a story attached to them) to make the way pleasant to my guests as we saunter the borders? ... Where be all these gone? – sacrificed to the exigencies of ribbon beds ... What a charming bond of union between a whole circle of neighbours to communicate to each other with their new acquisitions. How different now! ... What good to my neighbour a cartload of my thousand bedding out plants – he has another thousand just the same.

By this date, too, fond fantasies of the past were beginning to interest not only gardeners; painters began to play with rosy ideas of eighteenth-century gardens, inhabited by eighteenth-century figures indulging in sulks, courtship, and so on. None of it was particularly authentic, nor even of particularly high quality. Although vast attention was paid to arms and armour, clothes, furnishing and so on, the inhabitants' features are always in the currently fashionable Victorian mode, and many of the plants shown in the borders were still in China or Brazil in the eighteenth century.

Architects, too, were looking at old things with increasingly misty eyes. Architecture (and interior decoration), had been marching hand in hand with garden design for a century or more already, and had even run more or less in parallel during the wildest flights of the bedding craze. Even by 1820, with the discovery that classical Greek and Roman buildings had been brilliantly coloured, colour had become deeply respected, and the slightly later discovery that the greyest and purest of Gothic buildings had also once been painted all over only confirmed the enthusiasm. Architects, set free from the chasteness of mono-chrome, began to colour their buildings (usually using different building materials rather than mere paint).

All this was comparable to the colourful cut-out beds on the lawn. Ruskin and others at first admired big simple masses of colour; circles, squares and so on, just as circular beds of flowers were thought the most elegant. By 1850 an increasing taste for complexity in planning design and decoration, especially of flat surfaces, mirrored the growth of ribbon bedding and the new complexities of bed planting.

By the 1860s the most advanced of architects, and the most reactionary of gardeners, had developed a distaste for fanciful and elaborate polychromy, and were looking for more restrained images. Influential books of this period included Kerr's *The English Gentleman's House* of 1864 and C. L. Eastlake's *Hints on Household Furniture* of 1868. This last marked the move away from heavily Gothic or Graeco-Roman furniture (and therefore the parterre outside the Gothic or Grecian windows of the drawing-

54. A picture used by Robinson to refute Blomfield's assertion that formality is the only possible style.

room), and a move towards simple and undecorated cottage things, true to their materials, and often derived from seventeenth- and eighteenth-century domestic English buildings and their interiors. Architects like Philip Webb began to find new interest in the charming but rather naïve brick versions of 'classical' architecture of the same centuries, and suddenly elegant and quite expensive versions of vernacular houses and furnishing began, at least for the prosperous and fashionable, to appear, and were labelled 'Queen Anne'.

But the undoubted charms of 'Queen Anne' houses were dulled if they were just set among unromantic carpet bedding, or Jacobethan parterres in scarlet, yellow and sky blue. The architects, realizing that they needed a clear architectural frame to set the houses off to advantage, and feeling that garden design had become too much the province of the gardener, decided that their houses needed 'Queen Anne' gardens too, in which architectural elements like walls, elaborate gateways, garden pavilions and flights of steps formed a sumptuous framework for both house and plants. Architects began to write garden books to promulgate these ideas.

The thirty-six-year-old architect Reginald Blomfield published his wonderfully seductive book *The Formal Garden in England* in 1892. In this he wrote, not entirely correctly, that 'Till the end of the eighteenth century a tradition of good taste existed in England – a tradition not confined to any one class, but shown not less in the sampler of the village school than in the architecture of the great lord's house [and] it might be said to have lingered on into this century in sleepy country towns.' Neatly splitting the difference between cottager's sampler and lord's mansion, he goes on to suggest that there may be many trim lawyers' houses still with a 'delightful garden bright with old-fashioned flowers against the red brick wall, and a broad stretch of velvety turf set off by ample paths of gravel, and at one corner, perhaps, a dainty summer-house of brick, with marble floor and panelled sides; and all so private and sober, stamped with refinement which was once traditional, but now seems a special gift of heaven'. This, however exciting to prospective middle-class clients aiming to live refined and sober lives, was almost certainly merely a piece of charming literary fantasy. It was a good way of selling some expensive gatehouses, pavilions, gates, steps, and other architectural detailing to the new lawyers (and, naturally, members of all the other professions), who wanted to create for themselves this wonderful picture.

Blomfield, astute, also recognized that there was no point in purely architectural nostalgia; it had to embrace the garden's plants too. He mourned the fact (as many of us still do), that few gardeners ever plant apple trees, or any of our own delectable native trees, but are all hankering after monkey-puzzles or American conifers (nowadays it must be *Sorbus cashmiriana* or *Prunus* 'Amanogawa'). 'Again, the pear tree, the chequer tree, the quince, the medlar, and the mulberry are surely entitled in their beauty to a place in the garden. It is only since nature has been taken in hand by the landscapist and taught her proper position that these have been excluded ... ' Blomfield saw himself in reaction to the contemporary landscape gardeners' use of dahlias, magenta, asphalt; all, he thought, were in loud and pretentious bad taste.

However, it was by no means a blanket approval for any garden before 1725; Blomfield loved only the supposed simplicity of the middle decades of the seventeenth century, and bemoaned the increasing complexity of later seventeenth-century and early eighteenth-century gardens (yet he must have admired Hall Barn), remarking that it was as well that all this pomp was swept away. He passionately loved old-fashioned flowers, small-cale planning, and delight (and what gardener could gainsay him?).

Blomfield's alluring vision of a particular sort of seventeenth-century domestic design, though false, was to prove immensely powerful. Because it was also expensive to produce, it settled most frequently around country houses of middling size, though there must have been countless 'cottages' and landless manors whose gardens were soon surrounded by topiary, medlar trees, and filled with the perfumes of jasmine and old-fashioned pinks. The book had been splendidly illustrated by Inigo Thomas, and both he and Blomfield went on to design some quite stunning gardens, notably that of Athelhampton, where vast topiary pyramids are set amid rather French-looking terraces, pavilions, fountains and pools, all glimpsed through magnificent gateways. The ensemble is grouped around a magnificent old house, to which only the most successful lawyer could aspire (modern additions to the garden are of lesser quality).

Thomas and Blomfield between them, in numerous grand gardens from Mellerstane to Caythorpe and Parnham House, created a new 'mock' style, sometimes called neo-Georgian but perhaps better called neo-Kip and Knyff, after the topographical artists who produced dozens of ravishing illustrations of estates and gardens of the period so admired by Blomfield. Publications about the new ideas became themselves grander and grander, reaching a peak when H. Inigo Triggs, an architects' draughts-man, produced an extraordinary and glossy sequence of drawings and photographs under the title *The Formal Garden in England and Scotland* in 1902. This was really an augmentation of Blomfield's work, and intended partly as a source book of authentic formal detailing for those just about to throw out their verbenas. He included all sorts of formal gardens, showing some of the 1850s, like the supposed recreation at Belton House, and the remodelling (in the 1880s) of the upper levels of the ancient garden at Mel-bourne Hall. He also illustrated some of the lovely new formal gardens being developed in Scotland, including Balcaskie, where the terraces to the south of the seventeenth-century house had new balustrades and steps, and some rather dull bedding, Bal-carres (where the walled garden was supposed to have many of its original old flowers), Earlshall, with Lorimer's garden of 1891, supposedly based on old plans, and Lorimer's own wonderful and extant garden at Kellie.

Other, and non-architectural, writers took up the theme. One wrote in 1895: 'Again, the useful and the beautiful should be happily united, the kitchen and the flower garden, the way to the stables and outbuildings, the orchard, the winter garden, all having a share of consideration and connectedness; and if there be a chance for a filbert walk, seize it ... ' The writer hated the artistic delights of most conventional and contemporary house-holders, who were still not yet at all 'Queen Anne', and were even now attached to their 'flower-beds shaped as crescents and kidneys – beds like flying bats or bubbling tadpoles, commingled

55. Part French, part English, this is part of Mawson's version
of the 'Queen Anne' style.

with butterflies and leeches, stars and sausages, hearts and commas, monograms and maggots ... and the pretty flowers smile a sickly smile out of their comic beds ...'

Blomfield's style of 'architectural' gardening needed long borders to bask against the walls, and a number of entranced writers pointed out, correctly, that the ancient gardener wasn't obsessed by parterres, but also liked the 'border beds' that surrounded them. Even so, the new herbaceous borders, while laying claim to descent from seventeenth-century examples, still looked nothing like their ancestors even when filled with seventeenth-century flowers.

Writers looked for gardens that might tell them how old ones really looked. George Milner's garden book *Country Pleasures* describes an old long border as a ravishing mix of bulbs, paeonies, scented herbs and flowers, all overhung by ancient apple trees (such things sound wonderful on the page, but are less easy to make and maintain in real life). As to good taste in such things, he quoted the late seventeenth-century Sir William Temple's motto, 'the success is wholly in the gardener', continuing: 'The qualities to aim at in a flower-garden are beauty, animation, variety and mystery.' Gardens should be half common-sense and half romance; he should have added that it is the 'romance' that usually makes maintenance difficult. However, the phrase aptly describes such present-day wonders as Hidcote and Sissinghurst.

267

Amid this hazy and romantic nostalgia, William Robinson, fast becoming an important garden writer, and equally speedily becoming wealthy, thought at first that he had found a garden style to which he could pin his hopes (and his hatred of the bedding system). He quotes Robert Marnock (the design star of the mid-century) as saying: 'Again, I remember a beautiful old garden at Ockham Park in Dr Lushington's time, which was formal and yet beautiful, through the informality of the vege-tation ... ' Robinson began to encourage gardeners to examine some of the alternatives to the parterre. The first real attempt to do this was his book *The Wild Garden* of 1870, where he started to push the sort of flowers that were hardy, which could be left to their own devices in a rather sophisticated sort of wilderness, and would thrive without needing a fleet of gardeners.

The flora Robinson suggests for this sort of garden was very diverse, ranging from the wildlings in a ditch garden he admired near Dublin, to the brand new Jackman hybrids of *Clematis*, but he also wants the reader to grow thalictrums, anemones (like *A. appenina* and native ones, as well as the new *Anemone japonica* 'Honorine Jobert'), and a vast list of hardy herbaceous flowers from half-a-dozen sorts of *Erysimum* and the green-centred and wonderfully perfumed *Dianthus superbus*, to entirely familiar and old-fashioned things like *Muscari* and *Campanula*. He adds that 'Some are looking back with regret to the old mixed-border gardens; others are endeavouring to soften the harshness of the bedding system by the introduction of fine-leaved plants, but all are agreed that a great mistake has been made in destroying all our sweet old border flowers.' Given his mercurial temperament, and the speed with which the 'Queen Anne' style was catching on, such peace and quiet wasn't to last long.

Sentiment as well as dissent was beginning to thicken around ideas of the gardens of the past. Dean Hole, in *A Book about Roses* (1884), wrote that he had thrown out his ancient grottoes, the walks of laburnum, lilac and the rest, and replaced them with geometrical bedding. Now, he missed 'those borders and meandering walks, many a pleasant nook, where the aged might

56. A new 'long border' in full bloom at Campden, Gloucestershire.

rest, young men and maidens sigh their love, and happy children play ... '

Sentiment got thicker still with John Sedding, writing a garden book as he lay dying. *Garden Craft Old and New* appeared in 1895, five years after his death. Posing the question 'What is a garden?', he concludes (after some rather religiose musings) that it is a place where peace, formality and order are set in contrast to the noise, hurly-burly and dust of the outside world. That can, of course, be true, though he suggests rather expensive ways to its fulfilment; his ideal garden is all urns, octagonal steps, arched doorways; all, he felt, were 'Eden memories', though plainly that location had been designed by a fashionable architect.

Romancing further, he waxes lyrical about overgrown gardens filled with a sense of domestic harmony (he adds, too, the idea of 'trysts', as in the 'genre' paintings of the period). He remarks that

there is a wealth of quiet interest in an old garden. We feel instinctively that the place has been warmed by the sunshine of humanity; watered from the secret spring of human joy and sorrow. Sleeping echoes float across its glades; its leafy nooks can tell of felicities sweeter than the bee-haunted cups of flowers; of glooms graver than the midnight blackness of the immemorial yews ... We have before us the scenery of old home idylls, of old household reverences and customs, of old life's give and take ... The place is identified with the fortunes of old families ... the marvel of its cloistered grace has been God-reminder to the saint ... for [a] poets' retreat, as refuge for the hapless victim of broken endeavour, as enisled shelter for the tobacco-loving sailor-uncle with a wrecked fame.

Perhaps because of the increasingly high tone of all the sentimental writing accumulating around formal gardens, or perhaps because it so obviously delivered gardening into the hands of the architects (and the pretentious brickwork that they devised), William Robinson began to recoil from this new movement. As he began to fulminate against formalism, however, more and more ordinary gardeners were beginning to see through the passion for bedding; as with many other passions, the obsession was beginning to collapse into ashes.

Combined with the nostalgia for the old sorts of gardening was an increasing recognition of some of the faults of the bedding system; however brilliant or however luxuriously subtle, it had major disadvantages. As early as 1849, one writer put it: 'The mode of supplying beds of flowers now, is very different to what it was twenty years ago. The mixed flower garden where perennials..., biennials, annuals..., roses, bulbs and so forth, were all grown together is but seldom seen now, at least, to any extent. Yet the old method had its advantages.' One of these was that the ground was not bare for long periods, as it was with bedding. However, the writer does not yet go on to suggest a return to the old sort of flower garden, but suggests even more bedding, this time in winter (the winter bedding was to consist of ivies in pots, small conifers and various small evergreens – head gardeners must have been delighted).

A little later, in the 1850s, in spite of all the passion for verbenas and the other 'bedders', gardeners like David Fish were saying: '... I never read and carefully digest the articles on herbaceous plants by Mr Weaver, without wishing I was within elbow reach of him, and thinking of the times when flower-beds were kept gay all the spring and summer on the old mixed system ... ' By 1862 gardeners were becoming really alarmed. In the early summer of that year there had been a devastating late frost; it had decimated every bedding scheme throughout the country. The new advocates of hardy herbaceous plants were not too sorry, and even supporters of bedding were beginning to think that too many of their designs were flying rather in the face of nature. There was also a growing feeling that the bedding system was bad for gardeners too, who were so busy either continually propagating or planting that they had no time to study the rest of the garden flora. Any plant that wouldn't 'bed' was ignored.

A writer to the *Gardener's Chronicle* of that year felt that

You have not pronounced upon the ribbon beds a whit too soon. At the rate things were going, you might else ere long have had to put the 'garden' itself into your 'Hue and Cry' [this was a sort of gardening 'wants' column]. Some specimens of what a garden really is, may still survive in the more distant and little known parts of the kingdom, which the encroachments of fashion are slow to reach; but in the neighbourhood of London, and the civilized districts affected by its tone, the thing is already nearly gone. If something be not done to arrest their extinction ... not a garden will remain ... I remember a popular clergyman who was fond of fine words, talking in his sermon about 'the shrubberies of Eden' ... So it is with our gardeners; they have turned all our gardens into shrubberies and ribbon beds ...

By the early 1870s, popular writers like Forbes Watson were beginning to feel that the bedding system led to the constant subjection of the imaginative, or higher, to the sensuous, or lower, element of flower beauty ... we find flower-beds habitually considered too much as mere masses of colour, instead of as an assemblage of living beings. The only thought is to delight the eye by the utmost possible splendour ...

This constant revelling in a blaze of colour, without any proper relief, begets an indifference to the simple wildflower, which seems tame and insipid to eyes that have been injured by excessive stimulus ... the modern system tends to injure a healthy taste for flowers – I allude to the custom of putting out plants in the beds just for the period of bloom, and then removing them, as if both before and after flowering they were destitute of interest. A garden is, in fact, no longer the home of plants, where all the ages, the young, the mature, and the decayed, mix freely, and in easy dress. It has degenerated into a mere assembly room for brilliant parties, where childhood and age are both alike out of place.

More questionably, he associated wild or old-fashioned flowers with moral purity, and modern florists' flowers with depravity and corruption, quoting with approval part of a poem by John Clare:

> And where the marjoram once, and sage and rue
> And balm and mint, with curled-leaf parsley grew
> And double marigolds, and silver thyme
> And pumpkins 'neath the window used to climb;
> And where I often, when a child, for hours
> Tried through the pales to get the tempting flowers;
> As lady's laces, everlasting peas,
> True love lies bleeding, with the hearts at ease;
> And golden rods, and tansy running high,
> That o'er the pale top smiled at passer by;
> Flowers in my time which every one would praise
> Though thrown like weeds from gardens now-a-days.

Even the stolid and tolerant Alfred Smee could write that bedding plants

... are at once the blessing and the curse of a garden. They are a blessing, as they give to geometric flower beds a display of thousands of brilliant flowers ... they are a curse, as they are so easily grown that

57. A formal axis, but informal plantings; the look of things
to come in Alfred Smee's garden.

they have gradually superseded all those plants which our forefathers used to cultivate and admire ... At the present time all gardens look alike; the gaudy Scarlet Geranium flourishes to the exclusion of hundreds of little genera ...

Dean Hole, witty if vapid, mocked bedding schemes, even those of the nobility whom he usually admired. In *The Book about the Garden* (1892) he wrote:

I never wander in those charming grounds but I ask myself the question – Are we not making a tremendous sacrifice ... to the Gigantic Idol called 'Bedding Out'? Are not our modern gardens, and those close to our windows, fireworks and kaleidoscopes for three months in the year, with brown fallows for the remaining nine? Don't talk to me about your 'Winter Gardens', your golden hollies with eight leaves, your priggish little Irish yews, about as big as ninepins ... And I won't listen to any nonsense about 'grand display of bulbs in the spring'. The grand display costs a fortune and comes up 'patchy' after all. I looked out the other morning from the window of a grand house ... upon a magnificent but unhappy experiment ... there were to have been Maltese crosses in silver, and golden coronets upon cushions of purple. The idea was gorgeous but the result was this – I could scarcely shave for laughing! Puritanical mice had defaced the crosses and appropriated the Crown Jewels.

In the 1880s, those aspiring to 'trim lawyers' gardens' desperately needed the herbaceous flowers of the past as well as the douce and formal gardens in which to put them. Plant collectors were soon roused; although the seventeenth-century herbalist and gardener John Parkinson had himself felt nostalgia for the vanished flowers of his own childhood, the flowers that he admired and grew (and indeed the man himself) became the objects of sentimental regret. Most of his flowers had been out of the public eye only since the 1830s, but members of the Parkinson Society, founded by the energetic Mrs Ewing in the 1880s, as well as many more non-clubbable gardeners, began ardently to hunt for the old flora.

In America Parkinson's flowers had survived for slightly longer, and Andrew Jackson Downing could complain in 1849:

The mingled flower-garden, as it is termed, is by far the most common mode of arrangement in this country, though it is seldom well effected. The object in this is to dispose the plants in the beds in such a manner that while there is no predominance of bloom in any one portion of the beds, there shall be a generous admixture of colours and blossoms throughout the entire garden during the whole season of growth . . .

He gives a list of plants for borders, and includes all the nostalgia-drenched flora, from pasque flowers, hepaticas, violets and poly-anthus, to pulmonarias, white corydalis, lily-of-the-valley, *Iris florentina*, hemerocallis, *Campanula persicifolia* 'Flore Pleno', and the rest.

By the end of the century, garden theory in North America was now hardly much behind that of northern Europe, and its developments had thereby been telescoped. Hardly had Americans got used to bedding plants before, in 1896, Ellwanger was allying himself with Robinson and the new ideas. In *The Garden's Story* he wrote:

We should see more of this 'natural wilderness' in places whose extent and natural features are adapted to it, a source of far greater satisfaction than the flaring General Grant geranium beds that so often disturb the sense of repose . . .

The prim modern garden, too, almost always lacks a pleasing feature of the ancient garden when rightly carried out; it has so few spots to lounge in. There is a dearth of garden-seats, niches, and benches, and vine-draped arbours and cloistered summerhouses. And where has the old sun-dial disappeared, that used to count the time so leisurely and shadow the passing hours?

American gardeners too were suddenly remembering with regret the old farmstead gardens that once grew all sorts of lovely sweet-smelling things that could no longer be found, or would no longer grow 'in our gardens today'. Ellwanger's old-fashioned flora included snowdrops, daffodils, imperials, muscaris, larkspurs, campanulas, bachelor's buttons, monkshoods, double white poppies, sweet clover, snow pink (this was, and is, *Dianthus plumarius*), white phloxes, dicentras, sweet williams, tall yellow tulips, sword grass and ribbon grass, tradescantias, sweet peas, valerians, madonna lilies, white and purple stocks, lily-of-the-valley, briar rose, white day lily (he probably meant *Hosta*), tiger lilies, dahlias, hollyhocks, sunflowers, and all the European herbs. This old-fashioned American garden flora was practically the entire old European garden flora of the real 'Queen Anne' period, with only the tiniest smattering of new American garden plants.

And so, in both continents, it went on: nostalgia expanding into herbs, into folklore, into ancient kitchen recipes, and yet more romanticism about old houses and gardens. It all became a market in its own right, with writers (like George Milner and his *Country Pleasures*), whose work consisted of nothing but nostalgia. Naturally Milner, admiring his own herbaceous border with its collection of old herbaceous flowers, counted among his friends many of those artists who produced fake eighteenth-century genre scenes.

Even William Robinson, in *The English Flower Garden* of the same date, suggested the formation of a small herb garden inside each walled kitchen garden, of all the usual plants. One of his contributors to that work, and to his magazine *The Garden*, was Canon Kingsley, owner of Eversley. While this house once had fashionable bedding schemes, it soon became a wonderful 'cottage' garden. The borders were filled with phlox, delphiniums, alyssums, saxifrages, pinks, carnations and roses. The grass was dotted with wild white violets. Elsewhere there were picturesque tangles of roses, honeysuckle and quince. (Ironically, by 1905, his daughter Rose Kingsley was columnist for the *Guardian* and *Daily Telegraph*, and was writing nostalgically about the old ribbon plantings of her father when rector of Eversley in the 1840s and 50s, before nostalgia took over.) However, before that happened, Robinson had begun his long and bitter campaign against bedding, against formalism, against topiary, against garden architecture, indeed against almost anything that wasn't his. Capable as he was of sustained and immensely readable invective, his writings illuminate the entire period with their fretful glow. He had come to feel that what was wrong with present British gardens particularly was 'the desire to have everything trimmed, and shaven, and neat; hedges cut to a rectangular outline, creepers nailed to walls with the branches straight and at regular intervals; beds so many feet apart to an inch ... '

This, and much else, could be blamed upon the baleful influence of foreign ideas, rather than the soft theorizings of British 'practical men'.

There are from Versailles to Caserta, a great many ugly gardens in Europe, but it is at Sydenham that the greatest modern example of the waste of enormous means in making hideous a fine piece of garden is to be found. This has been called a great work of genius, but it is only the realization of a misguided ambition to outdo another sad monument of great means prostituted to a base use – Versailles.

In Victorian gardens, he claims, stonework had become the ultimate end.

The worst example Robinson knows of a posing-ground (a most lovely phrase of insult) is Witley Court, where the formal gardens are so overweening as to destroy the view. Witley, a late design by Nesfield, did indeed have remarkable amounts of gravel, stonework, vast terraces and ranks of pudding-shaped topiary. In feel it was far more the public park than a private Eden. Many lesser gardens were overwhelmed with stone too, some, like Keir (near Stirling), developing an almost funereal look. However, Robinson's hatred of all this grand Italianate stonework easily transferred itself to the more modest walls and steps of Blomfield's lawyers' gardens.

In the next decade Robinson was in full spate, especially after the appearance of Blomfield's book. In his counterblast, *Garden Design and Architects' Gardens* (1892), he says: 'Some formality is often essential in the plan of a flower garden near a house – NEVER as regards the arrangements of its flowers and shrubs.

To array things in lines or rings or patterns can only be ugly wherever done!' Blomfield soon pointed out that that wasn't at all what he was suggesting, but then weakened his own argument by attacking the sort of informal garden that Robinson hated just as much. Soon, everyone was thoroughly enraged. Robinson shouted that it was a shame that painters had retreated from the garden proper (he was busily commissioning them to come and paint his own) and could only be found in the pigsty. This wasn't in the least true, for there are dozens of painters of the period quite obsessed with cottages, cottagers, cottage gardens (though they may have been what Robinson thought of as pigsties – he wasn't much of a social liberal), and the formal gardens of manor and farmhouses. It was, however, a good line.

Robinson informed his readers that when he designed gardens he did away with all terraces, banks, lines, angles (they were all right in Italy, where the steep slopes of Tuscany meant that land had to be terraced). It was lawns that were essential to English houses, though they should never have been cut into beds. He hated Blomfield's idea that gardens should be separated from the grounds by high walls (however 'authentic' this may be for reproduction seventeenth-century houses), and he certainly treated the remains of old gardens on his own estate in a most cavalier way. When, at the end of his life, he came to write the story of the alterations he'd made at Gravetye, modern con-servationists might turn pale. He demolished ancient service and stable ranges to put in rather ordinary flower gardens, knocked down garden walls, filled in the medieval moats of the farmhouses, ripped out ancient windows for more light, cut down equally ancient orchards for much the same reason, and blocked up ancient rights of way.

The argument became ever muddier; Robinson claimed that Blomfield thought that he (Robinson) wanted gardens to look like Claude's landscapes, but he furiously denied this; he wanted to make them look like good English landscapes, far better than any painting, even by Claude. He was furious that Blomfield had (very sensibly) picked on his idea of dotting pampas grass and yuccas around on whatever lawn was to hand (Robinson has a lot to answer for). While doing all this, he avoided any direct reply to Blomfield's subsequent attacks, merely complaining that most modern houses were awful anyway and were ruining the countryside.

In old days gardens had to be set within the walls, hence they had to be formal in outline, though were often charming inside. To keep all that remains of such should be our first care; never to imitate them now! Many old gardens of this sort that remain to us are far more beautiful than the modern formal gardening, which by a strange perversity has been kept naked of plants or flower life!

The argument raged on. Blomfield blamed tropical bedding on Robinson (though Robinson hated it too, but for different reasons). Robinson blamed Blomfield for 'stone gardening', citing the Italianate gardens at the head of the Serpentine (Blomfield thought them ghastly as well). Robinson also hated, too, the fake seventeenth-century gardens of Worth Park; he'd espied a colourful bed of flowers, but, once closer, saw that it was made 'of pieces of broken brick, painted yellow, blue or red'! Blomfield shuddered just as much.

Gardens Robinson did like were the wrecked grounds of 'poor beautiful old Barrington [Court], now an ill-kempt farmhouse, with manure piled against the walls, and the ceiling of the dining room propped up with a fir pole!' Barrington was thereafter snapped up by a magnate and quite gloriously rebuilt, with Gertrude Jekyll keeping an eye on the iris garden and the new moated orchard, resulting in something that Blomfield would have liked too.

Robinson called the topiary so beloved of Blomfield's adherents 'Barber gardening', and maintained (falsely) that ' ... clipping leads to leprous disfigurement, disease, and death'. He even hated yew hedges – 'Alas! Many of our country-house gardens are disfigured by these hard black lines' – blaming these, and much else, on Italy, whose 'influence has been wholly evil ... the early Romans had no garden flora, a few trees and no gardeners. Great builders as they were, they aligned the trees and cut them into

58. The new 'wild garden', but with plants from every continent.

shapes to range with their buildings, and all through the Middle Ages, and for hundreds of years this system weighed like a nightmare on the gardens of Europe.' Perhaps he thought that the Romans would have liked pampas grass.

After a battle of extremes in which there has been no victory, synthesis must follow. From the ashes of yew hedges and topiary burnt by followers of Robinson, and from those of anthuriums, caladiums and palms burnt by the admirers of 'trim lawyer's gardens', a new sort of garden began to emerge. The first and perhaps the greatest exponent of the synthesis was undoubtedly Gertrude Jekyll. In 1896, in one of her early articles (a review of Blomfield and Thomas's book), she wrote:

> The formal army are architects to a man; they are undoubtedly right in upholding the simple dignity and sweetness and quiet beauty of the old formal garden, but they parade its limitations as if they were the end of all art; they ignore the immense resources that are the precious possession of modern gardeners and therefore offer no sort of encouragement to their utilization . . . All who love gardens must value Messrs Blomfield and Thomas's excellent and beautiful book . . . but those whose views are wider cannot accept their somewhat narrow gospel . . . The free gardener will do well to keep it at hand as a wholesome correction to the exuberance into which his vast resources are likely to tempt him . . .

The gardens Jekyll designed from the 1880s onwards, and especially the ones she made while working with the architect Edwin Lutyens, incorporated everything that the Victorian age had to offer. She made use of the newest and most modern of varieties, using all the most exciting asters, delphiniums, lupins, roses and phlox that the breeders could devise. Yet she also used native wildflowers, old and new introductions from all over the world, as well as garden plants familiar to gardeners for century upon century. Lutyens created some extraordinary garden architecture, using astonishingly detailed (and expensive) brick, tile and stonework. Many other designers, notably Oliver Hill and Thomas Mawson, did comparable things. Jekyll, too, loved gardens with fine walls, and often planned quite formal vistas to contrast with the exuberant and luscious planting that her borders contained. With her painter's eye she cared passionately about colour; while some earlier gardeners had preached the virtues of colour harmonies in the garden (even while the majority preferred

A HERTFORDSHIRE HOUSE AND GARDEN · · · · · T·H·MAWSON

59. New formal gardens were as expensive to maintain as high Victorian parterres; few remain.

contrasts), she emphasized the effectiveness of using a sequence of related colours combined with a dash of contrasting ones to give an exciting liveliness to the scene. Famous modern gardens have added little advance to her ideas.

Her planting schemes, too, were really only a modification of Victorian modes of bedding. Instead of verbenas or geraniums or echeverias, she used irises, asters and lupins. Instead of geometrical patches of flowers, she substituted slanted and irregularly shaped beds. The final effect, rich and lovely though it was, and totally unlike the tight bedding of previous decades, was also totally unlike the old borders that once surrounded real parterres. Modern garden design manuals and the back pages of grand nursery catalogues still produce Jekyllesque plans with amoeboid beds of herbaceous plants or erica (though they are generally schemes of much less refinement than hers).

Naturally, for colour schemes to work, the chosen planting needs to be isolated from other parts of the garden which might spoil it. In a large garden this is easily achieved if the space is split into distinct units, or garden 'rooms'. The currently fashionable desire for such plans, vaguely attributed to the influence of Sissinghurst, is only a slight modernization of the 'Queen Anne' gardens so persuasively designed by Blomfield, or of the garden areas designed by Gertrude Jekyll.

But then, almost everything in the most visited of today's gardens (and some are now so fashionable that they are beginning to be distorted and eroded by the intensity of public interest) is actually part of the late Victorian legacy, or is closely associated with that period's ideas. Coach-loads of tourists pour into vast car parks at Hidcote and Sissinghurst, into Cranborne and Crathes. Gates click ceaselessly at modern gardens like Barnsley House, Tyninghame, Tintinhull and East Lambrook. In almost every one of these gardens the late Victorian synthesis finds a marvellous fulfilment, or at least its continuation. Clipped yew hedges, topiary, formal walks or walks of filberts, quinces or laburnum, 'cottage' gardens, neat box parterres, quiet green theatres, luscious borders filled with a haze of soft colours, or of one colour alone, formal pools, carefully mossed steps, gilded gates, a tasteful scattering of obelisks or urns – all delight the onlooker.

Elsewhere, Victorian influence lingers. In hundreds of other gardens, flat Victorian roses seem to captivate all the hearts (except when there is a bad summer) of gardeners who cannot bear hybrid teas. Countless herb nurseries supply a vastly greater range of species than are ever needed for the kitchen to a rapidly increasing infinity of domestic herb gardens. 'Cottage Garden' societies burgeon, and interest in old-fashioned flowers grows apace. Dried flowers, pot-pourri (full of suspect colours and odours), sachets of lemon verbena leaves, tiny pots of medlar jelly swamp shop counters everywhere. Brand new magazines are founded, and find success, on the Victorian fantasy that all country dwellers, pink-cheeked, live in rose- and clematis-clad cottages of which even 'Rosa' would have approved. Yet among all these delights (real or false), and however lovely were the compromises worked out for late Victorian country gardens (whether around castle or cottage), it is perhaps more surprising how much of early and mid-Victorian gardening still persists unaltered, not only in actual great Victorian gardens that survive, but in the way that many of us still garden.

Much of vernacular gardening is still solidly high Victorian:

village gardeners still prune laurels, ericas, even unsuitable things like flowering currants and philadelphuses into rounded pudding shapes; front gardens all over the country still have diamond-shaped beds, or rockeries made from shells and piles of stones. Every ironmonger and garden centre still sells 'bedding plants', and if those are now F_1 hybrid *Begonia semperflorens* or petunias of exaggerated scale, then the underlying principle is still just as it was in 1850.

Victorian gardening is alive and well in almost every public park. Most of the parks that exist are of that date, so it is not surprising that the 'Parks Department' (and indeed most horticultural colleges') idea of gardening is therefore a 'fossilized' thing, associated with the birth of the institution, which propagates itself from each generation of park gardener to the next. In parks, even if the local authority has cut the budget and the glasshouses are clad in unbreakable plastic panels, time has stood almost still, and though the roses are modern, the way that they are put together still influences public taste.

In the popular garden press too, Victorian attitudes to colour, to the garden as a place for endless 'products', all new, all patented, all bright and shiny, and to notions of tidiness and over-elaborate garden craftsmanship, all survive totally intact. The names, at least, of several Victorian garden magazines are still in use. Further up the market, grand garden books show photographs of modern herbaceous borders or sophisticated 'cottage gardens', many of which date, either in fact or in inspiration, to the late Victorian period. A surprising number of big and still heavily Victorian private gardens actually exist, or have only just failed, and it is not uncommon to come across ones that can still send fresh figs and cherries to table throughout the year, constant supplies of orchids to the drawing-room, and have substantial bedding schemes. While there seem no longer to be many that have garden staffs of twenty or thirty men, some manage to look trim and elegant even though some of the parterres may have been grassed over, showing only as patterns on the lawn in dry summers or after a light fall of snow.

A few Victorian nurseries and seedsmen survive, mostly among

60. The new look of 1883, to which many gardeners still aspire.

the middle ranks but also in great firms like Suttons, Thompson and Morgan, Hilliers. Some still sell substantial numbers of plants collected or bred during the nineteenth century.

Survivals among Victorian gardening clubs and societies are more common. Some have had name changes, and the most august can now boast of being 'Royal'; the London Horticultural Society and the Gardeners' Benevolent Society are two of them. The latter now looks after retired gardeners (many of whom worked in the last of the fully Victorian gardens) in comfortable buildings in Surrey.

In many other aspects of life, beyond the garden walls, there is now a powerful vogue for things Victorian, whether it is for clothes, houses, literature, music or social mores. Within the garden, there are innumerable and poor recreations of Victorian conservatories, aluminium reproductions of seats once made of iron, and reconstituted stone jardinières and bird baths, all of which may mock the craftsmanship and solidity of the originals but probably give their owners just as much pleasure.

It all adds up to the greatest legacy of all – the fact that so many people are so interested in gardening, are able to indulge that interest, and make us almost an entire nation of gardeners.

GAZETTEER OF IMPORTANT GARDENS

T HE VICTORIAN PERIOD WAS A GREAT AGE FOR garden building, and there are still tens of thousands of gardens, of all sizes, whose bones are unaltered. Of the great country house and urban park gardens, many have vanished or been changed beyond recall. Some, still as they were, are determinedly private. However, a surprising number can easily be visited, and the gazetteer consists mainly of these. Some lost or private gardens have been included if they have been mentioned extensively in the text.

Opening times, liable to change from season to season, have not been given in detail. It is advisable to check with the garden, or with one of the garden publications that deal with such things, before planning a visit.

ABBOTSFORD HOUSE
Melrose, Borders region.
March to October.
Mrs P. Maxwell-Scott (Tel: 0896 2043).
Mostly early nineteenth century, but an important early example of formal planning near house. Marvellous site, and plenty of Scott planting.
Designer(s): Sir Walter Scott, *c.* 1820.

ALBURY PARK
Albury, Guildford, Surrey.
May to September.
Country Houses Association Ltd.
Exotic country house by Pugin, gardens with plenty of contemporary feel.
Worth seeing.

ALTON TOWERS
Nr Alton, Staffordshire.
March to October.
Alton Towers Ltd (Tel: 0538 702449).
Away from the modern addition lie a myriad late Georgian and Victorian
delights, including wonderful Chinoiserie, rockeries and spectacular plantings.
Designer(s): various from 1820.

ARLEY HALL AND GARDENS
Nr Northwich, Cheshire.
April to October.
The Hon. M. L. W. Flower (Tel: 056 585 353).
Handsome walled gardens, one with early herbaceous borders (now much
replanted) with yew buttresses dividing their length. Much else to see. 1850.

ARLINGTON COURT
Barnstaple, Devon.
All year.
The National Trust (Tel: 027 182 296).
Late Georgian house, but with gardens with handsome formal Victorian
terracing, and much Victorian planting.

ASCOTT
Wing, Buckinghamshire.
Spring to Summer and occasionally at other times.
The National Trust (Tel: 0296 688242).
A Rothschild property from 1873. Now with orchards and lawns near house,
and terraces and formal garden beyond. Much fabulous planting. 1880.

ATHELHAMPTON
Athelhampton, Dorset.
April to October.
Lady Jennifer Cooke (Tel: 030 584 363).
Marvellous formal enclosures, a terrace with pavilions, and magnificent topiary
pyramids. Sumptuous architecture; mostly modern planting.
Designer(s): Inigo Thomas, 1891.

BARRINGTON COURT
Ilminster, Somerset.
April to September.
The National Trust (Tel: 0460 41480/40601).
Gardens of 1920, around ancient house, and in the late Victorian formal manner; of great quality. Jekyll advised on planting. Moated orchard, canals etc. 1920.

BATSFORD
Moreton-in-Marsh, Gloucestershire.
April to October.
The Batsford Foundation (Tel: 0386 700409 or 0608 50722).
Lord Redesdale's Japanese garden of the 1890s; statues, lanterns, magnolias and cherries. All on a landscape scale. Recently reclaimed and augmented. Designer(s): Lord Redesdale, 1890–1910.

BATTERSEA PARK
London.
All year.
An important location, though now with only fragments of its grand past. Worth a look at the 1860s lake, and the grand rockery.

BELLE ISLE
Windermere, Cumbria.
May to September.
Mrs E. S. C. Curwen (Tel: 096 62 3353).
Handsome en-isled nineteenth-century arboretum, by late Georgian house.

BELTON HOUSE
Nr Grantham, Lincolnshire.
April to October.
National Trust (Tel: 0476 66116).
The Victorian recreation of the seventeenth-century gardens still reasonably intact, and worth seeing. The house is lovely, and the contemporary landscape park grand. 1850s.

BELVOIR CASTLE
Nr. Melton Mowbray, Leicestershire.
March to October.
His Grace the Duke of Rutland (Tel: 0476 870262).
From the 1850s, famous for very colourful bedding schemes then widely admired, now gone. Also a vast natural rockery, still to be seen. 1850s.

BIDDULPH GRANGE
Nr Congalton, Staffordshire.
Small parties by arrangement (Tel: 0782 513149).
Now being restored; a surprising amount of the original detail survives in the
hospital grounds – where you're more likely to encounter garden historians
than anyone else. From the 1820s.

BLENHEIM PALACE
Woodstock, Oxfordshire.
March to October.
His Grace the Duke of Marlborough (Tel: 0993 811325).
Amid earlier glories sits a fine late Victorian water and box-work parterre,
though designed in 1920 by Achille Duchesne – formality still at full throttle.
Designer(s): Duchesne, 1920.

BORDE HILL GARDEN
Haywards Heath, West Sussex.
March to October.
(Tel: 0444 450326).
Vast landscaped garden developed from 1890, with very grand arboretum
and pinetum now fully mature. Contemporary borders, and some modern
developments. 1890.

BOWOOD
Calne, Wiltshire.
April to September.
The Earl of Shelburne (Tel: 0249 812102).
In front of the orangeries, the grandiose Italian terraces designed by Kennedy
(1851); and in the park, an almost grander 'geographical' arboretum by
Spencer.
Designer(s): Kennedy, Spencer, 1850.

BRANTWOOD
Coniston, Cumbria.
All year.
Brantwood Educational Trust (Tel: 0966 41396).
Ruskin's estate, with his thoughts on planting woodland and shrubberies now
being restored. The bank of rhodos is also his. Stunning site.
Designer(s): John Ruskin, 1870s.

BROUGHTON CASTLE
Banbury, Oxfordshire.
May to September.
The Lord Saye and Sele (Tel: 0295 62624).
Wonderful old house, once with the earliest Victorian herb gardens, with 'Ye
Herbe Garden' in clipped santolina. Now with lush Jekyll-ish borders. 1890s.

BROUGHTON HALL
Skipton, North Yorkshire.
Open by appointment.
H. R. Tempest Esq. (Tel: 0756 2267).
Quite tremendous garden by Nesfield, 1850s, conservatories, courtyards, pavilions and a magnificent parterre.
Designer(s): Nesfield, 1850s.

CARDIFF CASTLE
Cardiff, South Glamorgan.
All year.
Cardiff City Council (Tel: 0222 822083).
Gardens laid out between 1871 and 1891, mostly by Andrew Pettigrew, and mostly in the landscape mode.
Designer(s): Pettigrew, 1870–90.

CASTLE ASHBY
Northampton.
Open occasionally and by arrangement.
Marquess of Northampton (Tel: 060129 234).
Among much older and grander work, the Victorian parterre is now called the 'Italian Garden'. Jekyll admired the bedding. There's a good orangery.
Designer(s): Sir Digby Wyatt, 1860s.

CASTLE KENNEDY
Stranraer, Dumfries and Galloway.
April to September.
The Earl and Countess of Stair (Tel: 0776 2024).
The tremendous seventeenth-century scheme replanted using monkey-puzzles and New Zealand flame trees and ilex. Much other Victorian planting around contemporary house.
Designer(s): in part Fowler, 1840–70.

CHARLECOTE PARK
Warwick.
April to October.
The National Trust (Tel: 0789 840277).
Brown's landscape was pushed aside for a vast expanse of bedding (20,000 plants for the forecourt alone) and fine terracing and architecture. Much remains.

CHATSWORTH
Bakewell, Derbyshire.
April to November.
Chatsworth House Trust (Tel: 024688 2204).
The site of Paxton's most exciting works. A pity about the conservatory (now

blown up), but the wall cases still have camellias, and the water is stunning.
Designer(s): Paxton from 1850.

CLIVEDEN
Taplow, Buckinghamshire.
Most of the year.
The National Trust (Tel: 062 86 5069).
Barry's astonishing house and terracing of 1850–51 remain, together with much other work from the Astor ownership from the 1890s.
Designer(s): Barry, Fleming, 1850–90.

CLUMBER PARK
Nr Worksop, Nottinghamshire.
All year.
The National Trust (Tel: 0909 476592).
The house, once directly in the landscape, was given an astonishing pair of terraces, one still with its parterre, overlooking the lake. Urns and stone herons.
Designer(s): Gilpin, 1840s?

COMPTON WYNYATES
Tyne, Warwickshire.
Private.
Handsome topiary of the 1880s still in good shape, though now with fewer surrounding flowers, but still a fine foil to the ancient house. 1885.

CRAGSIDE HOUSE
Rothbury, Northumberland.
All year.
The National Trust (Tel: 0669 20333).
Lord Armstrong's garden, from 1864, is almost the apotheosis of the rock garden, with the vast house set amid rhodo-strewn rock. Now some marvellous trees. 1860s.

CRYSTAL PALACE
Sydenham, London.
Daily.
Still a popular venue, though the palace and much of the gardens have vanished. Some remarkable remains (many of the monsters are from 1854), and an enormously important site.

DALKEITH PARK
Nr Edinburgh, Lothian Region.
March to October.
The Buccleuch Estates (Tel: 031 663 5684).
Fantastic, now partly derelict, conservatory by William Burn, 1840. The site of some famous rustic pavilions. Now a pleasant country park. 1840s.

DOCHFOUR GARDENS
Inverness, Highlands region.
April to October.
Lord and Lady Burton (Tel: 046 386 218).
A Highland estate; 15 acres of Victorian gardens, with water gardens and vast terraces. Arboretum and much else.

DRUMLANRIG CASTLE
Thornhill, Dumfriesshire.
April to August.
His Grace the Duke of Buccleuch and Queensberry (Tel: 0848 30248).
On top of the grandiose seventeenth-century terracing, Thomson designed elaborate sand and flower parterres – still visible in dry summers.
Designer(s): Thomson, 1860s.

DRUMMOND CASTLE
Muthill, Tayside region.
May to August.
The Grimsthorpe and Drummond Castle Trust Ltd (Tel: 076 481 257).
The parterre designed by George Kennedy, and possibly completed for the Queen's arrival, now much simplified, if not improved. Extraordinary among seventeenth-century works of greater quality.
Designer(s): Kennedy, 1838–42.

DUNROBIN CASTLE
Golspie, Highlands region.
June to September.
The Countess of Sutherland (Tel: 040 83 3177).
Various parterres remain from Barry's remodelling of the house from 1835, though now with modern plants.
Designer(s): Barry, 1835–50.

DYFFRYN GARDENS
St Nicholas, nr Cardiff, South Glamorgan.
March to October.
Mid and South Glamorgan County Councils (Tel: 0222 593328).
Among modern developments are remains of the formal garden of Thomas Mawson, with canal, bedding and rose gardens. Here, carpet bedding is still alive.
Designer(s): Mawson, 1906–14.

EARLSHALL CASTLE
Leuchars, Fife region.
Easter to September.
Major and Mrs D. R. Baxter (Tel: 033 483 205).

Nostalgic recreation of the seventeenth century by Lorimer in 1890, filled with topiary, hedges, and elegant gateways. Exceptionally attractive.
Designer(s): Lorimer after 1890.

EASTNOR CASTLE
Nr Ledbury, Herefordshire.
Infrequently from May to September.
(Tel: Ledbury 2305).
An early and very fine 'picturesque' (as opposed to taxonomic) arboretum, much from the 1840s. Some superb and unique conifers, and rare broad-leaves. 1840s.

ELVASTON CASTLE
Nr Derby.
By appointment only.
Derbyshire County Council (Tel: 0332 71342).
One of the major Victorian sites, with vast avenues, lushly planted dells, and vast formal gardens (once with 11 miles of hedges), Moorish gardens, and much, much more. From 1840.

FRIAR PARK
Henley on Thames, Berkshire.
Private.
Sir Frank Crisp's strange model of the Matterhorn, and many of the various jokes with which he amused himself, still exist, if overgrown.
Designer(s): various, 1900s.

GAWTHORPE HALL
Padiham, Lancashire.
April to November.
The National Trust (Tel: 0282 78511).
A conservative restoration by Barry of an Elizabethan house. He added an equally good four-square parterre at the garden side.
Designer(s): Barry, 1850.

GLENDURGAN GARDEN
Helford River, Cornwall.
March to October.
The National Trust (Tel: 032 623 481).
A fine laurel maze of the 1830s. The garden developed over the succeeding decades. It's now very fine. 1830s.

GODINTON PARK
Ashford, Kent.
June to September.
Alan Wyndham Green, Esq. (Tel: 0233 20773).

Eighteenth-century landscape, improved and extended by Sir Reginald Blomfield. Topiary and formal gardens.
Designer(s): Blomfield, 1890s.

GRAVETYE MANOR
Sharpthorne, East Grinstead, West Sussex.
Daily.
Gravetye Manor Hotel (Tel: 0342 810567).
William Robinson's beloved estate, neglected after his death but now once
again cared for. Some original planting remains.
Designer(s): William Robinson, 1880s.

HAREWOOD HOUSE
Leeds, West Yorkshire.
April to October.
The Earl of Harewood (Tel: 0532 886225).
A Brown landscape, with Barry's terrace of the 1840s giving the best views.
It's now being grandly restored.
Designer(s): Barry, 1840s.

HARLAXTON MANOR
Grantham, Lincolnshire.
By appointment.
University of Evansville (Tel: 0476 645541).
Exuberantly fake Elizabethan terraces around the Salvin house. A 'strapwork'
conservatory by Burn. Great fun.

HATFIELD HOUSE
Hatfield, Hertfordshire.
March to October.
The Marquess of Salisbury (Tel: 070 72 62823).
Amid old and new is the Victorian garden, maze of 1840s, terraces. See text.
Designer(s): 2nd Marquess, 1840s.

HOLKER HALL
Cark-in-Cartmel, nr Grange-over-Sands, Cumbria.
Easter to October.
Mr and Mrs Hugh Cavendish (Tel: 044853 328).
A lush garden indeed, part the work of Paxton from the 1850s, but with many
later things including a sunk garden and pergola by Thomas Mawson (1912).
Fine.
Designer(s): Paxton, Mawson, 1850–1900s.

HOLME PIERREPONT HALL
Radcliffe-on-Trent, nr Nottingham.
Easter to August.

Mr and Mrs Robin Brackenbury (Tel: 06073 2371).
Attractive courtyard parterre of 1875, and in good shape. 1875.

HOOLE HOUSE
Nr Chester, Cheshire.
Private.
The extraordinary early Victorian rockery still just about exists. See text.

IFORD MANOR
Bradford-on-Avon, Wiltshire.
Infrequently from May to August.
Mr and Mrs Hignett (Tel: 02216 3146 or 2840).
Turn-of-the-century formalism, with handsome terraces, steps and statuary,
fine plantings. The designer, Harold Peto, was also the owner.
Designer(s): Harold Peto, 1900s.

KEIR
Dunblane, Stirling.
Occasionally open.
His Excellency Mahdi Altajir (Tel: 0786 82267).
Topiary and rhododendrons, but especially fine and copious stonework, with
bridges and tunnels. Exciting, if slightly funereal.

KELLIE CASTLE
Nr Pittenweem, Fife.
All year.
National Trust for Scotland (Tel: 033 38 271).
Lovely and loving recreation of what was thought of as an old-fashioned Scots
garden, surrounding even finer old house.
Designer(s): R. Lorimer, 1900.

KILLERTON HOUSE
Nr Exeter, Devon.
April to October.
The National Trust (Tel: 0392 881345).
An early arboretum, associated with the Veitch family. The first redwood
seedlings and much else, including vast wellingtonias and even Lawson's
cypresses! From the early 1800s.

KNEBWORTH HOUSE
Knebworth, Hertfordshire.
May to September.
The Hon David Lytton-Cobbold (Tel: 0438 812661).
Ancient house revamped in the 1830s; new gardens in 1847, to match, but
askew. Later, Lutyens and Jekyll did much near the house – with their work
being restored.

KNIGHTSHAYES COURT
Nr Tiverton, Devon.
April to October.
The National Trust (Tel: 0884 254665).
Vast Victorian house; the contemporary yew hedges (wonderfully enclosing ponds and statuary) and trees remain from the 1860s.

LAMPORT HALL
Northampton.
Easter to September.
Lamport Hall Trust (Tel: 060 128 272).
The old gardens got a rock garden in 1848, soon inhabited by some of the first gnomes by the 1890s, as well as by other fauna.
Designer(s): Sir Charles Isham.

LANHYDROCK HOUSE
Nr Bodmin, Cornwall.
April to October.
The National Trust (Tel: 0208 3320).
Lovely formal terraces of 1857 around a house almost rebuilt after fire. Near the house, some fine box-edged flower-beds. Altogether lovely. From 1850s.

LEVENS HALL
Kendal, Cumbria.
Easter to October.
O. R. Bagot, Esq. (Tel: 076 87 72287).
Eighteenth century topiary garden, but totally recut in the early part of the nineteenth century and vastly admired since then. The ancient park re-landscaped in 1890.

LONG CROSS VICTORIAN GARDENS
Nr Wadebridge, Cornwall.
Easter to October.
Mr and Mrs R. Y. Warrillow (Tel: 0208 880243).
Interesting late Victorian scheme still intact. Some good trees.

LOSEHILL HALL
Castleton, Derbyshire.
Occasionally open.
Peak National Park Centre (Tel: 0433 20373).
Nice mid-range Victorian gardens, with formal area, a good arboretum.

LYME PARK
Disley, Cheshire.
May to September.
The National Trust (Tel: 066 32 2023).

A good late nineteenth-century Italian (though thought of as 'Dutch') garden, with sunk pool, box-edged parterres, still handsomely bedded out.

MELBOURNE HALL
Melbourne, nr Derby, Derbyshire.
April to September.
Marquess of Lothian (Tel: 033 16 2502).
An odd mix of original formality and Victorian lily-gilding. Much nineteenth-century tree planting, along old lines. A nice Victorian grotto.

MELLERSTAIN HOUSE
Duns, Borders region.
May to September.
The Earl of Haddington (Tel: 057 381 225).
About the Adam house is the astonishing formal landscape designed by Blomfield in 1909. Vistas, marvellous stonework and topiary. The parterres only are gone.
Designer(s): Blomfield, 1909.

MUNCASTER CASTLE
Ravenglass, Cumbria.
Easter to September.
P. Gordon-Duff-Pennington (Tel: 065 77 614).
Astonishing eighteenth-century terraces, now through 300 acres of Victorian and more recent rhododendrons. Stupendous views.

NUNEHAM COURTENAY PARK
Nuneham Courtenay, nr Oxford.
Occasionally open.
University and Rothmans International plc (Tel: 086738 551).
A famous flower garden in the eighteenth century; Gilpin started up the magnificent arboretum in the 1830s, and much remains.
Designer(s): Gilpin, 1830s.

NYMANS GARDEN
Handcross, West Sussex.
April to October.
The National Trust (Tel: 0725 400321 or 400002).
Borders (and their topiary) designed by William Robinson. The owners in the 1890s made some of the first Japanese and erica gardens.
Designer(s): Robinson, Messel, 1890s.

OSBORNE HOUSE
Cowes, Isle of Wight.
March to October.
English Heritage (Tel: 0983 200022).

Prince Albert's taste in the Italian style, both for house and garden. Neither is convincing, but both perfectly maintained.

OXBURGH HALL
Swaffham, Norfolk.
April to October.
The National Trust (Tel: 036 621 258).
Unique 'French' parterre of 1845, using coloured gravel and box. The Victorian 'wilderness' is being restored. 1845.

PACKWOOD HOUSE
Hockley Heath, Lapworth, Warwickshire.
April to September.
The National Trust (Tel: 056 43 2024).
The supposedly ancient topiary mostly dates from 1850. Handsome even so. With charming formal gardens, pools and marvellous parterres.

PARNHAM HOUSE
Beaminster, Dorset.
April to October.
Mr and Mrs John Makepeace (Tel: 0308 862204).
Gardens mostly designed by Inigo Thomas, though now being replanted.

PENCARROW HOUSE
Bodmin, Cornwall.
Daily.
The Molesworth-St Aubyn family (Tel: 020 884 369).
The 1840s saw the construction of a vast jumbled rockery, and an excellent American garden; Italian ones too. Lovely.
Designer(s): Sir William Molesworth, 1840s.

PENSHURST PLACE
Tunbridge Wells, Kent.
April to October.
The Rt. Hon. Viscount De L'Isle, V.C., K.G. (Tel: 0892 870307).
Marvellous house, sympathetically restored from 1850, and given gardens to match based on Kypp's drawings. Italian, sunken, and parterre gardens in full fig.
Designer(s): George Devey, 1850–80.

PRINCES PARK
Liverpool 8.
Daily.
Handsome public park, still with a nice Victorian feel and with plenty of the original detail.

RABY CASTLE
Staindrop, Darlington, Durham.
Easter to September.
The Lord Barnard T. D. (Tel: 0833 60202).
The site from which numerous Victorian garden plants were named. Walled gardens and some excellent nineteenth-century tree planting.

SCONE PALACE
Perth.
April to October.
The Rt. Hon. Earl of Mansefield (Tel: 0738 52300).
A fabulous pinetum of 1848, with grand walks, and trees now in perfection. Beware of the peacocks. 1850.

SHEFFIELD PARK
Nr Uckfield, East Sussex.
April to November.
The National Trust (Tel: 0825 790655).
Brown designed the lakes, but much of the lush late-Victorian-looking planting dates from 1909, though of very high quality.

SHRUBLAND PARK
Nr Needham Market, Suffolk.
Private.
The vast mansion by Barry surrounds earlier houses. The terraces, not quite the Villa d'Este but impressive, remain. The gardens were much simplified by William Robinson, but are still exciting.

SOMERLEYTON HALL
Nr Lowestoft, Suffolk.
Easter to October.
The Lord and Lady Somerleyton (Tel: 0502 730237).
Ornate mid-Victorian gardens with a maze by Nesfield, as well as terraces. Most of the parterres have gone, though colonnades and pergolas remain. Designer(s): Nesfield, 1850s.

STANDEN
East Grinstead, West Sussex.
April to October.
The National Trust (Tel: 0342 23029).
An attractive house of the 1890s, with a matching half-formal Queen Anne garden of the same date. Now being restored. 1890s.

SUDELEY CASTLE
Winchcombe, Gloucestershire.
April to October.

The Lady Ashcombe (Tel: 0242 602308).
Wavy bastions of yew, battlemented and tunnelled, enclose a formal garden, mostly of the 1850s. Very atmospheric. 1850s.

SYON HOUSE
Brentford, Middlesex.
April to September.
His Grace the Duke of Northumberland, K.G., G.C.V.O., P.C. (Tel: 01 560 0881).
The famous and extant conservatory overlooked the rockery, which reminded Londoners who should have known better of the Scottish Highlands. Little remains.

TAPELEY PARK
Instow, Devon.
Easter to October.
Mrs Rosamund Christie (Tel: 0271 860528).
A fine late Victorian site, with steeply terraced Italian garden, walled kitchen garden, exotic-looking palm trees and much more. 1890–1919.

TATTON PARK
Knutsford, Cheshire.
All year.
The National Trust (Tel: 0565 54822).
Italian terrace, pools and balustrades, probably by Paxton. Also one of the finest of all fern houses, and a nice Japanese garden of 1910.
Designer(s): Repton, Paxton.

THE ROYAL BOTANIC GARDEN, KEW
Kew, Richmond, Surrey.
Daily.
(Tel: 01 940 1171).
An important site. Nowadays, some interesting bedding still to be seen, and a good source of ideas if you feel encouraged to try your hand.

THORESBY HALL
Nr Newark-on-Trent, Nottinghamshire.
June to August.
(Tel: 0623 822301).
See text. Salvin terraces still with brilliant half-hardy bedding and grand statuary. Gazebos, marvellous trees, and a fake castle in formal gardens.
Designer(s): Salvin, Nesfield.

TOROSAY CASTLE
Isle of Mull, Strathclyde region.
May to September.

David Guthrie-James of Torosay, M.B.E., D.S.C. and the Hon. Mrs James
(Tel: 068 02 421).
House by Bryce, and a vast Italian garden by Lorimer. Some good statuary,
all recently splendidly restored.
Designer(s): Lorimer, 1890s.

TRENGWAINTON GARDEN
Penzance, Cornwall.
March to October.
The National Trust (Tel: 0736 64153).
The walled garden here grows tender plants on banked beds, once widely
seen, now all vanished. Battersea once looked like this. 1860–70s.

TRENTHAM GARDENS
Trentham, Stoke-on-Trent, Staffordshire.
Daily.
J. L. Broome (Tel: 0872 657341).
Much of the prodigy garden remains, terraces, lake, beds, bedding and all.
Probably the most important remaining site. The house has gone.
Designer(s): Barry, Nesfield, Flem, 1840s.

WADDESDON MANOR
Nr Aylesbury, Buckinghamshire.
March to October.
The National Trust (Tel: 0296 651211 or 651282).
Fantastic French château of 1877–89, with stupendous matching gardens still
in good condition, packed with topiary, statues, rockeries, aviaries. Superb.
Designer(s): Louis Laine, 1880s.

WARWICK CASTLE
Warwick, Warwickshire.
Daily.
(Tel: 0926 495421).
Brown landscape but with additions by Marnock, notably a parterre now being
reconstructed.
Designer(s): Marnock, 1864.

WEST DEAN GARDENS
Nr Chichester, West Sussex.
April to September.
The Edward James Foundation (Tel: 024363 301).
Fine Victorian kitchen garden, with contemporary glasshouses filled with
historical material. Colonnades, arboretum, and much else of interest.

WESTONBIRT ARBORETUM
Tetbury, Gloucestershire.

Daily.
Forestry Commission (Tel: 066 688 220).
Marvellous site, developed from 1829, with tremendous specimens of all the main Victorian conifers and broad leaf trees. Developments continue. 1830s.

WESTONBIRT SCHOOL
Tetbury, Gloucestershire.
Occasionally open.
This is the house and nearby garden. A wonderful Italian garden, quite as good as the arboretum. Also a lake, and plenty of 'rustic' work.

WIMBLEDON HOUSE
The last of many grand houses on this site vanished in 1939, though fragments of the park and gardens remain.

WREST PARK
Silsoe, Bedfordshire.
April to September.
English Heritage (Tel: 0525 60718).
Among exciting older work, the house and nearby gardens are in the French style and date from 1839. Statues from the Great Exhibition added, and some fine parterres from the 1850s.

BIBLIOGRAPHY

ADAMS, S. AND S. (1825): *Complete Servant*

ANON. (1842): *The Flower Garden, etc.*

ANON. (1880): *Famous Parks and Gardens, 1880*

BARRY, A. (1867): *Sir Charles Barry*

BEETON, S. O. (1862): *The Book of Garden Management*

BLOMFIELD, R. (1892): *The Formal Garden in England*

BRIDGEMAN, C. (1866): *The American Gardener's Assistant* (ed. Todd)

BUIST, J. (1843): *Queen Victoria in Scotland*

BURBIDGE, F. W. (1865): *The Book of the Scented Garden*

BURBIDGE, F. W. (1874): *The Domestic Floriculture; Window Gardening, etc.*

BURBIDGE, F. W. (1877): *Horticulture*

DELAWARE, E. S. (1855): *The Kitchen Garden*

DON, D. (1831): *General System of Gardening and Botany*

DOUGLAS, J. (1880): *Hardy Florists' Flowers*

DOWNING, A. J. (1849): *A Treatise on the Theory and Practice of Landscape Gardening*

EARLE, M. T. (1897): *Pot-Pourri from a Surrey Garden*

EASTLAKE, C. L. (1868): *The English Gentleman's House*

ELLWANGER, G. H. (1896): *The Garden's Story*

FERRIS, C. F. (1837): *The Parterre*

FORTUNE, R. (1847): *Wanderings in China*

FORTUNE, R. (1863): *Visits to the Capitals of Japan and China*

GLENNY, G. (1847): *Gardening for the Million*

GLENNY, G. (1852): *The Flower Garden*

HENDRIE, R. (1842): *Two Letters to an Amateur ... on Pictorial Colours and Effect*

BIBLIOGRAPHY

HIBBERD, S. (1856): *Rustic Adornments for Homes of Taste, etc.*

HIBBERD, S. (1857): *Garden Favourites*

HIBBERD, S. (1859): *The Town Garden*

HIBBERD, S. (1869): *The Fern Garden, etc.*

HIBBERD, S. (1870): *New and Rare Beautiful-Leaved Plants*

HOBDAY, E. (1877): *Cottage Gardening*

HOBDAY, E. (1887): *The Villa Gardener*

HOLE, S. R. (1884): *A Book about Roses*

HOPE, F. J. (1881): *Gardens and Woodlands*

HOWARD, E. (1898): *Tomorrow: A Peaceful Path to Real Reform*

JEKYLL, G. (1896): *Gardens and Garden Craft* (in *Edinburgh Review*, Vol. 184, p. 161)

JEKYLL, GERTRUDE (1899): *Wood and Garden*

JEKYLL, GERTRUDE (1908): *Colour Schemes for the Garden*

JESSE, E. (1847): *Favourite Haunts and Rural Studies*

KEMP, E. (1864): *How to Lay Out a Garden*

KINGSLEY, R. G. (1907): *Eversley Garden and Others*

LOUDON, J. (1840): *Instructions on Gardening for Ladies*

LOUDON, J. (1850): *The Villa Gardener, etc.*

LOUDON, J. C. (1838): *The Suburban Gardener*

LOUDON, J. C. (1838): *The Villa Gardener*

LOUDON, J. C. (1842): *Cottage, Farm & Villa Architecture*

LOUDON, J. C. (1843): *On the Laying Out ... of Cemeteries, etc.*

MCINTOSH, C. (1853): *The Book of the Garden*

MILLER, PHILIP (1754): *The Gardener's Dictionary*

MILNER, G. (1881): *Country Pleasures; the Chronicle, etc.*

MOORE, T. (1881): *Epitome of Gardening*

OLMSTED, F. L. (1861): *Journeys and Explorations in the Cotton Kingdom*

PATERSON, A. (1832): *The Manse Garden*

PAXTON, J. (1852): *The Cottager's Calendar of Garden Operations*

PIGGOTT, F. T. (1892): *The Garden of Japan*

RENNIE, J. (1834): *Handbook of Gardening*

ROBINSON, W. (1869): *Gleanings from French Gardens*

ROBINSON, W. (1871): *The Subtropical Garden*

ROBINSON, W. (1878): *Parks and Gardens of Paris*

ROBINSON, W. (1881): *The English Flower Garden*

ROBINSON, W. (1883): *The Wild Garden* (2nd edition)

ROBINSON, W. (1892): *Garden Design and Architects' Gardens*

ROBINSON, W. (1911): *Gravetye Manor, or Twenty Years' Work, etc.*

ROBINSON, W. (1914): *Home Grounds*

SEDDING, J. D. (1895): *Garden Craft, Old and New*

SMEE, A. (1872): *My Garden*

THOMSON, DAVID (1868): *The Handy Book of the Flower Garden*

TRIGGS, I. (1902): *The Formal Garden in England and Scotland*
WALSH, J. H. (1857): *A Manual of Domestic Economy*
WATSON, F. (1872): *Flowers and Gardens*
WAUGH, F. A. (1911): *Kemp's Landscape Gardening* (American edition)
WROTH, W. (1896): *London Pleasure Gardens of the Eighteenth Century*

MAGAZINES

The Cottage Gardener, 1848–60
The Floral Cabinet, 1837–80
The Florist, 1848–61
The Garden, 1871–1900
The Gardener, 1867–82
The Gardener's Chronicle, 1841–1905
The Gardener's Magazine, 1826–43
Gardening Illustrated, 1879–1900
The Horticultural Register, 1831–6
Memoirs of the Caledonian Horticultural Society, 1813–29
Paxton's Magazine of Botany, 1834–49
The Scottish Gardener, 1852–9

MODERN SOURCES

ALLAN, M. (1982): *William Robinson: Father of the English Flower Garden*
BERRALL, JULIA S. (1978): *The Garden, an Illustrated History*
BONIFACE, P. (1982): *The Garden Room*
BROWN, JANE (1982): *Gardens of a Golden Afternoon*
CARTER, TOM (1984): *The Victorian Garden*
CHADWICK, G. F. (1961): *The Works of Sir Joseph Paxton*
COATS, ALICE M. (1953): *Garden Shrubs and their Histories*
COATS, ALICE M. (1956): *Flowers and Their Histories*
FLEMING, LAURENCE AND GORE (1979): *The English Garden*
FORSYTH, A. (1983): *Yesterday's Gardens* (H.M.S.O.)
GIROUARD, M. (1977): *Sweetness and Light: the 'Queen Anne' Movement*
GOTHEIN, M. L. (1928): *A History of Garden Art* (translation from the German)
HADFIELD, M. ET AL. (1980): *British Gardeners*
HOLE, S. R. (1982): *A Book about the Garden*
HUXLEY, ANTHONY A. (1978): *Illustrated History of Gardening*
McFADYEN, D. (1933): *Sir E. Howard and the Town Planning Movement*
MUTHESIUS, S. (1978): *The High Victorian Movement*
MUTHESIUS, S. (1982): *The English Terraced House*
SCOTT-JAMES, ANNE (1981): *The Cottage Garden*
STUART, DAVID (1979): *Georgian Gardens*
STUART, DAVID (1984): *The Kitchen Garden*

BIBLIOGRAPHY

STUART, DAVID AND SUTHERLAND, J. (1987): *Plants from the Past*
TAYLOR, G. (1952): *The Victorian Flower Garden*
THACKER, CHRISTOPHER (1979): *The History of Gardens*
YOUNG, G. M. (1934): *Early Victorian England*

ILLUSTRATION
ACKNOWLEDGEMENTS

Illustrated London News (1851): 51
Jones' Catalogue (1901–2): 49
Journal of Horticulture, Vol. 32: 52
The Kitchen Garden, E. S. Delamer (1855): 46
My Garden, Alfred Smee (1872): 43, 50, 57
Parks and Gardens of Paris, William Robinson (1878): 48
Paxton's Magazine of Botany (1834): 16
Paxton's Magazine of Botany (1838): 25
Paxton's Magazine of Botany (1839): 36
Rustic Adornments for Homes of Taste, Shirley Hibberd (1856): 15,
    27, 39, 41
Suburban Gardener, J. C. Loudon (1832): 3, 8, 13
The Villa Garden, Jane Loudon (1850): 6, 24
The Wild Garden, William Robinson (1870): 58

Thanks must be given to the Librarian of the Lindley Library of
    the Royal Horticultural Society for allowing photography.
Photographer: Geoff Howard
Picture Research: Susan Rose-Smith

PHOTOGRAPHIC ACKNOWLEDGEMENTS

The colour photographs were taken from the following sources:
1 from the National Trust Photographic Library; 2, 5, 16 from
The Amateur's Flower Garden, Shirley Hibberd, 1875; 3, 17, 18,
from *Familiar Garden Flowers*, Hulme and Hibberd, 1879–87; 4,
12, 27 from *The Gardener's Assistant*, Robert Thompson, revised
Thomas Moore, 1878; 6, 26 from *Garden Favourites*, Shirley
Hibberd, 1858; 7, 8, 9, 10, 23, 24 from *The Gardens of England*, E.
Adveno Brooke, 1857; 11 from *The Parlour Gardener*, anon. 1863;
13 from *The Gardener's Chronicle*, 31 May 1862; 14 from *A Handbook for Ladies on Indoor Plants*, E. A. Maling, 1867; 15 from *The
New Practical Window Gardener*, John R. Mollison, 1877; 19, 22,
29 from *Cassell's Popular Gardening*, ed. D.T. Fish, 1884; 20, 25
from *Flora and Pomona*, Charles McIntosh, 1829; 21 from Grosv-
enor Museum, Chester; 28 from *The Gardener's Assistant*, 1873.

INDEX

INDEX